Designing Inclusion

D1550325

An inclusion failure has become highly visible in the advanced economies of the West. Too many able-bodied people are subject to chronic joblessness and, when employed, cannot earn a living remotely like that in the mainstream of the population. One policy response has been to give such workers a range of goods and services without charge, another has been to single out some groups for tax credits tied to their earnings. However, many of the welfare programs actually weaken people's incentive to participate in the labor force and wage-income tax credits appear to have made hardly a dent in joblessness. This timely volume brings together leading economists to present four studies of methods to rebuild self-sufficiency and boost employment: a graduated employment subsidy, a hiring subsidy and subsidies for training and education. It is of interest to anyone with a serious interest in the economics of subsidies to raise inclusion.

EDMUND S. PHELPS is McVickar Professor of Political Economy and Director of the Center on Capitalism and Society at Columbia University.

Designing Inclusion

*Tools to Raise Low-end Pay and Employment
in Private Enterprise*

edited by

Edmund S. Phelps

CAMBRIDGE
UNIVERSITY PRESS

PUBLISHED BY THE PRESS SYNDICATE OF THE UNIVERSITY OF CAMBRIDGE
The Pitt Building, Trumpington Street, Cambridge, United Kingdom

CAMBRIDGE UNIVERSITY PRESS
The Edinburgh Building, Cambridge, CB2 2RU, UK
40 West 20th Street, New York, NY 10011–4211, USA
477 Williamstown Road, Port Melbourne, VIC 3207, Australia
Ruiz de Alarcón 13, 28014 Madrid, Spain
Dock House, The Waterfront, Cape Town 8001, South Africa

http://www.cambridge.org

First published 2003

Printed in the United Kingdom at the University Press, Cambridge

Typeface Plantin 10/12 pt.   *System* LATEX 2$_\varepsilon$ [TB]

A catalogue record for this book is available from the British Library

ISBN 0 521 81695 5 hardback

Contents

List of figures   *page* vii
List of tables   ix
List of contributors   xi

Introduction   1
EDMUND S. PHELPS

1 Low-wage employment subsidies in a labor-turnover
   model of the "natural rate"   16
   HIAN TECK HOON AND EDMUND S. PHELPS

2 Taxes, subsidies and equilibrium labor market outcomes   44
   DALE MORTENSEN AND CHRISTOPHER PISSARIDES

3 Learning-by-doing versus on-the-job training: using
   variation induced by the EITC to distinguish between
   models of skill formation   74
   JAMES J. HECKMAN, LANCE LOCHNER AND
   RICARDO COSSA

4 Unemployment vouchers versus low-wage subsidies   131
   J. MICHAEL ORSZAG AND DENNIS J. SNOWER

Index   161

Figures

1.1	Wealth supply and asset demand	*page* 23
1.2	Labor, product and capital market equilibrium	27
1.3	Effects of a flat subsidy	30
1.4	Comparison of flat and graduated subsidies	32
1.5	Effects of a flat subsidy on hiring and employment	38
2.1	Equilibrium market tightness and reservation productivity	56
3.1	Earned Income Tax Credit	75
3.2	Simulated effects of EITC on investment (OJT model)	107
3.3	Simulated effects of EITC on hours worked (OJT model)	107
3.4	Simulated effects of EITC on human capital (OJT model)	108
3.5	Simulated effects of EITC on wage rates (OJT model)	108
3.6	Simulated effects of EITC on wage income (OJT model)	109
3.7	Simulated effects of EITC on hours worked (LBD model)	115
3.8	Simulated effects of EITC on human capital (LBD model)	115
3.9	Changes in hourly wages owing to increases in hours worked (LBD model)	117
3.10	Simulated effects of EITC on wage income (LBD model)	117
4.1	The structure of the model	137
4.2	The effect of changes in wages and employer firing propensity (ϕ) on the reward to work	141
4.3	The effect of changes in wages and employer firing propensity (ϕ) on unemployment	141
4.4	The effect of changes in the discount factor on the reward to work	142
4.5	The effect of changes in risk aversion (γ) on the reward to work	142
4.6	The value to dead-end workers of being employed with and without an unemployment voucher	144
4.7	The value to dead-end workers of being employed with and without a wage subsidy	144
4.8	The value to dead-end workers of being unemployed with and without an unemployment voucher	145

4.9   The value to dead-end workers of unemployment at different
      durations with a low-wage subsidy   145
4.10 Change in employment at different durations with an
      unemployment voucher   146
4.11 Change in unemployment at different durations with an
      unemployment voucher   147
4.12 Change in unemployment at different durations with a
      low-wage subsidy   147
4.13 Change in employment at different durations with a
      low-wage subsidy   148
4.14 The value to upwardly mobile workers of being employed
      with and without an unemployment voucher   149
4.15 The value to upwardly mobile workers of being
      unemployed with and without an unemployment voucher   150
4.16 Optimal duration-dependent balanced-budget payroll
      policy with flat wages   151
4.17 Optimal duration-dependent balanced-budget payroll
      policy with increasing wages   151

Tables

2.1	Baseline parameter values	*page* 60
2.2	Outcomes: high skill ($p = 1.4$)	62
2.3	Outcomes: low skill ($p = 0.75$)	62
2.4	Effects of an employment subsidy	65
2.5	Effects of a hiring subsidy	65
2.6	Effects of a "low-skill" subsidy and "high-skill" surtax	68
3.1	Earned Income Tax Credit for 1994	90
3.2	Distribution of households qualifying for the EITC	91
3.3	Distribution of earnings for working female high-school dropouts over the EITC schedule (household heads with children)	92
3.4	Distribution of earnings for working female high-school graduates over the EITC schedule (household heads with children)	93
3.5	Estimated lifecycle progression through the EITC schedule (OJT simulations based on 1994 EITC schedule for two children)	106
3.6	Effects of EITC (OJT model)	109
3.7	Annual compensation necessary to make people indifferent between employment and non-employment (OJT simulations based on 1994 EITC schedule for two children)	110
3.8	Employment rates and average human capital levels (OJT simulations based on 1994 EITC schedule for two children)	111
3.9	Effects of EITC on potential skill levels (OJT simulations based on 1994 EITC schedule for two children)	112
3.10	Effects of EITC on skills supplied to the market (OJT simulations based on 1994 EITC schedule for two children)	114
3.11	Estimated lifecycle progression through the EITC schedule (LBD simulations based on 1994 EITC schedule for two children)	116
3.12	Effects of EITC when imposed (LBD model)	118

3.13 Annual compensation necessary to make people indifferent
      between employment and non-employment (LBD simulations
      based on 1994 EITC schedule for two children)   118
3.14 Employment rates and average human capital levels (LBD
      simulations based on 1994 EITC schedule for two children) 119
3.15 Effects of EITC on potential skill levels (LBD simulations
      based on 1994 EITC schedule for two children)   120
3.16 Effects of EITC on skills supplied to the market (LBD
      simulations based on 1994 EITC schedule for two children) 121
3A.1 Definition of EITC regions for CPS calculations   126
3D.1 Parameter values for the OJT model   128
3D.2 Parameter values for the LBD model   128
3D.3 Goodness of fit (OJT model): weighted sum of squared
      differences   129
3D.4 Goodness of fit (LBD model): weighted sum of squared
      differences   129

Contributors

RICARDO COSSA, University of Chicago, USA

JAMES J. HECKMAN, University of Chicago and the American Bar Foundation, USA

HIAN TECK HOON, Singapore Management University

LANCE LOCHNER, University of Rochester, USA

DALE T. MORTENSEN, Northwestern University, USA

J. MICHAEL ORSZAG, Watson Wyatt, UK

EDMUND S. PHELPS, Columbia University, USA

CHRISTOPHER PISSARIDES, London School of Economics and Political Science, UK

DENNIS J. SNOWER, University of London, UK

Introduction

Edmund S. Phelps

Access to a career and to a livelihood in society's mainstream economy is again a topic of discussion among economists and sociologists. Great value is placed on working-age people having the opportunity to obtain rewarding work in the formal economy and to earn enough in such jobs to be self-sufficient. These are the twin conditions for what is sometimes termed *social inclusion*, or, more aptly, *economic inclusion*.

The central importance of jobs and self-support derives from several human needs. People need to engage their minds and, for most people, jobs are the main means by which they encounter new problems to solve, discover their talents and expand their capabilities. People gain satisfaction from achieving something and experience personal growth from working with others. A great many people also want involvement in their society and, for them, to work in a job in the economy's mainstream is to be a part of society's grand project. Last but not least, the pecuniary reward from working is of both material and symbolic value. People want the dignity brought by self-support and the autonomy brought by having a substantial income of their own to meet their special needs. Earning one's own way – making enough to support one's self at a decent level by society's standards and to be a part of community life – is hugely important for people's self-respect. For these reasons, the *availability* and the *quality* of a country's jobs as well as the wages employers can afford to pay, hence the *productivity* of work, are among life's "primary goods" in John Rawls's terminology. It is no wonder, then, that people want to be included. The recognition of inclusion, by the way, is not new to economics, which has long prized low unemployment, high job satisfaction and high productivity.

Until recent decades, the goal of inclusion was a rallying cry to break down the discriminatory barriers that were depriving women and many minorities from the ample access to the economy and the community that white males had long enjoyed. Commentators did not need to canvass moral philosophy to condemn these barriers. It was (and is) axiomatic that all persons having the same qualification – the same talent and preparation – ought to have the same career chances, regardless of race, religion or gender. And it was understood that the courts could pave the way, without benefit of economic theory and fiscal expertise. Those were simpler times.

Inclusion of the less advantaged

The deficiency of inclusion, remedies for which are the subject of this volume, is the tendency of a great number of the less advantaged, or less qualified, to be marginalized from society and possibly even from the labor force. Not all those whose labor in the market economy would be productive to some positive degree, however small, are found to be employed in the market, even those who would like to work and contribute if offered terms that society could afford.[1] Like the inclusion failure deriving from racial or ethnic or gender bias, this classic inclusion failure is quite old. It must have emerged (or intensified if it was already a problem) when impersonal private ownership of businesses began to pervade the market economy, so that a marginal worker in the family or in that of a neighbor would no longer be employed out of obligation or reciprocity.

The problem involves unequal treatment of persons of unequal marketability, which is philosophically different from unequal treatment of persons of equal ability and preparation. It is a great deal more difficult, since it is impossible to equalize rewards, such as wage rates, without deadening some of the incentives to prepare and to make an effort; more generally, it is impossible to pull up rewards to those on the bottom rung of the ladder without also pulling up rewards on the next rung and the rung after that, and so forth. So the problem cannot be usefully addressed by pretending that it is one of two homogeneous classes, proletarians and the rest; or even three such classes or several.

The marginalization of the less advantaged operates both through a paucity of jobs for them and through pay offers so remote from the earnings of those in the mainstream of the labor force that their morale is impaired or broken. Clearly the system called the market economy does not promptly deliver a viable job for everyone upon request – no matter

---

[1] Understandably, many would at once object to the idea that even people with just an epsilon of productivity should be brought into the market economy or else be deemed an inclusion failure. Thus, many will advocate a positive threshold level that people's productivity must exceed for us to count their non-employment as an inclusion failure. But moral philosophers have not suggested a solution to the problem of what an appropriate threshold level might be if not zero. As a practical matter, however, minimum wage laws remove the problem. One would not want to design and evaluate machinery to pull up wages from so low a level that they would remain below the statutory minimum wage.

how low a wage one is prepared to accept; there is involuntary unemployment. And, although some number of unemployed persons may be justifiable to concentrate the minds of employees on their jobs, the invisible hand is not thought to have restricted unemployment to the optimum level from this point of view. Even if that efficiency maximum prevailed, some workers might be so unlucky from entry to retirement that they never get a career going and earn their own support, which would be inequitable. That is a failure of inclusion. It is not enough to say that all workers had acceptable chances for a career and a decent living. And people cannot buy insurance against missing out on self-support and personal development – on having a life.

The way a market economy determines wage rates also affects inclusion. People are far from identical in their capabilities, and their productivity in terms of market value ranges over a vast spectrum from barely positive productivity at all to dazzling ability. There were times when a deficiency in capabilities did not translate into a deficiency of inclusion. A family farm might involve all the family members, even those only marginally productive. In the modern corporation, managers do not have much left after the demands of shareowners with which to subsidize some workers' employment – especially with the increased competition brought by globalization. As a result, the average pay check even a tenth of the way up the wage distribution is a small fraction of the average pay in the middle – about one-half in the United States and the so-called Anglo-Saxon countries generally. So workers in that region of the distribution, even when they are steadily employed, can hardly achieve the self-support and self-worth once thought to be attainable by all in the working class and have to live in poverty by the standards of the middle class. In turn, the meager pay available to these low-wage workers weakens their job attachment and their productivity, thus forcing up employers' costs. The effect is to reduce low-wage workers' wage rates further and also to reduce their employability, thus driving up their unemployment rate. So, to the deprivations of a low pay rate are added the economic and emotional burdens of joblessness.

A serious decline in the inclusion of less qualified workers swept over the advanced Western economies in the late 1970s and 1980s. None entirely escaped it and, in general, it was not fully offset by the higher employment and elevation of wages brought by the investment booms in several Western economies from 1996 to 2000; in any case, those booms have now largely subsided.[2] Compared with the 1960s, the pay

---

[2] The United States is not an exception to the decline of inclusion in either of its two dimensions. In the last years of the boom, 1998–2000, both relative wages and relative

gap between the low end of the labor market and the middle remains far wider, and, among less educated men, participation in the labor force is still lower and the unemployment rate still higher. (In Europe over the past two decades, France and Germany actually compressed the pay gap and Italy resisted a widening, but they appear to have paid the price with a far greater rise of unemployment and fall of participation among less educated men than elsewhere in Europe.)

One can summarize these observations by saying that the advanced economies have generally suffered an adverse shift of what may be called their *inclusion frontier*. That frontier relates the relative wage in the *lowest-paid* ranks to substantially these workers' absolute unemployment rate – or, more conveniently, their *employment* as a ratio of their number in the labor force. The unemployment rate is a measure of the frequency with which workers join or are discharged into the unemployment pool multiplied by the waiting time that entrants into the low-wage job pool must expect before being called to a job. These two data, the relative wage of the low paid and the proportion of the time they are employed, express their degree of inclusion.

Causes of the lost ground

Today, after considerable investigation, there is some degree of consensus that the deterioration of inclusion is, approximately at any rate, the result of structural forces operating through essentially non-monetary channels – both macro-structural forces and micro-structural ones. From this perspective it appears that most of the decline of inclusion in the Western economies can be explained by the evolution of three macro-structural forces: the economy's productivity growth, personal wealth and the world real rate of interest. The extraordinarily low jobless rates in the so-called "glorious years" from the mid-1950s to the early 1970s are now seen as the product of exceptional circumstances in all three respects. For one thing, the austere level of private wealth in relation to productivity that was a legacy of the war kept wage pressure low enough to permit very high employment; and the sprint of productivity, especially on the Continent where businesses moved to catch up with best technical practice in the

unemployment rates were much improved over their levels a decade earlier. But it is doubtful one could show that the bottom decile of wage earners could afford good housing, clothing and community participation to the same extent the corresponding group in, say, the 1960s could, since the relative wage as measured by the 10/50 ratio – the ratio between the 10th and 50th percentile wage rates in full-time jobs – declined so much over the preceding two and a half decades. Further, both high-school dropouts and (by a smaller margin) those workers with only a high-school diploma had higher reported unemployment in 1998 than in 1970 or 1965, notwithstanding the strong boom.

United States, caused wealth to lag further behind productivity, which lowered wage pressure more. Second, real interest rates throughout the world were low, thanks to the desire to reaccumulate wealth; this and the prospect of continued productivity growth at a fast rate served to lower the expected net cost of capital (net of expected productivity growth), which boosted the wage that businesses could afford to pay and thus the hiring they were willing to do. The United States and the United Kingdom were similarly blessed in some or all respects, though not to the same degree, and so their unemployment rates never reached the record lows recorded on the Continent. Yet the postwar structural boom could not last. Legislatures expanded welfare entitlements in the 1960s, and this rise in *social* wealth appears to have played a role over ensuing years as wages showed upward pressure and unemployment rates moved generally higher and profit shares generally lower. As the technical catch-up neared completion in one country after another in the 1970s, expected future productivity growth slowed from its breakneck speed to a normal pace; the resulting rise in the cost of capital (net of expected productivity growth) dampened hiring, and the resulting slowdown of paychecks relative to wealth generated upward wage pressure. Finally, a further rise of the cost of capital and still more wage pressure resulted from the sharp elevation of the world real rate of interest early in the 1980s. In the United States, of course, such a catch-up did not apply, but there was a substantial though lesser productivity slowdown from 1974 until 1994 and overseas interest rates became a regular object of American worry.[3]

This slump is distinctive not only in being largely structural in nature, but also in the severity of its relative impact on the less advantaged – say, for statistical purposes, those in the least educated group, the high-school dropouts. With few exceptions in the countries of the Organisation for Economic Co-operation and Development (OECD) over the 1980s and neighboring years, the *proportionate* increase in unemployment rate, not just the absolute increase, and the proportionate decrease in wage rates were both greatest in the lowest education category – and generally by a wide margin. Two of the macro-structural forces may have struck the earning power of the less educated with disproportionate force. The rise in the net cost of capital may have penalized the less educated if hiring them posed a greater investment cost relative to their wage than hiring more qualified workers did. And social wealth (social insurance and social assistance) rose steeply from the 1960s into the 1990s in most countries

---

[3] These views are developed and many of them tested in Phelps (1994), Hoon and Phelps (1997) and Phelps and Zoega (1997, 1998). Some of the same views (and others) are also found in Pissarides (1990), Layard, Nickell and Jackman (1991) and Blanchard (1997, 1999). A new perspective is offered in Greenwood (1997).

and the less advantaged got the lion's share of it. At the same time, poor families shared fully in the slowdown of productivity. As a result, particularly in low-productivity areas, work ceased to "pay" for as many as it did decades earlier. It is also plausible that the less advantaged suffered further reversals at the hands of some micro-structural forces: Globalization increased the reach of outsourcing by employers and information technology put an added premium on educated labor.[4]

To address the deficiency of inclusion through governmental action on a large scale – large enough to make a large difference – requires a paradigm shift in political economy that some policy makers are not yet ready to accept. So we are obliged to take up the philosophy of such a step and only then proceed to the business of this volume, which is the engineering of concrete fiscal programs to boost inclusion.

Political economy

A basic question here is whether the deficiency of inclusion among the less advantaged is, to any degree, a problem for society to address through the state. In the view of some observers, low inclusion, however regrettable, is *not* a phenomenon appropriate for *social intervention* – not something to be corrected through collective action by the state.

The reply to that position, a reply dating back to the eighteenth-century Enlightenment, is that a democratic country's formal economy is a project for citizens' mutual gain, so the accessibility of this project and the satisfactoriness of the terms it offers participants are a legitimate object of social policy. Some of the classical economists, with their notion of consumer surplus, suggested that in fact a mutual gain does result, an idea brought up in the Progressive era. A formulation is sometimes found in textbooks today: Just as the gains from foreign trade, which originate in the diversity of national resources, benefit everyone – or *could* be made to do so, if necessary with the help of redistributive taxes and subsidies – so likewise all workers interlinked in a large society's market economy enjoy wages rates superior to those they would earn if they worked alone or in homogeneous teams (at any rate, superior wage rates *could* be arranged through fiscal tools). So there is a "social surplus" that society can distribute in any one of a great many different ways to the diverse kinds of workers without leaving any group with no gain over what it could have if it broke away.[5]

---

[4] A less cursory discussion is in Phelps (1997a). See also Greenwood (1997).

[5] In Phelps (1997b) the economic doctrine of the Scottish Enlightenment is seen as a liberation movement prizing people's release from domestic work within the family or hamlet into the relative freedom, diversity and stimulus of the market economy. On the

The Progressive era first raised the question of the size of the surplus and – a matter of basic principle in any case – the appropriate uses of it. Most took the surplus to be nearly all of what is produced, suggesting, as did Hobhouse (1922), that one who does not collaborate or barter with others would not have any productivity to speak of.[6] Whatever its size, the surplus could be used to add to the rewards of participants who would otherwise earn a very low wage, taking away from others some or all of what the surplus had been adding to their relatively high rewards. Or it could be used to boost the educational preparation of persons who would otherwise be unable to earn more than a very low wage. With the surplus evidently in mind, Theodore Roosevelt sounded the theme of "distributive justice" in his 1912 re-election campaign.[7] Much later, in John Rawls's 1971 book, the surplus is viewed from its first pages as the rock on which any theory of economic justice must build. To his credit, the analysis takes fully into account that steadily boosting marginal tax rates to fund higher wages or education for the disadvantaged, in reducing the incentives of the others to work and save, would actually be lowering the surplus; and that, at some point, the marginal rates would be so high that no further boost in rates would succeed in moving more surplus to workers with the lowest wage. So it is not as if the surplus were some honey pot against which to measure the adequacy of public expenditures and subsidies aimed at a more equitable distribution of pay.

In present times, attention is more apt to be given to the *negative* interactions among people that may arise if an underclass is allowed to develop: *All* suffer a loss of amenities – unsafe streets, drug use among youth, public health hazards, high tax rates for social assistance, and so forth – if large numbers of working-age people are marginalized from work and self-support.[8] A central part of my book *Rewarding Work* (Phelps, 1997a)

social surplus, Paul Samuelson's textbook (1948, 4th edition, 1958: 445) cites Adam Smith's water–diamonds paradox and quotes Progressive era social theorist L.T. Hobhouse (1922: 162–163).

[6] Possibly the surplus is a smallish proportion of what is produced, since there is more behind labor productivity in a country than workers' diversity and specialization. Theoretical calculations by Gilles Saint-Paul and myself put the surplus at roughly 1 percent of the gross domestic product (GDP). (Phelps, 1997a: 141, also cites this result.) In judging the significance of that result, three points must be borne in mind. First, the neoclassical model used is just one model of the many that could be built for studying the question. The specialization of a heterogeneous labor force may produce Smithian learning and externalities. Second, it may produce a diversity of new ideas for new goods and methods. In any case, 1 percent of the GDP in the United States is close to US$100 billion, which far exceeds the net budgetary cost of the modest plan proposed in Phelps (1997a).

[7] Roosevelt's views on the economy are presented in a recent biography (Dalton, 2002).

[8] Although the occasional investigation fails to find an effect of unemployment rates on one or more social indicators, there are many successes. For example, Ernesto Felli and Giovanni Tria (1999) find that regional unemployment rates in Italy correlate pretty well with regional murder rates.

argues that the benefits from reducing these negative externalities through low-wage employment subsidies that draw the marginalized into regular work and self-support would come close to covering the cost of the subsidies.[9]

To commentators unmindful of the classic lines of thought reviewed above, however, deficient inclusion is nothing more than an instance of income inequality and, for some, not the most serious inequality either (if bad at all). On the seriousness issue, it is true that in several countries, upon controlling for a range of factors such as education, pay rates are estimated to discriminate against both women and blacks. Of course it rankles that there should be a systematic pay difference between two apparently equally prepared subgroups, and we must all be sensitive to the historical background of extreme racism and sexism. Yet the extant pay differentials of this kind are no longer garish and they appear to be still trending downwards.[10] By contrast, the inequality between the tenth percentile wage and the median wage is huge in the United States and quite wide in a great many other Western economies.[11]

On the basic issue, the reductionism that takes inclusion failure to be essentially an income inequality, the point is that a deficiency of inclusion – too few employed in society's central economic institution, the market economy, or too few of the employed able to support themselves by working, even full time – has social effects beyond income inequality, wage inequality and inequality in general.[12] Because having a job and earning enough in that job to be independent are crucial in their own

[9] See chapters 4 and 9 in Phelps (1997a).

[10] A paper by Sandra Black and Elizabeth Brainerd (1999) finds that the competition resulting from globalization has induced US companies to reduce costly discrimination against women.

[11] Finis Welch, in his Ely Lecture at the American Economic Association meetings in 1999, held that most Americans would prefer today's vast inequality to the more homogeneous income distribution of the late 1940s when racism and sexism blocked occupational choice and pay. Perhaps so. But the question, if there is one, is whether marginalization of the disadvantaged now is less serious than racism and sexism *now*, not *then*. Take the United States. The wage difference now between childless men and childless women ages 27 to 33 is put at less than 2 percent by the Independent Women's Forum of Washington, DC (*Wall Street Journal*, April 13, 1999, p. 1). In contrast, the wage ratio between the 10th and 50th percentiles of full-time jobs is put at 44 percent in 1986 by Gottschalk and Joyce (1992). In December 2001 the gap between the male unemployment rate and the female rate was equal to zero, whereas the gaps between the average unemployment rate in the bottom education group and the rate in each of the other education groups were very large.

[12] Empirically, inclusion difficulties add to income inequality. Theoretically, though, they might not do so. In a "lifecycle" model of the economy in which successive cohorts of homogeneous workers are born in the unemployment pool and emerge with lifetime jobs, there may be *lifetime equality* because *all* the young suffer *equally* from the inclusion difficulty (for such a model, see Phelps, 1998).

right – no matter how much non-wage income, including the benefits offered by entitlements, may be available – failure to achieve these objectives
is apt to deprive a person of gains in knowledge, information, achieve-
ments, personal growth and self-esteem that would otherwise have been
acquired.[13] The consequences in turn are that the unemployed and the
dependent make poor parents and neighbors, and when a community is
dominated by these problems the effects extend to drug trade and the loss
of public safety. One might think that all this is commonplace wisdom.
"Yet," as Derek Bok said, "we continue to talk . . . as if income statistics
captured the phenomenon in some meaningful way" (Domestic Strategy
Group, 1998: 18).

By its nature, then, the inclusion problem cannot be solved by
"throwing money" in the form of *transfer payments* to those not included.
Receiving income support from the state does not make one a contrib-
utor to society's economy and a member of society who works for what
he has. When the OECD governments expanded the system of entitlements offering transfer payments under various contingencies (illness,
reaching a certain age, etc.), they were meeting a desire of the electorate
for greater security – not for greater inclusion, which had been rising
in the postwar decades and which was already pretty broad in several
of these countries. Unfortunately, these programs have lessened inclusion. That must be so if recent studies are right in confirming that what
lies behind the inclusion difficulty faced by many working-age people –
their low pay rates in relation to their other resources, their low participation rates and their high unemployment rates as a result of their poor
morale – is their low marginal productivity after taxes and any subsidies
relative to the benefits from their private assets and their entitlements.
To legislate still more government transfer payments would worsen the
inclusion problem by making jobholding less competitive as a means
of supporting one's self and thus lowering participation and increasing

---

[13] Another unfortunate effect of viewing deficient inclusion as an instance of income inequality is that it burdens the discussion of inclusion with the baggage of controversy
and confusion about inequality. First of all, an increase in income inequality cannot be
judged out of context to be either good or bad. Yes, it may be that some non-inclusion is
theoretically needed (in the form of positive unemployment) to avoid serious inefficiency
in employee conduct, so there is a theoretical ambiguity there too; but there is a strong
presumption that inclusion at present is far from reaching a level at which it threatens
productivity. Second, many economists appear to think that existing taxation of high
incomes is about right, believing that continuing moderation in marginal tax rates at the
top is serving to pull up after-tax wage rates across the board – hence those of the least
advantaged – by energizing effort and innovation. (Some other economists muster no
interest in income equality whatsoever.) It is possible to stand in that camp, however,
and still believe that a great deal more inclusion, suitably achieved, would yield a pretty
general gain.

unemployment, especially among working-age people with relatively low earning power.

By the same logic, the spread of the underground economy does not solve the problem either. The underground economy, like the welfare state, shrinks and damages the formal economy by weakening performance incentives in formal jobs and weakening the incentive to participate in the formal economy. Working underground may be socially preferable to *welfare*, since at least something is produced, but it is a poor substitute for a job in the legitimate economy. Like the domestic economy of paid housework, the underground economy functions as an escape valve that drives unemployment in the legitimate economy above the level it would be if there were no such escape from unemployment.[14] If that is right, the underground, far from offering a welcome *cushion* of alternative work for people viewed as having irrevocably lost the possibility of employment in the formal sector, ultimately substitutes its inferior jobs – dead-end jobs, jobs with poor conditions that would once have been passed up, jobs that are viable only because of tax evasion and other criminal acts, all work activities that were once rejected – for the good jobs that would otherwise have been created in the formal economy. The personal and social effects of this development may be nearly as stultifying and pernicious as the effects of the entitlements of the welfare state. However, the toleration of both the explosion in welfare entitlements and the expansion of the underground economy is part of the *problem*, not a solution.

I would add that the value of careers in the formal economy depends on the stimuli provided by its organization along capitalist lines. Any country can achieve full employment and high relative wage rates at the low end by sacrificing private enterprise and forgoing decentralized wage-setting. The Soviets did it through central wage-setting and toleration by state enterprises of employee shirking, absenteeism and alcoholism. Yet that system could not offer the job satisfaction and personal growth obtainable

---

[14] When payroll tax rates and income tax rates were increased in the 1970s and 1980s, the *initial* response was a fall of employment in the form of both higher unemployment and lower labor-force participation. In the theoretical perspective of incentive-wage theory, wages were cut insufficiently to accommodate the cost shock because employers knew that further wage cuts, which would be needed to restore employment, would reduce pay *relative to wealth* to such low levels as to have disincentive effects that would actually leave production costs increased on balance. (The collective bargaining perspective tells a parallel story.) Yet, if there existed no underground economy, the *long-term* response would have been a fully accommodating decline of wealth and pay in equal proportion, triggered by the reduction of saving in response to the decrease of employment and earnings; this would have proceeded to the point where employers could afford to offer the same number of jobs as before. In offering escape into subterranean jobs the underground blocks the completion of that adjustment of wealth and wages, thus blocking full recovery of employment in the *formal* economy.

from stimulating jobs and motivating pay. In capitalism, owing to its unplanned and entrepreneurial nature, careers have unforeseeable turns. Most people relish and learn from the novel challenges and changing opportunities presented, and they compare such work favorably with jobs in the public sector. The right objective, therefore, is wide inclusion in *private enterprise*, not more work and better pay anywhere at all. And worthwhile inclusion requires jobs offering real engagement in firms – preferably career-track jobs and in any case full-time jobs, so there is serious involvement with the firm and its workforce rather than just a peripheral and ephemeral presence.

It should be commented that policy measures unshackling private enterprise from *harmful* regulations and harnessing their productivity through *helpful* regulations would for a time boost inclusion indirectly through a resulting expectation of productivity gains (as well as directly through the improvement of employees' absenteeism, shirking and turnover brought about by the resulting increase in the satisfactions from work). An acceleration of productivity in European business would bring a partial recovery of inclusion, just as the deceleration of productivity in Europe decades ago contributed to its decline. Yet it would be unrealistic to suppose that governments could find a way to return to the record-breaking productivity growth rates of the "glorious years." That is why another policy tool must be deployed.

Recent policy responses

The large setback in the inclusion of the less advantaged has posed the question of how governments might best respond. Until recently the discussion focused on the optimum position to assume on the two horns of the dilemma. One camp proposed dismantling union-set pay scales and statutory minimum wage rates propping up pay at the low end, saying that these "rigidities" destroyed jobs and thus operated to expand dependency or increase the underground economy. The other camp opposed moving to greater employment through increased "flexibility," saying that a fall of low-end pay rates or of social transfer payments would widen income inequality. Many in this camp boldly advocated that a statutory minimum wage be created if it did not already exist or be increased if already created as a means to help low-productivity workers as a group. The latter view accepts lower employment in return for higher pay at the low end, while the former would trade off some pay for more jobs. Some at the low end will lose from the one, others from the other.

It is now dawning on policy makers and commentators, in Europe and to some extent in the United States, that countries can engineer a reduction of unemployment *without* a sacrifice of low-end pay and a rise in low-end pay rates *without* a sacrifice of employment – or some of both. This can be done by means of tax-subsidy measures producing a favorable *shift* of the inclusion locus. Already several countries have introduced, some many years ago, fiscal programs aimed to do just that. The Luxembourg Summit of 1999, with its agreement of governments to submit annual reports on progress made and new initiatives taken, has served to intensify governmental attention on the matter.

France, for example, has taken steps starting as far back as 1994 to decrease markedly the payroll tax on the low paid. The size of that part of the social contribution paid by the employer (rather than the employee) now shows a cumulative reduction amounting to about 10 percent of the employer's total wage cost per employee at the lowest (minimum wage) level. The tax paid by low-wage earners for their health insurance, which was about 4 percent of the employee's wage, has also been lifted, with the tax burden shifted to the general social contribution faced by all income receivers. Finally, a flat subsidy of FFr4,000 per employee per year affecting relatively low-wage employees has recently been introduced in connection with the 35-hour workweek. In France as in other economies in recent years, many things have been going on at the same time, so any inference of cause and effect is risky. Nevertheless, there has been a gain relative to trend in employment in the past several years and this gain is weighted toward the low end of the market.

Important initiatives in the same direction have also been taken in the Netherlands. The payroll tax on workers who were unemployed when hired has been reduced by 10 percent for a period of two years and reduced by 13 percent for employees who had been unemployed for more than four years. The traditional exemption in the personal income tax law has been abolished and replaced by a tax credit that taxpayers may apply against the personal income tax liability on their wage income. This "earned-income" tax credit is not politicized, so far at any rate: it applies to older workers as well as younger ones, couples as well as those who are single, the childless as well as parents, men as well as women. This credit amounts to some 9,000 guilders (US$3,000–4,000).

On the other hand, efforts in this direction in some other countries have been far more limited. Typically, those efforts are targeted at one or more relatively narrow groups in the low-wage population. An extremely selective sort of program started up around 1980 in the United States (the Earned Income Tax Credit) and in the United Kingdom (the Family Credit). The original intent of such tax credits was to lift from low-wage people the burden of the proportional tax imposed to finance retirement and other old-age benefits (if only because the working poor had low survival rates). However, a combination of political forces could agree only on tax credits to parents of dependent children having low earned income, the selling point being that the recipients would claim even more money if left in the "welfare trap" than they would if induced to work.

This volume's studies

This volume presents four studies of fiscal instruments – subsidies of one kind or another – that are or might be aimed at boosting employment and pay rates among the relatively low paid. The first of these, by Hian Teck Hoon and myself, examines the effects in our incentive-wage model of a graduated employment subsidy – one offering a higher subsidy the smaller the wage rate, gross or net. Both the open economy and the closed economy and both the short run and the long run are considered. Hoon and I study the theoretical effects on pay rates and employment from bottom to top of the labor force. In every case, we find, the result is a lift to employment as well as to paychecks at the low end of the market. Special attention is paid to the effects on near-bottom wage earners. These effects of the employment subsidy are then contrasted with the effects of a hiring subsidy.

The next chapter, by Dale Mortensen and Christopher Pissarides, uses their version of the search and matching model to study the theoretical effects of a range of fiscal tools that might be legislated in the name of employment creation. It is found, for example, that a hiring subsidy reduces the average duration of unemployment but has an ambiguous effect on the employment rate. The authors also explore the "optimum" mix of the fiscal tools, each one responding to one or more of the market's imperfections.

For some, there is a side-effect of employment subsidies or wage subsidies that could be a serious, possibly fatal, drawback. Their very success in making low-wage jobs more plentiful and better paid might greatly slow the growth of their human capital and thus their future earnings growth. The chapter by James Heckman, Lance Lochner and Ricardo Cossa conducts simulations based on microdata estimates to analyze the outcomes of one kind of subsidy, the Earned Income Tax Credit. Two models of skill formation are used and the outcomes for skill formation are quite sensitive to the model selected. In the standard Becker–Ben Porath model, where skill formation is gained by schooling, the subsidy to wage earnings increases schooling's opportunity cost (the present earnings forgone) without generally increasing the benefit (the gain in future earnings) as much. In a model of "learning-by-doing," which receives more empirical support, the subsidy actually increases skills among the lowest-wage workers whose earnings remain in the phase-in region of the credits schedule. So apparently there may be no tradeoff between boosting wages and boosting skill formation after all.

The chapter by Michael Orszag and Dennis Snower contrasts the effects of low-wage subsidies exhibited in their model with another fiscal instrument, the unemployment voucher – a voucher that unemployed workers can present to the firm hiring them in order to defray some of the hiring costs. As the authors show, both programs operate in their different ways to combat unemployment and to reduce the poverty of the working poor. Which one is better depends upon how much relative weight one puts on raising pay and how much on raising employment.

Those with an interest in ways to raise the inclusion of the least advantaged in the working-age population, and hence an interest in how subsidies of one or another kind would work, will discover a wealth of findings in the four diverse chapters of this volume.

References

Black, S. and E. Brainerd (1999). "Importing Equality? The Effects of Increased Competition on the Gender Wage Gap," Federal Reserve Bank of New York, Staff Report 74, Research and Market Analysis Group, April.

Blanchard, O.J. (1997). "The Medium Term," Brookings Papers on Economic Activity No. 2, 89–141.

(1999). *European Unemployment: The Role of Shocks and Institutions*. Rome: Banca d'Italia.

Dalton, K. (2002). *Theodore Roosevelt: A Strenuous Life*. New York: Alfred Knopf.

Domestic Strategy Group (1998). *Work & Future Society: Where Are the Economy and Technology Taking Us?* Washington, DC: The Aspen Institute.

Felli, E. and G. Tria (1999). "Productivity and Organized Crime in Italy," mimeo, Rome, Università Tor Vergata, June.

Gottschalk, P. and M. Joyce (1992). "Is Earnings Inequality Also Rising in Other Industrialized Countries?" typescript, Boston College, October.

Greenwood, J. (1997). *The Third Industrial Revolution: Technology, Productivity and Income Inequality*. Washington, DC: American Enterprise Press.

Hobhouse, L.T. (1922). *The Elements of Social Justice*. New York: Holt.

Hoon, H.T. and E.S. Phelps (1997). "Growth, Wealth and the Natural Rate: Is Europe's Jobs Crisis a Growth Crisis?" *European Economic Review* **41**: 549–557.

Layard, R., S. Nickell and R. Jackman (1991). *Unemployment: Macroeconomic Performance and the Labour Market*. Oxford: Oxford University Press.

Phelps, E.S. (1994). *Structural Slumps: The Modern Equilibrium Theory of Unemployment, Interest and Assets*. Cambridge, MA: Harvard University Press.

(1997a). *Rewarding Work: How to Restore Participation and Self-Support to Free Enterprise*. Cambridge, MA: Harvard University Press.

(1997b). "A Strategy for Employment and Growth: The Failure of Statism, Welfarism and Free Markets," *Rivista Italiana degli Economisti* **2**(1): 121–128.

(1998). "Moral Hazard and Independent Income in a Modern Intertemporal-Equilibrium Model of Involuntary Unemployment and Mandatory Retirement," in G. Chichilnisky (ed.), *Markets, Information and Uncertainty: Essays in Economic Theory in Honor of Kenneth J. Arrow.* Cambridge: Cambridge University Press.

Phelps, E.S. and G. Zoega (1997). "The Rise and Downward Trend of the Natural Rate," *American Economic Review* **87**(May): 283–289.

(1998). "OECD Unemployment and Natural Rate Theory," *Economic Journal* **108**(May): 782–801.

Pissarides, C.A. (1990). *Equilibrium Unemployment Theory.* Oxford: Blackwell.

Rawls, J. (1971). *A Theory of Justice.* Cambridge, MA: Harvard University Press.

Samuelson, P.A. (1948). *Economics: An Introductory Analysis.* New York: McGraw-Hill, 4th edn, 1958.

Welch, F. (1999). "In Defense of Inequality," *American Economic Review Papers and Proceedings* **89**(May): 1–17.

1 Low-wage employment subsidies in a labor-turnover model of the "natural rate"

Hian Teck Hoon and Edmund S. Phelps

Abstract

This paper models two kinds of wage subsidy in a model of the natural rate having a continuum of workers ranked by their productivity – a flat wage subsidy and a graduated wage subsidy, each financed by a proportional payroll tax. In the small open economy case, with the graduation as specified, we show that both schemes expand employment throughout the distribution; for those whose productivity is sufficiently far below the mean, take-home pay is unambiguously up, though the tax financing lowers take-home pay at the mean and above. For any particular class of workers paid the same amount of the wage subsidy under the two plans, the graduated plan expands employment more. In the closed economy case, employment is increased for workers whose productivity levels are below or equal to the mean but the interest rate is pulled up, and that may cause employment to fall at productivity levels sufficiently far above the mean.

There is considerable agreement that the extraordinarily low commercial productivity of active-age persons in the lower reaches of the distribution relative to median productivity is the number one social problem of our time. In creating a huge wage gap it makes the less productive incapable of supporting a family, or in some cases themselves (in a way that meets community standards of decency at any rate), and having access to mainstream community life. In reducing the wage incentives that private enterprise can afford to offer low-wage workers relative to their other resources and attractions, it worsens unemployment and non-participation. Both sets of effects operate in turn, especially in areas where there is a high concentration of these effects, to increase dependency on welfare and property crime, spread drug use and violence, widen illegitimacy and blight the upbringing of children (Murray, 1984; Phelps, 1994b, 1997; Freeman, 1996; Wilson, 1996).

There is far less agreement on what, if anything, would be useful to do about it. An important line of thinking, however, looks to wage subsidies

This chapter is a revised version of a paper presented at a conference on low-wage employment subsidies sponsored by the Russell Sage Foundation, New York, December 1997.

of one kind or another. The pioneers were Cecil Pigou (1933) and Nicholas Kaldor (1936), who studied the conditions for employment subsidies to be self-financing. Targeted hiring subsidies were championed by Daniel Hamermesh (1978), Michael Hurd and John Pencavel (1981) and Robert Haveman and John Palmer (1982). The employment-expanding effects of a constant employment subsidy were studied by Richard Jackman and Richard Layard (1986). Phelps argued informally for a graduated employment subsidy to raise low-end wage rates (Phelps, 1994a) and to reduce unemployment (Phelps, 1994b) as a counterweight to the welfare system. A hiring subsidy targeted at the long-term unemployed has been championed by Dennis Snower (1994). Wage subsidies were urged to counter the effects of payroll taxes by Jacques Dréze and Edmond Malinvaud (1994). Christopher Pissarides (1996) has studied the effects of such tax relief.

These analyses focus on the subsidies' near-term effects. None of the papers expressly argues that there would be a permanent effect on unemployment. Some of the authors may have thought the effect was only temporary but a way to buy valuable time. To study the long-term effects, however, requires an intertemporal model in which workers accumulate wealth and firms invest in capital of one or more kinds according to expectations of the future and interest rates.

As a comparative exercise, the first section undertakes a neoclassical analysis of the effects in the steady state of a flat (constant) subsidy, financed by a proportional payroll tax on the equilibrium level of man-hours supplied. We show that wealth decumulation serves ultimately to eliminate the employment decline first brought by the tax, and wealth accumulation operates to eliminate all the employment gains brought by the subsidy. The employment effect is ultimately neutralized, although the take-home wage is increased for low-wage workers.

We then shift to the theory of the natural rate of unemployment. Using our labor-turnover model, with its incentive wage, we study two employment subsidies: a flat (constant) subsidy and a graduated subsidy that decreases with the wage rate and vanishes asymptotically at the top – each program financed by a flat-rate payroll tax (as if resulting external benefits brought no revenue gains). In this model (Phelps, 1968, 1994c; Hoon and Phelps, 1992), quitting by employees poses an incentive problem for the firm, since it must invest in the firm-specific training of workers to make them functioning employees and such an investment is lost whenever an employee quits. The problem prompts firms to drive up the going wage. This leads in turn to involuntary unemployment in labor-market equilibrium. Our 1992 paper posited worker-savers in overlapping cohorts to obtain a general equilibrium framework with which to endogenize the rate of interest or the accumulation of net foreign assets. This chapter introduces a continuum of workers differentiated by productivity in each cohort.

The gist of our findings can be indicated. Owing to incentive-wage considerations, the two schemes permanently expand employment in the long run. The proportional payroll tax used to finance the subsidy is neutral for employment. With employment unchanged, the payroll tax lowers take-home pay in the same proportion for every type of worker but non-wage income is also reduced by the same proportion. As a result, the incentive-wage condition is invariant to the proportional payroll tax in the long run. The subsidy, however, is non-neutral. If, before, a penny increase in hourly labor compensation by the firm had a marginal benefit equal to marginal cost at the original employment rate, it must now have a marginal benefit less than the marginal cost because, with take-home pay up, since it drives a wedge between take-home pay and hourly labor compensation (net of subsidy) that additional penny now has a smaller impact on quitting. Hence firms cut their hourly compensation, and as a result employment is expanded throughout the distribution in the long run.

For low-wage workers, there is an added boost to employment in the short run. Given net wealth and the interest rate, the higher take-home pay induces a decline in the propensity to quit. The result is a rightward shift of the zero-profit curve and an additional rightward shift of the incentive-wage curve on top of the wedge caused by the subsidy. In the long run, wealth accumulation leads to a proportionate rise of non-wage income at given employment, thus shifting the zero-profit curve back to its original position. The incentive-wage curve also shifts leftward but not by enough to eliminate the added boost. The net result, then, for low-wage workers is that the expansionary effect on employment is even larger in the short run than in the long run.

The long-run question in the closed economy case is the subsidies' effect on the rate of interest and the effect in turn on wages and employment. Here we find that, if the zero-profit curve is elastic, aggregate wealth supply is increased, but it increases by less than the increase in asset demand. The result is a rise in the rate of interest. However, for workers whose productivity levels are below or equal to the mean, employment is expanded; at productivities far enough below the mean, take-home pay is also increased.

We also found that the graduated scheme, besides having (for the same subsidy rate at the bottom) a lighter budgetary burden than the constant subsidy, has an extra downward impact on hourly labor cost, as firms moderate wage rates above the bottom to win a larger subsidy, with the result that employment receives an extra boost. Such an effect raises the fear that some middle-wage workers would see their wage reduced on balance. We show, however, that unless the subsidy tapers off too fast no such wage effect occurs. Finally, we show that the gross hiring rate is increased the most for low-wage workers.

The paper is organized as follows. Section 1 analyzes the effects of a flat (constant) subsidy in a neoclassical model. Section 2 presents the basic features of the labor-turnover model with a continuum of workers exhibiting constant marginal training cost. Section 3 studies the incidence of the subsidies in the steady-state, general equilibrium model of the small open economy, and section 4 analyzes the closed economy case. Section 5 briefly discusses the case of rising marginal training cost in the small open economy case. Section 6 concludes.

1   Neoclassical theory

We follow the treatment by Olivier Blanchard (1985) of finitely lived agents with no bequest in a one-sector setup (see Kanaginis and Phelps, 1994, and Phelps, 1994c: ch. 16.) In each cohort, the workers form a continuum when ranked by their respective potential productivity levels. The productivity, or ability, of worker input at location i in this continuum is measured by a labor-augmenting, hence Harrod-neutral, parameter denoted Λ_i. There is a known and unvarying distribution of Λ_i in the working population, which we normalize to one. The proportion of workers with productivity level Λ_i or less is $G(\Lambda_i)$ and the density function is $g(\Lambda_i) = G'(\Lambda_i)$. We call a worker with productivity level Λ_i a type-i worker.

Each agent of type i derives utility from consumption and leisure, which we assume are additively separable and take the log form. He or she has a finite life and faces an instantaneous probability of death θ that is constant throughout life. Solving the agent's problem, and denoting aggregate variables by capital letters, we obtain $C_i = (\theta + \rho)[H_i + W_i]$ and $(\bar{L} - L_i)/C_i = 1/v_i^{\mathrm{h}}$, where C_i is consumption, L_i is labor supply, H_i is human wealth, and W_i is nonhuman wealth per member of the type-i workforce. Here ρ is the time preference parameter, $\bar{L}$ is total time available, and v_i^{h} is the real hourly household wage received by a type-i worker, which is related to the hourly labor cost to the firm of a type-i worker, v_i^{f}, by $v_i^{\mathrm{f}} \equiv (1 + \tau)v_i^{\mathrm{h}} - s_i$, τ being the proportional payroll tax rate. Under the flat subsidy scheme, s_i equals s^{F}, a constant. Under a graduated subsidy scheme, s_i is a decreasing function of the wage paid by the firm to each type-i worker, denoted $s_i = S(v_i^{\mathrm{f}})$, and tapers off asymptotically. We impose throughout the conditions $S'(v_i^{\mathrm{f}}) < 0$ and $|S'(v_i^{\mathrm{f}})| < 1$.

In the small open economy, the path of the domestic interest rate conforms to the exogenously given world interest rate, r^*: $r = r^*$, r^*

a constant > 0. The level of net external assets adjusts endogenously to bring about this condition. The steady-state H_i equals $v_i^h L_i/(r^* + \theta)$ and non-wage income of a type-i worker is given by $y_i^w \equiv (r^* + \theta)W_i$, θW_i being actuarial dividend. In the steady state, setting $\dot{C}_i = 0$, we also have $r^* = \rho + [\theta(\theta + \rho)W_i/C_i]$. This can be rewritten, after some substitutions, as

$$r^* = \rho + \frac{\theta}{1 + \left(\frac{v_i^h \bar{L}}{y_i^w}\right)\left(\frac{L_i}{\bar{L}}\right)}. \tag{1.1}$$

The steady-state labor supply relation in manhours can also be expressed as

$$\frac{L_i}{\bar{L}} = \frac{1 - \left[\frac{\theta+\rho}{r^*+\theta}\right]\left(\frac{v_i^h \bar{L}}{y_i^w}\right)^{-1}}{1 + \left[\frac{\theta+\rho}{r^*+\theta}\right]}. \tag{1.2}$$

Turning to the production side, let the production function be written as $Y = [\int_{\underline{\Lambda}}^{\infty} \Lambda_i L_i g(\Lambda_i) d\Lambda_i] f(K/\int_{\underline{\Lambda}}^{\infty} \Lambda_i L_i g(\Lambda_i) d\Lambda_i)$, where $\underline{\Lambda}$ is the minimum productivity level and K is capital stock. Firms' optimal choice of labor and the capital–labor ratio, $k \equiv (K/\int_{\underline{\Lambda}}^{\infty} \Lambda_i L_i g(\Lambda_i) d\Lambda_i)$, imply

$$\frac{v_i^f}{\Lambda_i} = f(k) - kf'(k); \tag{1.3}$$

$$r^* = f'(k). \tag{1.4}$$

The given world interest rate, r^*, pins down the optimal capital–labor ratio, k. Consequently, the wage paid by the firm, v_i^f, is pinned down, being directly proportional to Λ_i. Observe that the wage-to-non-wage income ratio in (1.1) is an implicit function of r^* at each L_i:

$$\frac{v_i^h \bar{L}}{y_i^w} = \Upsilon\left(r^* - \rho, \frac{L_i}{\bar{L}}\right); \quad \Upsilon_1 < 0, \; \Upsilon_2 < 0. \tag{1.5}$$

Using this in (1.2), we obtain a reduced-form labor supply relation in the steady state:

$$\frac{L_i}{\bar{L}} = \frac{1 - \left[\frac{\theta+\rho}{r^*+\theta}\right]\left[\Upsilon\left(r^* - \rho, \frac{L_i}{\bar{L}}\right)\right]^{-1}}{1 + \left[\frac{\theta+\rho}{r^*+\theta}\right]}. \tag{1.6}$$

This equation uniquely determines the labor supply in manhours and is independent of the tax and subsidy rates. It is also independent of Λ_i.

To understand this result, we notice that the labor demand curve in the $(L_i/\bar{L}, v_i^f)$ plane is infinitely elastic. With wealth and hence y_i^w given, the labor supply schedule is upward sloping. Under a balanced-budget policy, the flat subsidy case yields a convenient expression for the tax rate, namely, $\tau = s^F/v^h_{\text{mean}}$, where $v^h_{\text{mean}} \equiv \int_{\underline{\Lambda}}^{\infty} v^h_i g(\Lambda_i)d\Lambda_i$. For an employee whose $\Lambda_i < \Lambda_{\text{mean}}$, the tax liability (τv^h_i) is therefore less than the subsidy (s^F). Hence, at given y^w_i, low-wage workers increase their equilibrium labor supply. Wealth accumulation then brings their y^w_i up until the original v^h_i/y^w_i is restored. On the other hand, for employees whose $\Lambda_i > \Lambda_{\text{mean}}$, their v^h_i is reduced. Such high-wage workers decumulate wealth until once again the original v^h_i/y^w_i is restored. Thus, in the long run, the tax-subsidy scheme is neutral for employment for all workers throughout the distribution. A similar argument holds for the graduated subsidy scheme.

In the closed economy case, the essential task is to endogenize the rate of interest. One approach to the problem is to work toward a diagram involving an asset demand curve and a wealth supply schedule, the intersection giving us the general equilibrium rate of interest. Using the following two conditions:

$$r = \rho + \frac{\theta}{1 + \left(\frac{v^h_i \bar{L}}{y^w_i}\right)}, \tag{1.7}$$

$$\frac{L_i}{\bar{L}} = \frac{1 - \left[\frac{\theta+\rho}{r+\theta}\right]\left(\frac{v^h_i \bar{L}}{y^w_i}\right)^{-1}}{1 + \left[\frac{\theta+\rho}{r+\theta}\right]}, \tag{1.8}$$

we prove in the appendix that we can write $L_i/\bar{L}$ as a decreasing function of r, given ρ and θ, that is,

$$\frac{L_i}{\bar{L}} = \psi(r;\rho,\theta); \quad \psi'(r) < 0. \tag{1.9}$$

Using the firm's optimal condition $r = f'(k)$ and (1.9), the aggregate asset demand given by

$$A = k\int_{\underline{\Lambda}}^{\infty} \Lambda_i \bar{L}\psi(r)g(\Lambda_i)d\Lambda_i \tag{1.10}$$

is decreasing in r.

The average supply of wealth per member of the type-i workforce is obtained by substituting $y^w_i \equiv (r+\theta)W_i$ in (1.8):

$$W_i = \left[\frac{(v^h_i \bar{L})\left(\frac{L_i}{\bar{L}}\right)}{r+\theta}\right]\left[\frac{r-\rho}{\theta+\rho-r}\right]. \tag{1.11}$$

Excluding the case where $r - \rho > \theta$, we have a well-defined steady state with the righthand side of (1.11) being unambiguously positive. Observe that the first bracketed term in (1.11) is simply human wealth per type-i

worker and, for a given after-tax real wage $(v_i^h L_i)$, human wealth, H_i, is decreasing in r. On this account, W_i falls as r rises. On the other hand, a rise of r has a positive effect on W_i on account of the second bracketed term, W_i/H_i. The total supply of wealth per worker is given by $W \equiv \int_{\underline{\Lambda}}^{\infty} W_i g(\Lambda_i) d\Lambda_i$. Using (1.11), we obtain

$$W = \left[\frac{r - \rho}{(\theta + \rho - r)(r + \theta)} \right] \int_{\underline{\Lambda}}^{\infty} v_i^h L_i g(\Lambda_i) d\Lambda_i.$$

Under a balanced budget, we get

$$W = \left[\frac{r - \rho}{(\theta + \rho - r)(r + \theta)} \right] \int_{\underline{\Lambda}}^{\infty} v_i^f L_i g(\Lambda_i) d\Lambda_i. \tag{1.12}$$

Using $(v^f/\Lambda_i) = f(k) - kf'(k)$ and (1.9), and noting that k is a decreasing function of r, we obtain an expression of total wealth supply as a function of the rate of interest:

$$W = \left[\frac{r - \rho}{(\theta + \rho - r)(r + \theta)} \right] \int_{\underline{\Lambda}}^{\infty} [f(k) - kf'(k)] \psi(r) \bar{L} \Lambda_i g(\Lambda_i) d\Lambda_i. \tag{1.13}$$

What is the shape of the supply of wealth? There are two opposing forces. In the general equilibrium, an increase of r lowers the real wage as well as the supply of manhours; and, as remarked above, it lowers the present value of these expected earnings. So human wealth is reduced. However, the second bracketed term in (1.11) works to increase the desired supply of wealth as r rises. At r sufficiently low that W_i is at or near zero, the former effects are outweighed by the latter, though at sufficiently high r the opposite may occur. Hence the per worker supply of wealth schedule is upward sloping initially but at very high r may bend backward. In the same plane, per worker demand for the domestic assets is downward sloping. We will suppose that the equilibrium r is unique or that only the lowest equilibrium r is empirically relevant (see figure 1.1). The important thing to observe from (1.10) and (1.13) is that the pair of equations are independent of the tax-subsidy parameters. Hence the balanced-budget tax-subsidy policy is neutral for the rate of interest and, consequently, also neutral for employment.[1] Nevertheless, for low-wage workers, their take-home pay is increased.

---

[1] Another way to see that the policy is neutral for the rate of interest is to use the requirement that aggregate supply be equal to aggregate demand. Equating the aggregate demand to aggregate supply in the equation, $(r - \rho) \int_{\underline{\Lambda}}^{\infty} C_i g(\Lambda_i) d\Lambda_i = \theta(\theta + \rho) \int_{\underline{\Lambda}}^{\infty} W_i g(\Lambda_i) d\Lambda_i$, we obtain, $r = \rho + [\theta(\theta + \rho)k/f(k)]$, which, noting that k is decreasing in r, determines the general equilibrium r independently of the tax-subsidy parameters.

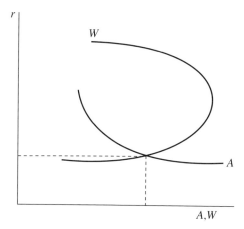

Figure 1.1 *Wealth supply and asset demand*

2 Basic features of the economy in modern equilibrium theory

The preceding neoclassical theory has difficulty explaining why, under plausible assumptions, the policy shift and other aggregate shocks experienced in recent decades should cause large changes in equilibrium labor input and national income. That is in part because the theory does not allow for *unemployment*; rather, changes in labor input are attributable entirely to variations in the work week.

To study the effects of the tax-subsidy schemes on the equilibrium path of unemployment, we need to draw on modern equilibrium theory, which sees unemployment as structural in nature and traces its vicissitudes to changes in the structure of the economy (Phelps, 1994c). At the center of this theory is the relationship between the firm and the employee arising from their incentives in the modern setting of asymmetric information. The economics of incentive (or efficiency) wages plays a key role in generating involuntary unemployment and shaping its equilibrium path.

There are many identical firms. For convenience we may think of them as fixed in number (normalized to one) and equal in size. Consider the representative firm j. Its problem is to choose the wage and hiring–training policies that maximize

$$\int_0^\infty \int_{\underline{\Lambda}}^\infty N_{jit}\{\Lambda_i[1-\beta h_{jit}]-v_{jit}^{\mathrm{f}}\}g(\Lambda_i)e^{-\int_0^t r_v dv}d\Lambda_i dt,$$

which is the present value of the stream of real quasi-rents, subject to

$$\dot{N}_{jit} = N_{jit}\left[h_{jit} - \zeta\left(\frac{z_{it}^{he}}{v_{jit}^{h}}, \frac{y_{it}^{w}}{v_{jit}^{h}}\right) - \theta\right]$$

and given N_{ji0}. Note that s_i is implicit in v_{ji}^{h} and v_{ji}^{f}, given τ. (Since to simplify we will initially work with constant marginal training cost, we also assume that h_{jit} is bounded, $0 \le h_{jit} \le \bar{h}$.) Here, N_{jit} is the stock of type-i employees at the representative firm j taken as a ratio to the type-i workforce (equivalently, the rate of employment among type-i workers), βh_{jit} is the fraction of their working time type-i employees devote to training new hires, h_{jit} is the gross hiring rate of new type-i recruits, ζ similarly measured is the quit rate, and z_{it}^{he} is a proxy for the expected value of real wage earnings of a type-i worker employed at firm j if he or she quits.[2]

We may write the current-value Hamiltonian as

$$\int_{\Lambda}^{\infty} \Big\{ \Lambda_i[1 - \beta h_{jit}] - v_{jit}^{f}$$
$$+ q_{jit}\big[h_{jit} - \zeta\big(z_{it}^{he}/v_{jit}^{h}, y_{it}^{w}/v_{jit}^{h}\big) - \theta\big]\Big\} N_{jit}g(\Lambda_i)d\Lambda_i,$$

where q_{jit} is the co-state variable.[3] It measures the shadow value of a type-i worker after training by the employer. First-order necessary conditions (which are also sufficient under our assumptions) are given by

$$\left.\begin{array}{ll} h_{jit} = \bar{h} & \text{if } q_{jit} > \Lambda_i\beta; \\ h_{jit} = 0 & \text{if } q_{jit} < \Lambda_i\beta; \\ h_{jit} \in [0, \bar{h}] & \text{if } q_{jit} = \Lambda_i\beta; \end{array}\right\} \qquad (1.14)$$

$$N_{jit}\left\{-1 + q_{jit}\left[\left(\frac{z_{it}^{he}}{v_{jit}^{h2}}\right)\zeta_1 + \left(\frac{y_{it}^{w}}{v_{jit}^{h2}}\right)\zeta_2\right]\frac{dv_{jit}^{h}}{dv_{jit}^{f}}\right\} = 0; \qquad (1.15)$$

$$\dot{q}_{jit} - r_t q_{jit} = -\left\{\Lambda_i - v_{jit}^{f} - q_{jit}\left[\zeta\left(\frac{z_{it}^{he}}{v_{jit}^{h}}, \frac{y_{it}^{w}}{v_{jit}^{h}}\right) + \theta\right]\right\}; \qquad (1.16)$$

$$\lim_{t\to\infty} \exp^{-\int_0^t r_v dv} q_{jit} N_{jit} g(\Lambda_i) = 0. \qquad (1.17)$$

The equations represented by (1.14) characterize the optimal number of new hires. In the case arising in the steady-state analysis below, the shadow

---

[2] The quit rate function has the following first derivatives: $\zeta_1 > 0$ and $\zeta_2 > 0$. By virtue of the firm's second-order condition for maximization, $\zeta_{11} > 0$ and $\zeta_{22} > 0$. We also make the assumption that an increase in the non-wage income raises a worker's marginal propensity to quit with respect to wage prospects elsewhere, that is, $\zeta_{12} > 0$.

[3] The flow of output at firm j is then given by $\int_{\Lambda}^{\infty} \Lambda_i[1 - \beta h_{jit}] N_{jit}g(\Lambda_i)d\Lambda_i$.

value of a trained worker is equal to the marginal training cost in output terms. Equation (1.15) gives the optimal tradeoff between real wage and turnover cost, equating the marginal cost of raising v_i^f to the marginal benefit. Equation (1.16) relates the shadow value of functional employees to the total marginal benefit of having one more employee. The transversality condition is in (1.17). These equations summarize the conditions that have to be satisfied for the typical firm.

To move to the equilibrium conditions, we use the Salop–Calvo approximation for z_{it}^{he}, namely, $z_{it}^{he} = N_{it}^e v_{it}^{he}$. (Using the exit rate from the unemployment pool would not differ in the steady state.) On any equilibrium (correct expectations) path with identical firms, $v_{jit}^h = v_{it}^h = v_{it}^{he}$ and $N_{jit} = 1 - u_{it} \equiv N_{it} = N_{it}^e$. Hence we obtain a subsystem of equations in the equilibrium path of the economy. For any exogenously given path of the instantaneous real interest rates, this subsystem is

$$\dot{q}_{it} = q_{it}\left[\zeta\left(N_{it}, \frac{y_{it}^w}{v_{it}^h}\right) + \theta + r_t\right] - \left[\Lambda_i - v_{it}^f\right]; \tag{1.18}$$

$$\dot{N}_{it} = N_{it}\left[h_{it} - \zeta\left(N_{it}, \frac{y_{it}^w}{v_{it}^h}\right) - \theta\right]; \tag{1.19}$$

$$N_{it}\left\{-1 + q_{it}\left[\left(\frac{N_{it}}{v_{it}^h}\right)\zeta_1 + \left(\frac{y_{it}^w}{v_{it}^{h2}}\right)\zeta_2\right]\frac{dv_{it}^h}{dv_{it}^f}\right\} = 0. \tag{1.20}$$

3 Open-economy incidence of tax subsidy schemes

In steady state, $\dot{N}_{it} = 0$. This and (1.19) give the steady-state employment (SSE) condition that hires balance quits and mortality:

$$h_i = \zeta\left(N_{it}, \frac{y_{it}^w}{v_{it}^h}\right) + \theta. \tag{1.21}$$

This implies that $q_i = \Lambda_i\beta$.

With $\dot{q}_{it} = 0$ in (1.18) and $q_i = \Lambda_i\beta$, the zero-profit (ZP) condition that quasi-rents cover interest and depreciation on training becomes

$$\frac{v_i^f}{\Lambda_i} = 1 - \beta\left[\zeta\left(N_i, \frac{y_i^w}{v_i^h}\right) + \theta + r^*\right], \tag{1.22}$$

where r^* is substituted for the domestic interest rate. Since quitting is increasing in N_i and y_i^w, the zero-profit wage must be decreasing in those variables.

Assuming that the employment rate is always strictly positive, we obtain from (1.20) the incentive-wage (IW) condition for the hourly compensation that minimizes compensation plus training cost. The cost per employee of paying a penny more in annual wages is one. The cost saving, or benefit, per employee of doing so is the opportunity cost of replacing each defector, $\beta\Lambda_i$, times the number of annual quits per employee that would be saved. Equating these two gives

$$1 = \beta\Lambda_i \left[N_i\zeta_1 + \left(\frac{y_i^w}{v_i^h}\right)\zeta_2 \right] \left[\left(\frac{1}{v_i^h}\right)\left(\frac{dv_i^h}{dv_i^f}\right) \right]. \tag{1.23}$$

The flat (constant) subsidy case gives

$$1 = \beta\Lambda_i \left[N_i\zeta_1 + \left(\frac{y_i^w}{v_i^h}\right)\zeta_2 \right] \left[\frac{1}{1+\tau} \bigg/ \frac{v_i^f + s^F}{1+\tau} \right]$$

$$= \beta\Lambda_i \left[N_i\zeta_1 + \left(\frac{y_i^w}{v_i^h}\right)\zeta_2 \right] \left[\frac{1}{v_i^f + s^F} \right], \tag{1.24}$$

since $dv_i^h/dv_i^f \equiv 1/(1+\tau)$ and $v_i^h \equiv (v_i^f + s^F)/(1+\tau)$. The graduated subsidy case gives

$$1 = \beta\Lambda_i \left[N_i\zeta_1 + \left(\frac{y_i^w}{v_i^h}\right)\zeta_2 \right] \left[\frac{1 + S'\left(v_i^f\right)}{v_i^f + S\left(v_i^f\right)} \right]. \tag{1.25}$$

Notice that (1.25) can be satisfied as an equality only if $|S'(v_i^f)| < 1$. If $|S'(v_i^f)| > 1$, each firm would find it profitable to drive the wage all the way down in order to gain a higher subsidy.

The third general equilibrium condition arises from the firms' assets. The assets are the investments in their employees, the ownership claims to which – the equity shares – generate non-wage income and have an equilibrium value. As before, we use the Blanchard–Yaari setup to generate, in steady state, the equation:

$$r^* = \rho + \frac{\theta}{1 + \left(\frac{v_i^h}{y_i^w}\right) N_i}. \tag{1.26}$$

This condition makes the non-wage-income-to-wage ratio an implicit function of the unemployment rate and of the interest rate:

$$\frac{y_i^w}{v_i^h} = \Omega(r^* - \rho, N_i), \quad \Omega_1 > 0, \Omega_2 > 0. \tag{1.27}$$

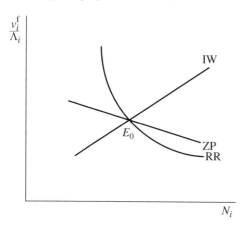

Figure 1.2 *Labor, product and capital market equilibrium*

3.1 Long-run effects of the flat subsidy

Substituting (1.27) into (1.22) and (1.24) gives the reduced-form system in the flat subsidy case:

$$\frac{v_i^f}{\Lambda_i} = 1 - \beta[\zeta(N_i, \Omega(r^* - \rho, N_i)) + \theta + r^*], \tag{1.28}$$

$$\frac{v_i^f}{\Lambda_i} + \frac{s^F}{\Lambda_i} = \beta[N_i \zeta_1(N_i, \Omega(r^* - \rho, N_i))$$
$$+ \Omega(r^* - \rho, N_i)\zeta_2(N_i, \Omega(r^* - \rho, N_i))]. \tag{1.29}$$

Suppose that initially the ad valorem payroll tax rate is zero and the subsidy is also zero. Equation (1.28) can be represented as a downward-sloping zero-profit schedule and (1.29) can be depicted as an upward-sloping wage curve in the Marshallian plane shown in figure 1.2. Examining (1.26), and recalling that in the absence of the tax-subsidy scheme $v_i^* \equiv v_i^f$, notice that we can also draw a family of hyperbolas in figure 1.2 with each hyperbola lying north-east corresponding to a higher level of y_i^w. Note also that when the ZP curve cuts the hyperbola from below, as we have drawn in figure 1.2, the labor cost elasticity of labor demand is implied to exceed one. (In that case, as we shall see, the proportionate increase of N_i effected by the subsidy exceeds the proportionate decrease of v_i^f/Λ_i that the increased N_i induces so that, on balance, the product $(v_i^f/\Lambda_i) N_i$ is up.) The algebraic slope of the zero-profit curve is given by $-\beta[\zeta_1 + \zeta_2 \Omega_2]$, which, in the absence of any other factors leading to diminishing returns to labor, depends only on the sensitivity of the quit function to the economy-wide rate of employment (or unemployment). The zero-profit curve slopes downward both because a lower rate of unemployment implies a tighter labor market, which induces higher quits, and because it implies a higher non-wage income-to-wage ratio, which also raises the propensity to quit. For the United States over the period 1931–1962, Eagly (1965) obtains an estimate of the elasticity of the quit rate with respect to the unemployment rate that is equal to -0.634.[4] If we accept that, in the equilibrium steady-state scenario we are considering, the quit rate does not vary much with movements in the employment rate, the zero-profit curve will be somewhat flat, that is, the labor cost elasticity of the zero-profit curve will be high. We also notice that the same diagram (figure 1.2) represents the equilibrium for every type-i worker. The employment rate, N_i, the real effective wage, v_i^f/Λ_i, and the non-wage income taken as a ratio to productivity level, y_i^w/Λ_i, are the same for every type-i worker, so the real wage, v_i^f, is twice as high for a worker who is twice as productive as another worker.[5] The non-wage income, y_i^w, corresponding to the hyperbola passing through E_0 is also twice as high for a worker who is twice as productive as another worker.

Consider now the long-run employment effects of a flat (constant) subsidy. The derivative of N_i with respect to s^F is calculated to be

$$\frac{dN_i}{ds^F} = \frac{\Lambda_i^{-1}}{\beta[2(\zeta_1 + \zeta_2\Omega_2) + N_i(\zeta_{11} + \zeta_{12}\Omega_2) + \Omega(\zeta_{21} + \zeta_{22}\Omega_2)]} > 0 \tag{1.30}$$

for every type i. The argument that this inequality is unambiguously positive is the following. Assume that there was no change in unemployment so that we were at an unchanged point (N_i, v_i^f) on the zero-profit curve and firms have returned to the original point that they were at before. The proportional payroll tax, taken by itself, has two effects. First, a penny

---

[4] Looking at the effects of wage differentials on quits, Krueger and Summers (1988: 280) find that "at the mean the elasticity of quits with respect to the wage premium is $-.07/.26 = -.27$." They reason that, taken together, "these results imply that a 10 per cent increase in the wage differential brings about a .3 per cent increase in output through reduced quits alone. This suggests that although turnover does adversely affect output, reductions in turnover alone are not sufficient to justify wage premiums of the magnitude actually observed unless fixed costs of hiring are very high or labor's share in output is very low."

[5] The equalization of unemployment rate result depends on the assumption that the marginal training cost in *manhours*, β, is the same across all types of workers. If we have $\beta_i > \beta_j$, then it can be shown that the unemployment rate for type-i workers will be higher than that for type-j workers. Note that this assumption is consistent with $\Lambda_i\beta_i < \Lambda_j\beta_j$, that is, although the marginal training cost for type-i workers is higher when measured in manhours, it could be lower when measured in terms of output on account of its lower productivity.

increase in v_i^f increases v_i^h by only a fraction of a penny, namely, $1/(1+\tau)$. This lowers the marginal benefit of a penny increase in v_i^f. Second, the proportional payroll tax lowers v_i^h and, under correct expectations, v_i^{he}, in the same proportion for every type i. With the employment rate unchanged, y_i^w would also be reduced by the same proportion. Then each additional penny received by an employee now has a greater impact on v_i^h taken as a ratio to expected real wage earnings elsewhere and taken as a ratio to non-wage income, so that the salutary effect on quitting is increased. Through this channel the marginal benefit of a penny increase in v_i^f is increased. If, instead of financing the subsidy, the proceeds from the payroll tax were, say, thrown into the sea, the two effects would exactly cancel out, leaving employment unaffected. There is, however, a third effect arising from the presence of the constant subsidy. In the presence of the subsidy, an additional penny received by an employee has a smaller impact on v_i^h/v_i^{he} and v_i^h/y_i^w, so that the salutary effect on quitting is reduced. In the general equilibrium involving correct expectations and long-run capital market equilibrium, the incentive-wage condition can be written as

$$1 = \beta\Lambda_i[N_i\zeta_1 + \Omega(r^* - \rho, N_i)\zeta_2]\left[\frac{1}{1+\tau}\bigg/\frac{v_i^f + s^F}{1+\tau}\right].$$

We can see from the righthand side of this equation that the two effects arising from the presence of $(1+\tau)$ exactly cancel out. This implies that in the long run, after wealth has fully adjusted, the payroll tax is neutral for employment. It follows that, if a penny increase in v_i^f had a marginal benefit equal to marginal cost at the original employment rate, it must now have a marginal benefit less than the marginal cost. Hence firms cut their v_i^f and employment is expanded as a result.

We can see that, with the same dollar amount of wage subsidy given to each type-i worker, less productive workers enjoy a higher subsidy relative to their productivity level. In figure 1.3 we show that the employment effect is larger for less productive workers as their wage curve is shifted further down than that for more productive workers.

Consider now the long-run wage effects of the flat subsidy. We note that, under a balanced-budget policy, the following relationship holds:

$$\int_{\underline{\Lambda}}^{\infty} s^F N_i g(\Lambda_i)d\Lambda_i = \int_{\underline{\Lambda}}^{\infty} \tau v_i^h N_i g(\Lambda_i)d\Lambda_i.$$

As noted earlier, around an equilibrium with no tax subsidy, N_i is equal for every type i. It follows that the budget constraint can be simplified to $\tau = s^F/v_{\text{mean}}^h$, where $v_{\text{mean}}^h \equiv \int_{\underline{\Lambda}}^{\infty} v_i^h g(\Lambda_i)d\Lambda_i$. Using this, and noting that around a zero tax-subsidy equilibrium $(v_i^h/v_{\text{mean}}^h) = (\Lambda_i/\Lambda_{\text{mean}})$, it

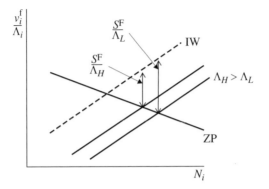

Figure 1.3 *Effects of a flat subsidy*

is straightforward to show that

$$\frac{dv_i^h}{ds^F}\bigg|_{\tau=0} = \frac{\eta_{ZP}}{\eta_{ZP}+\eta_{IW}} - \frac{\Lambda_i}{\Lambda_{mean}}, \tag{1.31}$$

where η_{ZP} and η_{IW} are the elasticities of the zero-profit and wage curves, respectively. For a worker whose Λ_i is sufficiently low, say $\Lambda_i \to \underline{\Lambda} \to 0$, the derivative of v_i^h with respect to s^F is unambiguously positive. But employment is expanded everywhere.

3.2   Short-run effects of the flat subsidy

Consider now briefly the short run in which wealth and y_i^w are given. Here the subsidy provides an additional boost to employment. With net wealth and interest unchanged, the increased take-home pay leads workers to value their job more highly. This has the effect, at any employment rate, of raising the firm's real demand wage as the propensity to quit is reduced. Around a zero tax-subsidy equilibrium, the vertical shift of the iso-y_i^w ZP curve is given by

$$\frac{dv_i^f}{ds^F}\bigg|_{ZP} = \frac{\beta\Lambda_i\zeta_2\left(\frac{y_i^w}{v_i^{h2}}\right)\left[1-\frac{\Lambda_i}{\Lambda_{mean}}\right]}{1-\beta\Lambda_i\zeta_2\left(\frac{y_i^w}{v_i^{h2}}\right)},$$

which is positive for any worker whose productivity is below the mean.[6] The decreased propensity to quit on account of the reduced non-wage income relative to wage ratio also has the effect of shifting down the

[6] Around a zero tax-subsidy equilibrium, $1-\beta\Lambda_i\zeta_2(\frac{y_i^w}{v_i^{h2}}) = \beta\Lambda_i N_i/v_i^h > 0$.

incentive-wage curve, which is on top of the shift owing to the wedge caused by the subsidy. The vertical shift of the iso-y_i^w IW curve is given by

$$\left.\frac{dv_i^f}{ds^F}\right|_{IW} = \frac{-1 - \beta\Lambda_i\left(\frac{y_i^w}{v_i^{h2}}\right)\left[\zeta_2 + N_i\zeta_{12} + \left(\frac{y_i^w}{v_i^h}\right)\zeta_{22}\right]\left[1 - \frac{\Lambda_i}{\Lambda_{mean}}\right]}{1 + \beta\Lambda_i\left(\frac{y_i^w}{v_i^h}\right)\left[\zeta_2 + N_i\zeta_{12} + \left(\frac{y_i^w}{v_i^h}\right)\zeta_{22}\right]},$$

which is unambiguously negative for a worker whose productivity level is below the mean. From (1.26) we see that, at given N_i, the non-wage income, y_i^w, is increased by the same proportion as the rise in v_i^h for the low-wage worker. Hence, in the long run, wealth accumulation ultimately shifts the ZP curve back to its original position and the IW curve also shifts up as wealth catches up to the increased take-home pay. However, a wedge remains, implying that employment is expanded throughout the distribution in the long run, as shown earlier. For low-wage workers, there is an additional boost to employment in the short run.

3.3 Long-run effects of the graduated subsidy

Now the graduated subsidy: Equation (1.29) is replaced by

$$\frac{v_i^f + S(v_i^f)}{\Lambda_i[1 + S'(v_i^f)]} = \beta[N_i\zeta_1(N_i, \Omega(r^* - \rho, N_i))$$

$$+ \Omega(r^* - \rho, N_i)\zeta_2(N_i, \Omega(r^* - \rho, N_i))]. \quad (1.32)$$

Around a zero tax-subsidy equilibrium, the response of N_i to a small change in $s^* \equiv S(v_i^{f*})$ is then calculated to be

$$\left.\frac{dN_i}{ds^*}\right|_{\tau=0}$$

$$= \frac{\Lambda_i^{-1} + \Lambda_i^{-1}\left\{\frac{[v_i^{f*}S''/(1+S')]\tilde{\eta}_{IW}}{(1 - [v_i^{f*}S''/(1+S')])\tilde{\eta}_{IW} + \eta_{ZP}}\right\}}{(1 + S')\beta[(\zeta_1 + \zeta_2\Omega_2) + N_i(\zeta_{11} + \zeta_{12}\Omega_2) + \Omega(\zeta_{21} + \zeta_{22}\Omega_2)] + \beta[\zeta_1 + \zeta_2\Omega_2]}, \quad (1.33)$$

where

$$\tilde{\eta}_{IW} = \frac{\Lambda_i\beta[(\zeta_1 + \zeta_2\Omega_2) + N_i(\zeta_{11} + \zeta_{12}\Omega_2) + \Omega(\zeta_{21} + \zeta_{22}\Omega_2)]N_i}{v_i^f/(1 + S')} > 0.$$

Expressing $\eta_{IW} \equiv \{(1 + S') - [v_i^f S''/(1 + S')]\}\tilde{\eta}_{IW}$, the condition that the wage curve be positively sloped in the (N_i, v_i^f) plane is that $S'' < (1 + S')^2/v_i^f$. Given the restriction that $|S'(v_i^f)| < 1$, a sufficient condition for a graduated subsidy scheme paying $s^* = s^F$ to give an extra boost to

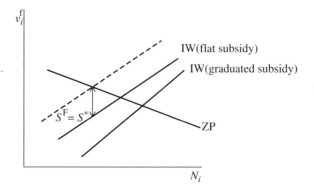

Figure 1.4 *Comparison of flat and graduated subsidies*

employment is therefore that $0 < S'' < (1 + S')^2/v_i^f$. With graduation, there are two effects at work when compared with the constant subsidy case, as shown in figure 1.4. First, with graduation firms are induced to moderate wage rates above the bottom in order to gain a larger subsidy. For $s^* = s^F$, figure 1.4 shows that the wage curve is shifted further down under a graduated scheme. Second, graduation changes the slope of the wage curve. Whereas a constant subsidy scheme has no effect on the slope of the wage curve (there being a parallel shift), with a graduated scheme the new wage curve becomes steeper at higher wages. The restriction on S'' is sufficient to ensure that the "shift" as well as the "slope" effects of graduation give a bigger boost to employment compared with the constant subsidy case. Note also that, by designing a subsidy plan such that the subsidy asymptotically reaches zero as v_i^f is increased, we ensure that employment is raised throughout the distribution, although the expansionary effect is smaller at higher v_i^f.

Consider now the long-run wage effects. We can show that, around a zero tax-subsidy equilibrium, the following derivative holds:

$$\left.\frac{dv_i^h}{ds^*}\right|_{\tau=0} = \left\{ \frac{\eta_{ZP} - \left[\frac{v_i^{f*}S''}{1+S'}\right]\tilde{\eta}_{IW}}{\left(1 - \left[\frac{v_i^{f*}S''}{1+S'}\right]\right)\tilde{\eta}_{IW} + \eta_{ZP}} \right\} - \left[\frac{\Lambda_i}{\Lambda_{mean}}\right]\left[\frac{dS}{ds^*}\right],$$

$$(1.34)$$

where $S \equiv \int_{\underline{\Lambda}}^{\infty} S(v_i^f)g(\Lambda_i)d\Lambda_i$ and $dS/ds^* > 0$. If we further restrict the value of S'' such that $0 < S'' < (1 + S')^2/v_i^f - (\eta_{IW}/\eta_{ZP})(1 + S')/v_i^f$, the first curly brace term in (1.34) is unambiguously positive. Notice from (1.33) that employment is increasing in S''. If we strike a balance in our choice of S'' with regard to the extra expansionary employment effect on the one hand and the wage effect on the other hand, we can obtain a higher take-home wage for a worker whose Λ_i is sufficiently low along with higher employment.

3.4   Long-run effects of a hiring subsidy

Before concluding our analysis of the small open economy, let us examine the effects of a hiring subsidy in our model. Suppose that an ad valorem payroll tax is used to finance a flat hiring subsidy of s^{HF} for each new recruit hired. It is straightforward to show that our two fundamental equations giving the reduced-form ZP and IW schedules become, respectively,

$$\frac{v_i^f}{\Lambda_i} = 1 - \left[\beta - \frac{s^{HF}}{\Lambda_i}\right][\zeta(N_i, \Omega(r^* - \rho, N_i)) + r^* + \theta]; \qquad (1.35)$$

$$\frac{v_i^f}{\Lambda_i} = \left[\beta - \frac{s^{HF}}{\Lambda_i}\right][N_i\zeta_1(N_i, \Omega(r^* - \rho, N_i))$$
$$+ \Omega(r^* - \rho, N_i)\zeta(N_i, \Omega(r^* - \rho, N_i))]. \qquad (1.36)$$

Such a policy shifts the ZP curve up but shifts the IW curve down, leading to an unambiguous expansion of equilibrium employment but possible decline of the product wage, v_i^f. (In contrast, under both the flat and graduated subsidy plans, the before-tax wage of the workers, $v_i^f + s_i$, unambiguously rises.) The take-home wage would accordingly fall further as the payroll tax is applied, though this must be set against the subsidy that each new recruit receives when hired. We obtain the following derivative:[7]

$$\left.\frac{d[v_i^f/(1+\tau) + (r^* + \theta)s^{HF}]}{ds^{HF}}\right|_{s^{HF}=0}$$

$$= (\zeta + \theta)\left[\mu - \left(\frac{\Lambda_i}{\Lambda_{mean}}\right)\right] + (1+\mu)r^*$$

$$+ \theta - (1 - \mu)[N_i\zeta_1 + \Omega\zeta_2],$$

where

$$0 < \mu \equiv \frac{(\zeta_1 + \zeta_2\Omega_2) + (\zeta_{11} + \zeta_{12}\Omega_2)N_i + (\zeta_{21} + \zeta_{22}\Omega_2)\Omega}{2(\zeta_1 + \zeta_2\Omega_2) + (\zeta_{11} + \zeta_{12}\Omega_2)N_i + (\zeta_{21} + \zeta_{22}\Omega_2)\Omega} < 1.$$

---

[7] The balanced-budget condition with a hiring subsidy simplifies to $\tau = [(\zeta + \theta)s^{HF}/v_{mean}^h]$ around a zero hiring subsidy equilibrium, noting that in the steady state the hiring rate equals $\zeta + \theta$ for every type of worker.

4   Closed economy incidence

We confine our analysis to a flat subsidy in the closed economy financed by a proportional payroll tax. For any r, our reduced-form ZP and IW curves are written respectively as

$$\frac{v_i^f}{\Lambda_i} = 1 - \beta[\zeta(N_i, \Omega(r - \rho, N_i)) + \theta + r], \tag{1.37}$$

$$\frac{v_i^f}{\Lambda_i} + \frac{s^F}{\Lambda_i} = \beta[N_i\zeta_1(N_i, \Omega(r - \rho, N_i))$$
$$+ \Omega(r - \rho, N_i)\zeta_2(N_i, \Omega(r - \rho, N_i))], \tag{1.38}$$

where we have again substituted for y_i^w/v_i^h the function $\Omega(r - \rho, N_i)$ obtained from the Blanchardian relationship expressed as

$$r = \rho + \frac{\theta}{1 + (v_i^h/y_i^w)\,N_i}. \tag{1.39}$$

We note from (1.37) and (1.38) that, by equating the required incentive wage to the demand wage, we can express the employment rate of any type-i worker as an implicit function of the interest rate and the subsidy relative to productivity level, namely,

$$N_i = \epsilon(r; (s^F/\Lambda_i)); \; \epsilon_1 < 0; \; \epsilon_2 > 0. \tag{1.40}$$

The function ϵ is interpretable as the demand for the stock of employees in steady state. The value of the total stock of employees, which are the only form of asset in the closed economy, is $A \equiv \int_{\underline{\Lambda}}^{\infty} \beta\Lambda_i N_i g(\Lambda_i)d\Lambda_i$ because each employee is worth $\beta\Lambda_i$. By (1.40), A is a decreasing function of the rate of interest:

$$A = \int_{\underline{\Lambda}}^{\infty} \beta\Lambda_i\epsilon(r; (s^F/\Lambda_i))g(\Lambda_i)d\Lambda_i. \tag{1.41}$$

An expression for the average supply of wealth per member of the type-i workforce is obtained from (1.39) as

$$W_i = \left(\frac{v_i^h N_i}{r + \theta}\right)\left[\frac{r - \rho}{\theta + \rho - r}\right]. \tag{1.42}$$

As before, excluding the case where $r - \rho > \theta$, we have a well-defined steady state, with the righthand side of (1.42) being unambiguously positive. The total supply of wealth per worker, under a balanced budget, is given by

$$W = \left[\frac{r - \rho}{(\theta + \rho - r)(r + \theta)}\right]\int_{\underline{\Lambda}}^{\infty} v_i^f N_i g(\Lambda_i)d\Lambda_i. \tag{1.43}$$

Further, using (1.37) and (1.40) in (1.43), we obtain an expression giving us the total desired supply of wealth as a function of the rate of interest:

$$W = \left[\frac{r - \rho}{(\theta + \rho - r)(r + \theta)} \right] \int_{\underline{\Lambda}}^{\infty} \left\{ 1 - \beta \left[\zeta \left(\epsilon \left(r; \frac{s^{F}}{\Lambda_i} \right) \right), \right. \right.$$

$$\left. \left. \Omega \left(r - \rho, \epsilon \left(r; \frac{s^{F}}{\Lambda_i} \right) \right) + r + \theta \right] \right\} \epsilon \left(r; \frac{s^{F}}{\Lambda_i} \right) \Lambda_i g(\Lambda_i) d\Lambda_i.$$

$$(1.44)$$

Suppose that initially the subsidy and payroll tax are zero. In that case, we note from (1.37) and (1.38) that setting $s^{F} = 0$ implies that N_i and y_i^{w}/v_i^{h} are equal across all types of workers. Consequently, the quit rate is initially identical across all types of workers. As in our earlier discussion in the neoclassical case, we can argue that the per worker supply of wealth is upward sloping initially, but at very high r may bend backward as in figure 1.1.[8] In the same plane, per worker demand for the domestic assets in value terms is downward sloping. We suppose that the equilibrium r is unique or that only the lowest equilibrium r is empirically relevant.

To see how the tax-subsidy policy affects the rate of interest, it will help to have a sharper characterization of this equilibrium. Since the quit rate is equal across all types of workers in the neighborhood of the zero-subsidy equilibrium, we can simplify the equilibrium condition to

$$W \equiv \left[\frac{r - \rho}{(\theta + \rho - r)(r + \theta)} \right]$$

$$\times \left\{ 1 - \beta \left[\zeta \left(\epsilon \left(r; \frac{s^{F}}{\Lambda_i} \right) \right), \Omega \left(r - \rho, \epsilon \left(r; \frac{s^{F}}{\Lambda_i} \right) \right) + r + \theta \right] \right\}$$

$$\times \int_{\underline{\Lambda}}^{\infty} \epsilon \left(r; \frac{s^{F}}{\Lambda_i} \right) \Lambda_i g(\Lambda_i) d\Lambda_i$$

$$= \beta \int_{\underline{\Lambda}}^{\infty} \epsilon \left(r; \frac{s^{F}}{\Lambda_i} \right) \Lambda_i g(\Lambda_i) d\Lambda_i \equiv A. \qquad (1.45)$$

The equilibrium r is therefore given by

$$\left[\frac{r - \rho}{(\theta + \rho - r)(r + \theta)} \right] \left\{ 1 - \beta \left[\zeta \left(\epsilon \left(r; \frac{s^{F}}{\Lambda_i} \right) \right), \right. \right.$$

$$\left. \left. \Omega \left(r - \rho, \epsilon \left(r; \frac{s^{F}}{\Lambda_i} \right) \right) + r + \theta \right] \right\} = \beta. \qquad (1.46)$$

---

[8] Although the increase in r leads to a decline in the real demand wage, the fall in N_i acts to lower the quit propensity and hence indirectly acts to offset the fall in wage. We assume that the direct effect dominates.

Thus we see that a tax-subsidy policy involving a small change in s^F financed by a proportional payroll tax ultimately has an influence on the interest rate only via its influence on the quit rate. The effects of introducing a small subsidy are as follows. At the original r, the subsidy, in expanding the demand for employees of all types, shifts the domestic asset demand schedule in figure 1.1 to the right (see the righthand side of (1.45)). Workers, finding the probability of obtaining employment improved, step up their saving accordingly, so that the supply of wealth schedule is also shifted to the right (see the lefthand side of (1.45)). In fact, both rightward shifts are equal in magnitude, leaving the interest rate unchanged. But the rise in each N_i acts to tighten the labor market of each type-i worker. The resulting increase in the propensity to quit reduces the demand wage. This leads to a leftward shift of the supply of wealth schedule, causing the interest rate to rise.[9] (When the zero-profit curve is horizontal, however, this effect would be zero.) But clearly this effect can only moderate the net expansionary effect on employment of low-Λ_i workers. To show this we may calculate the total derivative of $\epsilon(r; (s^F/\Lambda_i))$ evaluated at a low Λ_i with respect to s^F.

Taking the total derivative in (1.45), we obtain

$$\frac{dr}{ds^F} = \frac{(\zeta_1 + \zeta_2\Omega_2)\epsilon_2}{\left\{\left[\frac{\theta(\theta+\rho)}{(r-\rho)^2} - \zeta_2\Omega_1\right] - (\zeta_1 + \zeta_2\Omega_2)\epsilon_1\right\}\Lambda_{\text{mean}}}. \tag{1.47}$$

In the appendix, we show that a necessary condition for the aggregate supply of wealth schedule to be positively sloped under the proviso that the labor cost elasticity of the zero-profit curve exceeds unity is that $[\theta(\theta + \rho)/(r - \rho)^2] > \zeta_2\Omega_1$.[10] Hence the tax-subsidy scheme raises the rate of interest. To prove that, for low-Λ_i workers, the rise of r only moderates but does not overturn the expansionary employment effect of s^F,

---

[9] In the appendix, we calculate the extent of the horizontal shifts of the total supply of wealth and total asset demand schedules. When the labor cost elasticity of the zero-profit curve is greater than one, the net shift of the total supply of wealth schedule is rightward. When this elasticity is less than one, the net shift is leftward.

[10] The inequality could (but need not necessarily) be reversed when the labor cost elasticity of the zero-profit curve is less than one. If the inequality is reversed but the aggregate supply of wealth schedule remains positively sloped, there is an increased upward pressure on the interest rate. If the inequality is reversed and the aggregate supply of wealth becomes negatively sloped, there is the theoretical possibility that the rate of interest is lowered as a result of the tax-subsidy scheme. In such a case, employment is unambiguously expanded for workers of all types.

we calculate the following derivative:

$$
\frac{dN_i}{ds^F} = \epsilon_1 \left(\frac{dr}{ds^F} \right) + \frac{\epsilon_2}{\Lambda_i}
$$

$$
= \frac{-(\zeta_1 + \zeta_2 \Omega_2)\epsilon_1 \epsilon_2 \left(\Lambda_i^{-1} - \Lambda_{\text{mean}}^{-1} \right) + \left[\frac{\theta(\theta+\rho)}{(r-\rho)^2} - \zeta_2 \Omega_1 \right] \epsilon_2 \Lambda_i^{-1}}{\left\{ \left[\frac{\theta(\theta+\rho)}{(r-\rho)^2} - \zeta_2 \Omega_1 \right] - (\zeta_1 + \zeta_2 \Omega_2)\epsilon_1 \right\} \Lambda_{\text{mean}}}.
$$

$$(1.48)$$

In the homogeneous case, the tax-subsidy scheme unambiguously expands employment for everyone. In the heterogeneous case, all workers whose Λ_i is either below or equal to the mean find their employment expanded. It is straightforward to obtain an expression for the derivative of v_i^h with respect to s^F:

$$
\left. \frac{dv_i^h}{ds^F} \right|_{s^F=0} = 1 - \frac{\Lambda_i}{\Lambda_{\text{mean}}} - \Lambda_i \beta \left[(\zeta_1 + \zeta_2 \Omega_2) \frac{dN_i}{ds^F} + \zeta_2 \Omega_1 \frac{dr}{ds^F} \right].
$$

$$(1.49)$$

We see that, for workers whose Λ_i is sufficiently low, their v_i^h will rise as well.

5   The case of rising marginal training cost

We will confine our discussion here to the case of the small open economy. Suppose that the fraction of a type-i employee's working time devoted to training new hires is given by $\Phi(h_i)$, where $\Phi'(h_i) > 0$ and $\Phi''(h_i) > 0$. Solving the Hamiltonian problem, we would have $q_i = \Lambda_i \Phi'(h_i)$. With a flat (constant) subsidy, the two fundamental reduced-form ZP and IW relationships would now be given by

$$
\frac{v_i^f}{\Lambda_i} = 1 - \Phi(h) + h\Phi'(h) - \Phi'(h_i)[\zeta(N_i, \Omega(r^* - \rho, N_i)) + \theta + r^*],
$$

$$(1.50)$$

$$
\frac{v_i^f}{\Lambda_i} + \frac{s^F}{\Lambda_i} = \Phi'(h_i)[N_i \zeta_1(N_i, \Omega(r^* - \rho, N_i))
$$

$$
+ \Omega(r^* - \rho, N_i)\zeta_2(N_i, \Omega(r^* - \rho, N_i))]. \quad (1.51)
$$

The steady-state employment (SSE) condition is that

$$
h_i = \zeta(N_i, \Omega(r^* - \rho, N_i)) + \theta. \quad (1.52)
$$

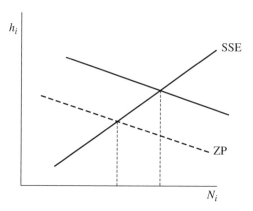

Figure 1.5 *Effects of a flat subsidy on hiring and employment*

From (1.51), we note that v_i^f/Λ_i is positively related to h_i and N_i and negatively related to s^F/Λ_i, written $v_i^f/\Lambda_i = V(h_i, N_i; s^F/\Lambda_i)$. Using this relation in (1.50), we obtain a downward-sloping schedule in the (N_i, h_i) plane. Equation (1.52), on the other hand, gives us a positively sloped schedule (see figure 1.5). Starting from a zero-subsidy equilibrium, it is now clear that the implementation of the flat subsidy scheme results in a rightward, and hence upward, shift of the ZP curve in this plane. The result is that employment is expanded along with a rise in steady-state hiring. Moreover, for the same dollar amount of subsidy, the expansion is greatest for low-wage workers.

6   Concluding remarks

The pay open to the less advantaged is now so inadequate for meaningful self-support and the participation rates and job attachment of the less advantaged, especially among men, are now so far from integrating poor communities in the nation's business life that, arguably, any remedy will require novel intervention. (If the goal is not far, just raising the level of familiar instruments may suffice to reattain it; if the goal is far, designing de novo a more tailored instrument may be cheaper.) Any such innovation, however, may open the law of unintended consequences, since we do not know the scale and perhaps the nature of all the effects. This uncertainty leads to hesitation and disagreement over the intervention to select. An investment in education that would hypothetically restore low-end wages to their late-1970s level has been calculated to cost nearly US$2 trillion (Heckman, 1993). But the radical uncertainty over exactly what education reforms and expenditures to make may be a bigger draw-back (along with the needed one-generation lead-time).

The employment subsidy instrument has the advantage that economists are familiar with the workings of corrective taxes and subsidies – although mainly at the partial-equilibrium level of the individual industry. Massive and perhaps permanent low-wage employment subsidies would not likely prove an exception to the law of unanticipated effects. This chapter has been addressed to the doubts over such subsidies that might arise at the level of general equilibrium. Is it theoretically possible in the context of our model of the natural rate that the rise of the wage rate relative to non-wage income initially achieved by the subsidies – recall that the increased payroll tax rate is ultimately neutral for that ratio – will induce worker-savers to build up non-wage income relative to the wage rate until incentive wages have been driven up and the demand wage rate driven down by enough to nullify the expansion of employment? As the chapter has shown, the adjustment of wealth in the small open economy does act to moderate the expansion of employment achieved by the subsidies in the "short run," but, in the long run, employment is increased throughout the distribution. In the closed economy case, the interest rate is pulled up, which moderates employment expansion. Nevertheless, employment unambiguously expands for all workers whose productivity level is below the mean.

Other uncertainties must be left for future work. One of these, obviously, is the net budgetary cost of wage subsidies. In principle, employment subsidies could be targeted at groups who, if their employment were not subsidized, would otherwise cost the government as much or more in public support – single parents (generally mothers) with dependent children, for example. In the United States, however, it may be the increased difficulty of self-support and the increased disengagement from business life among *men* that is fundamental, since that may lie behind the rise of single-parenting as well as the rise of crime, violence and drug abuse. And men are not as eligible as women for most welfare outlays. So employment subsidies had better be untargeted. And the argument that their net budgetary cost will be small enough to satisfy taxpayers has to rest on estimates of the indirect savings and revenues achieved when entire poor communities are made self-supporting through work: the savings in welfare, crime prevention, administration of justice, unemployment compensation and other social insurance programs (under existing benefit schedules), and the revenues from the additional collection of income and sales taxes (under existing rates).

An attractive feature of hiring subsidies is that they can be targeted at those potential workers currently depending on unemployment compensation or welfare benefits for their support. So the budgetary savings achieved by stimulating their employment may equal or exceed the gross budgetary outlay for the subsidies. This feature has been used by Dennis Snower in designing a program whereby unemployed workers create their own hiring subsidy by trading in their unemployment benefits in return for a job. We found, however, that subsidies to hiring might actually reduce wage rates at the low end, perhaps appreciably so, and this would be a serious drawback in the US context where, among the disadvantaged, low wages are as much in need of remedying as depressed employment. Furthermore, jobless American men receive little in entitlements that they could exchange for a job other than their unemployment compensation and those benefits are not long term and not broad based.

Uncertainty also hangs over the amount of abuse and fraud that wage subsidy programs would lead to. Hiring subsidies would apparently invite employers to swap employees, perhaps after the spell of unemployment required for eligibility, and to move employees more freely from corporation to corporation under the same parent company – all in order to collect increased hiring subsidies. An advantage of the employment subsidies studied here is that they would not encourage such abuses. However, employment subsidies (and possibly hiring subsidies too) would inspire firms, especially single-proprietor firms, to featherbed the payroll with phantom employees under the names of persons, such as family members, whose silence would be trusted. On balance, it might be advantageous for this as well as other reasons to restrict the subsidies to full-time jobs and to good-sized firms where whistle-blowers would be a deterrent, and to limit the subsidies to credits against the firms' tax liabilities. In another sort of abuse, the employer and employee would agree to a reduced wage, which would add to the subsidy earned, and a compensating increase in non-wage benefits, which, if undetected or not counted as compensation, would not add to the subsidy earned. For this reason, a graduated subsidy must decrease slowly with the wage rate so that this temptation is not too strong in relation to the monitoring powers of the tax authorities. Yet another abuse would draw upon the collusion of third parties. To earn increased employment subsidies an employer might reduce the wage rate of employees and compensate them with side jobs above their normal pay rates at a cooperating firm, which might do the same with the first firm or with other firms. Similarly, under the existing Earned Income Tax Credit program, which awards subsidies directly to the taxpayer reporting low earnings, the wage can be reduced and the employee compensated through special discounts obtained from third parties. It may be, however, that such abuses could be deterred by punishing them with the same severity meted out to other kinds of tax fraud.

Appendix

1. To prove that $L_i/\bar{L}$ is decreasing in r, we obtain from (1.7) the relation $r = R(v_i^h\bar{L}/y_i^w, L_i/\bar{L})$ with $R_1 < 0$ and $R_2 < 0$. Substituting the function R for r in (1.8), we obtain a variable-interest-rate labor supply schedule in the $(L_i/\bar{L}, v_i^h\bar{L}/y_i^w)$ plane, whose slope is given by

$$\frac{d\left(\frac{v_i^h\bar{L}}{y_i^w}\right)}{d\frac{L_i}{\bar{L}}}\Bigg|_{LS}$$

$$= \frac{1 + \left[\frac{\theta+\rho}{r+\theta}\right] + \left[\frac{\theta(\theta+\rho)}{1+(v_i^h\bar{L}/y_i^w)(L_i/\bar{L})}\right]}{\left[\frac{\theta+\rho}{r+\theta}\right]\left(\frac{v_i^h\bar{L}}{y_i^w}\right)^{-2}\left\{1 - \left[\frac{1}{(1+(r/\theta))(1+(v_i^h\bar{L}/y_i^w)^{-1}(L_i/\bar{L})^{-1})}\right]\right\}} > 0.$$

As we move north-east along the variable-interest-rate labor supply function, (1.7) tells us that the interest rate is declining.

2. To prove that, at given r, the tax-subsidy policy shifts the aggregate supply of wealth schedule to the right, we express (1.44) as $W = \psi(r, s^F)$. Taking a total derivative through (1.44) with respect to s^F, we obtain

$$\Psi_2 = B\{[1 - \beta(\zeta + r + \theta)] - \beta(\zeta_1 + \zeta_2\Omega_2)\epsilon\}\epsilon_2,$$

where $B \equiv (r - \rho)/[(\theta + \rho - r)(r + \theta)]$. The assumption that the labor cost elasticity of the zero-profit curve exceeds one implies that the reduced-form ZP curve cuts the hyperbola from below in the $(N_i, v_i^f/\Lambda_i)$ plane. The slope of the hyperbola is given by $-(v_i^f/\Lambda_i)N_i^{-1}$, which equals $-[1 - \beta(\zeta + r + \theta)]N_i^{-1}$ around the equilibrium, and the slope of the reduced-form ZP curve is given by $-\beta(\zeta_1 + \zeta_2\Omega_2)$. Hence,

$$[1 - \beta(\zeta + r + \theta)] > \beta(\zeta_1 + \zeta_2\Omega_2)\epsilon.$$

Accordingly, $\Psi_2 > 0$.

From (1.41), we can express total asset demand as $A = \Theta(r, s^F)$. We obtain the following derivative:

$$\Theta_2 = \beta\epsilon_2,$$

which is positive. Noting (1.45), it is clear that $\Theta_2 > \Psi_2$.

3. It is straightforward to show that

$$\Psi_1 = \beta B\left\{\epsilon\left[\frac{\theta(\theta+\rho)}{(r-\rho)^2} - \zeta_2\Omega_1\right] - \epsilon_1 B^{-1}[B\epsilon(\zeta_1+\zeta_2\Omega_2)-1]\right\}\Lambda_{mean}.$$

Noting (1.46), the condition

$$[1 - \beta(\zeta + r + \theta)] > \beta(\zeta_1 + \zeta_2\Omega_2)\epsilon$$

can be re-expressed as

$$B\epsilon(\zeta_1 + \zeta_2\Omega_2) > 1.$$

Thus, for Ψ_1 to be positive, it is required that

$$\left[\frac{\theta(\theta + \rho)}{(r - \rho)^2} - \zeta_2\Omega_1\right] > \frac{\epsilon_1}{\epsilon}\left[\frac{B\epsilon(\zeta_1 + \zeta_2\Omega_2) - 1}{B}\right] > 0.$$

Hence a necessary condition for the aggregate supply of wealth curve to be positively sloped when the labor cost elasticity of the zero-profit curve exceeds one is that $[\theta(\theta + \rho)/(r - \rho)^2] > \zeta_2\Omega_1$.

References

Blanchard, O.J. (1985). "Debt, Deficits and Finite Horizons," *Journal of Political Economy* **93**: 223–247.

Dréze, J.H. and E. Malinvaud (1994). "Growth and Employment: The Scope for a European Initiative," *European Economic Review* **38**: 489–504.

Eagly, R.V. (1965). "Market Power as an Intervening Mechanism in Phillips Curve Analysis," *Economica* **32**: 48–64.

Freeman, R.B. (1996). "Why Do So Many Young American Men Commit Crimes and What Might We Do about It?" National Bureau of Economic Research Working Paper No. 5451.

Hamermesh, D.S. (1978). "Subsidies for Jobs in the Private Sector," in John Palmer (ed.), *Creating Jobs: Public Employment Programs and Wage Subsidies*. Washington, DC: Brookings Institution.

Haveman, R.H. and J.L. Palmer, eds. (1982). *Jobs for Discouraged Workers*. Washington, DC: Brookings Institution.

Heckman, J.J. (1993). "Assessing Clinton's Program on Job Training, Workfare, and Education in the Workplace," National Bureau of Economic Research Working Paper No. 4428.

Hoon, H.T. and E.S. Phelps (1992). "Macroeconomic Shocks in a Dynamized Model of the Natural Rate of Unemployment," *American Economic Review* **82**(September): 889–900.

Hurd, M.D. and J.H. Pencavel (1981). "A Utility-Based Analysis of Wage Subsidies," *Journal of Public Economics* **15**: 185–201.

Jackman, R. and R. Layard (1986). "A Wage-Tax, Worker-Subsidy Policy for Reducing the 'Natural Rate of Unemployment,'" in Wilfred Beckerman (ed.), *Wage Rigidity and Unemployment*. Oxford: Basil Blackwell.

Kaldor, N. (1936). "Wage Subsidies as a Remedy for Unemployment," *Journal of Political Economy* **44**(December); reprinted in N. Kaldor, *Essays on Economic Policy*, New York: W.W. Norton, 1965.

Kanaginis, G. and E.S. Phelps (1994). "Fiscal Policy and Economic Activity in the Neoclassical Theory with and without Bequests," *Finanz Archiv* **51**: 137–171.

Krueger, A.B. and L.H. Summers (1988). "Efficiency Wages and the Inter-Industry Wage Structure," *Econometrica* **56**(March): 259–293.

Murray, C. (1984). *Losing ground.* New York: Basic Books.

Phelps, E.S. (1968). "Money-Wage Dynamics and Labor-Market Equilibrium," *Journal of Political Economy* **76**(July/August): 678–711.

(1994a). "Economic Justice to the Working Poor through a Wage Subsidy," in Dimitri Papadimitriou (ed.), *Aspects of Distribution of Wealth and Income,* 151–164. New York: St. Martins Press.

(1994b). "Low-Wage Employment Subsidies versus the Welfare State," *American Economic Review, Papers and Proceedings* **84**(May): 54–58.

(1994c). *Structural Slumps: The Modern-Equilibrium Theory of Unemployment, Interest and Assets.* Cambridge, MA: Harvard University Press.

(1997). *Rewarding Work: How to Restore Participation and Self-Support to Free Enterprise.* Cambridge, MA: Harvard University Press.

Pigou, A.C. (1933). *The Theory of Unemployment.* London: Macmillan.

Pissarides, C.A. (1996). "Are Employment Tax Cuts the Answer to Europe's Unemployment Problem?" London School of Economics, Centre for Economic Performance, January.

Snower, D.J. (1994). "Converting Unemployment Benefits into Employment Subsidies," *American Economic Review, Papers and Proceedings* **84**(May): 65–70.

Wilson, W.J. (1996). *When Work Disappears: The World of the New Urban Poor.* New York: Alfred Knopf.

2 Taxes, subsidies and equilibrium labor market outcomes

Dale T. Mortensen and Christopher A. Pissarides

Abstract

We explore the effects of taxes and subsidies on job creation, job destruction, employment and wages in the Mortensen–Pissarides version of the search and matching equilibrium framework. Qualitative analytical results show that wage and employment subsidies increase employment, especially of low-skill workers, and also increase wages. A job creation or hiring subsidy reduces unemployment duration but increases incidence, with an ambiguous effect on overall employment. A firing tax has the reverse effects but the same indeterminacy. In the special case of a competitive search equilibrium, the one in which search externalities are internalized, there is a first-best configuration: no tax on the wage, an employment subsidy that offsets the distortions on the job destruction margin induced by unemployment compensation and employment protection policy, and a hiring subsidy equal to the implicit tax on severance imposed by any form of employment protection, with the costs of these and other policies financed by a non-distortionary consumption tax. Computational experiments confirm this ideal also determines the direction in which marginal improvements can be made both in terms of efficiency and in terms of improving low-skill worker employment and wage outcomes.

1   Introduction

Our purpose is to consider various tax and subsidy effects on wages and unemployment within the search and matching labor market framework. This structure is the basis for the "flows" approach to aggregate labor market analysis. In Mortensen and Pissarides's (1994) version, an existing employment relationship commands quasi-rent as a consequence of search and recruiting investment, hiring and firing costs and other forms of match-specific human capital formation. The quasi-rents that accrue to any specific employer and worker pair are allocated between the parties by a wage contract. Given a particular wage determination rule, employers provide jobs and recruit workers while workers search for employment. At the same time, an existing employer–worker match ends when sufficiently bad news arrives about their expected future productivity.

44

These job creation and job destruction decisions generate worker flows into and out of employment that depend on the current value of the employed stock. When the two flows differ, employment dynamics are set in motion that, under a reasonable set of conditions, lead to a unique steady-state employment level.

The search and matching approach owes its origins to the pioneering works of Stigler (1961), Phelps (1968) and Friedman (1968) and was already at an advanced state when the Phelps et al. (1970) volume was published. The equilibrium analysis of the current vintage of models, however, did not start until the early 1980s, when models by Diamond (1982a, 1982b), Mortensen (1982) and Pissarides (1985, 1986) explored the properties of two-sided search and characterized the nature and welfare properties of market equilibrium. A key ingredient of the new approach was the use of the solution to the Nash bargaining game to determine wages. The Nash solution is appropriate in this context because of the assumptions of two-sided search and the symmetry that they introduce to the game. It is also flexible enough to enable the study of market equilibrium under a variety of assumptions about parameters, including policy ones.

The policy parameters studied in this chapter are a job creation subsidy, an implicit firing tax, and a linear wage tax and employment subsidy imposed on continuing job–worker matches. We investigate the effects of each on job creation, job destruction, employment and wages. Because analytical results are often ambiguous, we conduct computational experiments that illuminate the model's implications.

2   The framework

2.1   Basic concepts

The Mortensen–Pissarides model is founded on two constructs: a matching function that characterizes the search and recruiting process by which new job–worker matches are created; and an idiosyncratic productivity shock that captures the reason for resource reallocation across alternative activities. Given these concepts, decisions about the creation of new jobs, about recruiting and search effort, and about the conditions that induce job–worker separations can be formalized.

Job and worker matching is viewed as a production process. The flow of new matches that form is the output of the process, and the search and recruiting efforts of workers and employers are the inputs. The matching function gives the aggregate relationship between matching output and the inputs. Under the simplifying assumptions that all employers with a vacancy recruit with equal intensity and that unemployed workers search, also at a given intensity, aggregate matching inputs can be represented simply by the number of job vacancies, v, and the number of unemployed workers, u.

Let the function $m(v, u)$ represent the matching rate associated with every possible vacancy and unemployment pair. As in production theory, it is reasonable to suppose that this function is increasing in both arguments but exhibits decreasing marginal products to each input. Constant returns, in the sense that

$$m(v, u) = m\left(1, \frac{u}{v}\right)v \equiv q(\theta)v \quad \text{where } \theta = v/u, \quad (2.1)$$

is a convenient additional assumption, one that is consistent with available evidence.[1] The ratio of vacancies to unemployment, θ, *market tightness*, is an endogenous variable to be determined.

On average, a vacant job is taken by a worker at the rate $q(\theta)$ and workers find jobs at rate $\theta q(\theta)$. By the assumption of a concave and linear homogeneous matching function, $q(\theta)$ is decreasing and $\theta q(\theta)$ increasing in θ. $\theta q(\theta)$ is the *unemployment duration hazard*. The duration of unemployment spells is a random exponential variable with expectation equal to the inverse of the hazard, $1/\theta q(\theta)$, a decreasing function of market tightness. Analogously, $q(\theta)$ is the *vacancy duration hazard* and its inverse, $1/q(\theta)$, is the mean duration of vacancies.

An important source of job–worker separations is job destruction attributable to an idiosyncratic shock to match productivity. Empirically this is the main reason for job destruction (see Davis, Haltiwanger and Schuh, 1996). Initial decisions regarding location, technology and/or product line choices embodied in a particular match are irreversible in the sense that subsequent innovations and taste changes, not known with certainty at the time of match formation, shock the market value of the product or service output. For example, the initial decision might involve the choice of locating a productive activity on one of many "islands." In future, island-specific conditions that affect total match productivity, say the weather, may change. If the news about future profitability implicit in the shock is bad enough, then continuation of the activity on that particular island is no longer profitable. In this case, the job is destroyed and the match dissolves.

To model this idea, we assume that the output of each job is the product of two components: p, which is common to all jobs in a particular skill group, and x, which is idiosyncratic. The idiosyncratic component x,

---

[1] See the survey by Petrongolo and Pissarides (2001).

which takes values on the unit interval, arrives from time to time at the Poisson rate λ and is distributed according to the cumulative distribution function $F(x)$ given an arrival. Note that these assumptions satisfy the empirical properties of idiosyncratic job destruction; that is, the shocks have persistence and they appear to hit the job independently of the aggregate state or the skill of the worker (here represented by p). Furthermore, the sequence of shocks is independent identically distributed (iid).

The parameter p represents the common productivity of a particular skill group. A key assumption is market segmentation; that is, skill groups are not linked through migration, rivalry in the job search process or common wage-setting institutions. In other words, each skill group participates in a separate labor market with its own matching function, tax and subsidy structure and employment-wage equilibrium. Under this strong assumption, we can derive the equilibrium of one skill group without reference to others.[2] It will become obvious during the description of equilibrium why different skill groups experience different equilibrium employment-wage configurations.

Under our assumptions about the information structure and the behavior of firms and workers after the formation of a match, an existing match is destroyed if the idiosyncratic productivity shock falls below some reservation threshold, an endogenous variable denoted by R. Unemployment *incidence* is defined as the average rate of transition from employment to unemployment, $\lambda F(R)$, and increases with the reservation threshold.

Entrepreneurs are unconstrained with respect to initial location, technology and product choice and also have the same information about market conditions. Under the assumption that they know the product or service that commands the highest expected future profit, all will create jobs at the highest idiosyncratic productivity, $x = 1$. Given this property of the model and the assumption that future match product evolves according to a Markov process with persistence, the jobs that are still at initial productivity are the most productive for a given skill group. Note, however, this does not imply that new jobs have greater expected duration, which would violate the empirical facts. All jobs in our model, regardless of productivity, have the same expected duration, equal to the inverse of the job destruction rate, $1/\lambda F(R)$, given the assumption that the sequence of shocks is iid.

Because all workers are assumed to participate, the unemployed fraction of each skill group evolves over time in response to the difference

---

[2] Implicit in the statement is the additional assumption that the labor services of members of two different skill groups are not substitutes for one another. The consequences of relaxing this assumption are discussed in the final section of the chapter.

between the flow of workers who transit from employment to unemployment and the flow who transit in the opposite direction, i.e.

$$\dot{u} = \lambda F(R)(1 - u) - \theta q(\theta)u \qquad (2.2)$$

where $1 - u$ represents both employment and the employment rate in each skill group. The steady-state equilibrium unemployment rate is

$$u = \frac{\lambda F(R)}{\lambda F(R) + \theta q(\theta)}. \qquad (2.3)$$

As individual unemployment histories are described by a simple two-state Markov chain, the steady-state unemployment rate is also the fraction of time over the long run that the representative participant spends unemployed. It decreases with market tightness and increases with the reservation product, because the unemployment hazard, $\theta q(\theta)$, and the employment hazard, $\lambda F(R)$, are both increasing functions.

2.2   *Job creation and job destruction*

The sequence of events that lead to job creation and job destruction can be summarized as follows. A firm with a profit opportunity opens a job vacancy for a worker with skill indexed by p at a flow cost of recruiting equal to cp. Applications from workers begin arriving at hazard rate $q(\theta(p))$, and one is received on average $1/q(\theta(p))$ periods after the posting of the vacancy. When they meet, worker and employer bargain. After the initial wage, $w_0(p)$, is agreed to, *job creation* takes place: The firm pays setup cost pC, which includes the cost of hiring and training and other forms of match-specific investment. Production then takes place, until a productivity shock arrives. Wage renegotiation occurs, with wage outcome $w(x, p)$ prevailing on any continuing job, one that generally reflects the new information, x. However, if x falls below some reservation level $R(p)$, *job destruction* takes place: The firm pays firing cost pT and exits the market, and the worker enters unemployment. Here we have in mind an implicit firing tax, one imposed by employment protection regulations that restrict "employment at will," not a severance transfer from firm to worker.[3]

Note that the vacancy posting, job creation and job termination costs are assumed to be proportional to the worker skill parameter. This reflects the reasonable assumption that it is more expensive to the firm to maintain a skilled job vacant than a less skilled one and more expensive to train a

---

[3] In the case of the principal wage contract assumed, such a transfer has no allocation effect, for reasons pointed out by Lazear (1990) and Burda (1992).

more skilled worker to the special requirements of the job (because the job is more demanding). The termination cost is an implicit tax, and again the reasonable assumption is that it is more costly to get rid of a more skilled worker than a less skilled one. Of course, the assumption of proportionality is a simplification that may not hold precisely in all situations. For example, termination costs may increase with the wage rather than with productivity. Any other assumption, however, would complicate the model considerably and the simulations show that results with the proportionality assumption are reasonable.

The following policy parameters are studied. First, a *job creation* or *hiring subsidy*, denoted as pH, is defined as a payment made to the employer when a worker is hired. Second, a linear labor *tax-subsidy schedule*, $a + tw$, is imposed on employers. If $t = 0$, the schedule corresponds to a pure employment subsidy when $a < 0$ and a lump-sum employment tax when $a > 0$. If $t > 0$, the schedule corresponds to a progressive tax if $a < 0$ and a regressive one if $a > 0$. For $t < \tau$, where τ represents the underlying payroll tax, $\tau - t$ is a wage subsidy of the kind advocated by Phelps (1997). Third, as already indicated, we also consider an explicit *job destruction tax*, pT, as a policy instrument. Finally, we allow for an unemployment compensation payment equal to some fraction of the average wage for each skill group, $\rho\bar{w}(p)$, where the fraction ρ is the *replacement ratio*.

The policy-free equilibrium is one characterized by $H = T = a = t = \rho = 0$. Our assumptions about the policy parameters are that, in addition to the firing tax, the hiring subsidy is also proportional to productivity but the rates a, t and ρ are independent of productivity. H is modeled as a hiring subsidy that is proportional to productivity for convenience. Given the private cost of hiring, C, which is proportional to productivity, $p(C - H)$ is the *net* private job creation cost for each skill group p. That t and ρ are independent of productivity needs no explanation, because they are both rates that apply to equilibrium wage outcomes that depend on productivity. By making them constant we restrict ourselves to linear schedules. a is treated as a flat (lump-sum) employment subsidy for keeping a worker employed, regardless of skill.

In addition to unemployment compensation, $\rho\bar{w}(p)$, each unemployed worker enjoys imputed income during unemployment, $b > 0$. Crucially, this "income" is independent of skill. It is the imputed value of leisure (home production) to the worker, although it may include other incomes that must be given up when the worker moves from non-employment to employment. The critical assumption is that the value of home production to the worker is independent of market skill. This assumption is the reason that the employment-wage configurations that we derive depend on skill: More-skilled workers enjoy on average lower relative returns from home production, b/p, and so they should be expected, on average, to have higher employment rates. In a general utility-maximizing framework and in a (very) long-run equilibrium, b might depend on market productivity through wealth accumulation, a point emphasized by Phelps (see, for example, chapter 1 in this volume). We ignore such a dependence here.

A formal equilibrium model of unemployment requires specification of a production technology, preferences, expectations and a wage determination mechanism. Match output is proportional to employment where the factor of proportionality, px, varies with the worker's skill level, p, and the job's idiosyncratic shock, x. Both workers and employers maximize human wealth, defined as the expected present value of future net income streams conditional on current information. Forward-looking rational expectations are imposed. Wages are determined by bilateral bargaining after the firm and worker meet.

Given these assumptions, equilibrium market tightness – the ratio of vacancies to unemployment, $\theta(p)$ – satisfies the following job creation condition: The expected present value of the future return to hiring a worker equals the expected cost. Of course, a hiring decision, implicit in the act of posting a job vacancy, is taken by an employer. The equilibrium reservation product reflects the decisions of both parties to continue an existing employment relationship. Individual rationality implies that separation occurs when the forward-looking capital value of continuing to either party is less than the capital value of separation. For joint rationality, the sum of the values of continuing the match must be less than the sum of the values of separating, otherwise a redistribution of the pair's future incomes can make both better off. Whether these job destruction conditions also satisfy the requirements of joint optimality depends on the wage mechanism assumed. For a given wage determination mechanism, a *search equilibrium* is a pair $(R(p), \theta(p))$ for each skill level, p, that simultaneously solves these job creation and job destruction conditions. Given our assumptions of market segmentation along skill lines, we can ignore from now on in the notation the functional dependence of all equilibrium mappings on p.

A *wage contract*, formally a pair $(w_0, w(x))$, is composed of a starting wage, $w_0 \in \Re$ and a continuing wage function $w : X \to \Re$ that obtains after any future shock to match specific productivity. Implicit in this specification is the idea that a worker and an employer negotiate an initial wage when they meet and then subsequently renegotiate in response to new information about the future value of their match.[4]

---

[4] Note that contracts of this form are instantly "renegotiated" on the arrival of a new idiosyncratic shock. MacLeod and Malcomson (1993) persuasively argue that the initial wage need not be renegotiated until an event occurs that would otherwise yield

A continuing match has specific productivity, x, and the worker is paid a wage $w(x)$. Given that the match ends in the future if a new match-specific shock, z, arrives that is less than some reservation threshold R, its capital value to an employer, $\mathcal{J}(x)$, solves the following asset-pricing equation for each p:

$$r\mathcal{J}(x) = px - a - (1+t)w(x)$$
$$+ \lambda \int_R^1 [\mathcal{J}(z) - \mathcal{J}(x)]dF(z) + \lambda F(R)[V - pT - \mathcal{J}(x)],$$

(2.4)

where r represents the risk-free interest rate, V is the value of a vacancy and a, t and T are policy parameters. An analogous relationship implicitly defines the asset value of the same match to the worker involved, $W(x)$. Namely,

$$rW(x) = w(x) + \lambda \int_R^1 [W(z) - W(x)]dF(z) + \lambda F(R)[U - W(x)],$$

(2.5)

where U is the capital value of unemployment.

Given a match product shock, z, the employer prefers separation if and only if its value as a vacancy, V, exceeds the value of continuation, $\mathcal{J}(z)$, plus the firing cost, pT. Similarly, the worker will opt for unemployment if and only if its value, U, exceeds $W(z)$. Given that under our wage rule both $\mathcal{J}(z)$ and $W(z)$ are increasing (see below), separation occurs when a new value of the shock arrives that falls below the reservation threshold

$$R = \max\{R_e, R_w\},$$

(2.6)

where $\mathcal{J}(R_e) = V - pT$ and $W(R_w) = U$. Because in the bilateral bargain wealth is transferable between worker and employer, the separation rule should be jointly optimal in the sense that it maximizes their total wealth. The necessary and sufficient condition for joint optimization is that $R = R_e = R_w$, where $\mathcal{J}(R) + W(R) = V - pT + U$, a condition that holds for only an appropriately designed wage contract.

Although the idiosyncratic component of a new job match is $x = 1$, the expected profit from a new match may be different from $\mathcal{J}(1)$, as

an inefficient separation. Contracts of this form may well generate more realistic wage dynamics but job creation and job destruction decisions are the same under theirs and our specification, provided the initial wage does not violate any non-negativity or other (e.g. minimum wage) constraints. Hence, for the purpose at hand, there is no relevant difference. However, their observation does suggest a possible explanation within our framework for the observed "stickiness" of wage rates, which, nonetheless, is not a cause of "underemployment" equilibria.

defined in (2.4), because of the existence of the job creation cost, pC, and the policy parameters pH and pT. We therefore introduce the notation $\mathcal{J}_0$ for the expected profit of a new match to the employer and write the asset-pricing equation for the present value of an unfilled vacancy, V, as

$$rV = q(\theta)[\mathcal{J}_0 - V - p(C - H)] - pc, \tag{2.7}$$

where pc is the recruiting cost flow per vacancy held, pC is a fixed cost of hiring and training a new worker plus any other match-specific investment required and pH is the hiring subsidy given by the government. Similarly, the value of unemployment solves

$$rU = b + \rho\bar{w} + \theta q(\theta)[W_0 - U], \tag{2.8}$$

where b is the flow of imputed income during unemployment and $\rho\bar{w}$ is the unemployment compensation: ρ is a policy parameter and $\bar{w}$ is the mean wage for the skill group. Note that the opportunity cost of employment is invariant with respect to the worker's skill as reflected in the parameter p by assumption.

Given an initial wage equal to w_0, the asset-pricing relation implies that the initial value of a match to employer and worker, respectively, satisfies

$$rJ_0 = p - a - (1 + t)w_0$$
$$+ \lambda \int_R^1 (\mathcal{J}(z) - \mathcal{J}_0)dF(z) + \lambda F(R)[V - pT - \mathcal{J}_0], \tag{2.9}$$

and

$$rW_0 = w_0 + \lambda \int_R^1 (W(z) - W_0)dF(z) + \lambda F(R)[U - W_0],$$

$$\tag{2.10}$$

where $(\mathcal{J}(x), W(x))$ represents the values of match continuation defined above.

Free entry requires that new vacancies are created until the capital value of holding one is driven to zero, i.e.

$$V = 0 \Leftrightarrow \frac{pc}{q(\theta)} + p(C - H) = \mathcal{J}_0. \tag{2.11}$$

As the expected number of periods required to fill a vacancy is $1/q(\theta)$, the condition equates the cost of recruiting and hiring a worker to anticipated discounted future profit stream. The fact that vacancy duration is increasing in market tightness guarantees that free entry will act to equate the two.

2.3   Wage determination

The generalized axiomatic Nash bilateral bargaining outcome with "threat point" equal to the option of looking for an alternative match partner is the baseline wage specification assumption found in the literature on search equilibrium.[5] Given that the existence of market friction creates quasi-rents for any matched pair, bilateral bargaining after worker and employer meet is the natural starting point for an analysis.[6]

Given the notation introduced above, the starting wage determined by the generalized Nash bargain over the future joint income stream foreseen by worker and employer supports the outcome

$$w_0 = \arg\max\{[W_0 - U]^\beta (S_0 - (W_0 - U))^{1-\beta}\}$$

subject to the following definition of initial match surplus:

$$S_0 \equiv \mathcal{J}_0 - p(C - H) - V + W_0 - U. \tag{2.12}$$

In the language of axiomatic bargaining theory, the parameter β represents the worker's relative "bargaining power." Analogously, the continuing wage contract supports the outcome

$$w(x) = \arg\max\{[W(x) - U]^\beta (S(x) - (W(x) - U))^{1-\beta}\},$$

where continuing match surplus is defined by

$$S(x) \equiv \mathcal{J}(x) - V + pT + W(x) - U. \tag{2.13}$$

The difference between the initial wage bargain and subsequent renegotiation arises for two reasons. First, hiring costs are "sunk" in the latter case but "on the table" in the former. Second, termination costs are not incurred if no match is formed initially but must be paid if an existing match is destroyed.

The solutions to these two different optimization problems satisfy the following first-order conditions:

$$\beta(\mathcal{J}_0 - V - p(C - H)) = (1 - \beta)(1 + t)(W_0 - U) \tag{2.14}$$

---

[5] See Diamond (1981, 1982b), Mortensen (1978, 1982) and Pissarides (1986, 1990).
[6] See Binmore, Rubinstein, and Wolinsky (1986), Rubinstein and Wolinsky (1985) and Wolinsky (1987) for applications of Rubinstein's strategic model in the search equilibrium framework. Although the precise form of the wage contract can differ under alternative specifications of the strategic bargaining game, all outcomes that are efficient from the perspective of any employer–worker pair yield the same job destruction decisions. Job creation decisions, however, may differ, because they depend on the share of the surplus going to one side only.

and

$$\beta(\mathcal{J}(x) - V + pT) = (1 - \beta)(1 + t)(W(x) - U), \tag{2.15}$$

where β, the worker's "bargaining power," is the resulting worker's share of match surplus in the absence of taxes. But, when there is marginal taxation, the worker's share falls, because firm and worker realize that they can pay less tax (a net loss to the pair) by reducing the negotiated wage. As an immediate consequence of (2.15), it follows that the reservation threshold R, defined by equation (2.6), is jointly rational, i.e. it solves

$$S(R) = \mathcal{J}(R) - V + pT + W(R) - U = 0.$$

In order to solve for the equilibrium (θ, R) pair, we first use the asset value equations and the sharing rules to solve for initial wages and wages in continuing jobs:

$$w_0 = (1 - \beta)(b + \rho\bar{w})$$
$$+ \frac{\beta}{1 + t}[p - a + pc\theta - (r + \lambda)p(C - H) - \lambda pT] \tag{2.16}$$

and

$$w(x) = (1 - \beta)(b + \rho\bar{w}) + \frac{\beta}{1 + t}[px - a + pc\theta + rpT]. \tag{2.17}$$

The dependence of these wages on the policy parameters needs some explanation. Both wage functions depend on a and t, because all jobs pay these taxes. The employment tax, a, reduces job surplus directly, so it is simply deducted from the match product before the latter is shared. The marginal tax, t, influences the share going to each party in the bargaining outcome. Specifically, because t affects the marginal rate at which the surplus can be traded between worker and employer, the tax rate influences the net share of match product obtained by the worker. The similarity between the two wage functions, however, stops there. The net job creation cost $p(C - H)$ reduces the initial wage, because the cost is conditional on an agreement to form the match and hence must be shared. But, once the job is formed, the creation cost is sunk and as such does not influence wages in continuing jobs. The firing cost, pT, reduces expected match surplus at the creation date and so reduces the initial wage for that reason. However, once the job is formed, the firing tax is an employer liability if the job is destroyed. This fact strengthens the worker's hand in the wage bargain and so pushes the negotiated wage up for continuing workers.

Equation (2.17) reflects the fact that the second influence dominates the first, so the wage in continuing matches goes up by the introduction of the firing cost.[7]

3   The solution

3.1   Market equilibrium

It remains to substitute the wage equations into the asset value equations and the job creation and job destruction conditions, in order to derive overall market equilibrium. Substitution into the job value conditions yields

$$
\begin{aligned}
(r + \lambda)\mathcal{J}_0 = {} & (1 - \beta)[p - (1 + t)(b + \rho\bar{w}) - a] - \beta pc\theta \\
& + \beta(r + \lambda)p(C - H) + \beta\lambda pT \\
& + \lambda \int_R^1 \mathcal{J}(z)dF(z) - \lambda F(R)pT
\end{aligned}
\tag{2.18}
$$

and

$$
\begin{aligned}
(r + \lambda)\mathcal{J}(x) = {} & (1 - \beta)[px - (1 + t)(b + \rho\bar{w}) - a] - \beta pc\theta - \beta rpT \\
& + \lambda \int_R^1 \mathcal{J}(z)dF(z) - \lambda F(R)pT.
\end{aligned}
\tag{2.19}
$$

Jobs are destroyed when

$$
\mathcal{J}(R) + pT = 0.
\tag{2.20}
$$

Equations (2.18), (2.19) and (2.20) imply the job creation condition

$$
\mathcal{J}_0 = (1 - \beta)p\left(\frac{1 - R}{r + \lambda} - T\right) + \beta p(C - H),
\tag{2.21}
$$

and the job destruction condition

$$
R + \frac{\lambda}{r + \lambda}\int_R^1 (z - R)dF(z) = \frac{a + (1 + t)(b + \rho\bar{w})}{p} + \frac{\beta}{1 - \beta}c\theta - rT.
\tag{2.22}
$$

---

[7] From an accounting perspective, workers pay their share of the expected amortized cost of termination at the first shock, $\beta\lambda pT/(1 + t)$, in the form of a lower wage flow over the period prior to the first shock arrival. Subsequently, they earn the market return on the prior "forced saving," equal to $\beta rpT/(1 + t)$, as long as the match continues.

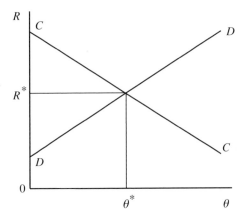

Figure 2.1 *Equilibrium market tightness and reservation productivity*

Finally, from (2.11) and (2.21), θ is the solution to

$$(1 - \beta)\left(\frac{1 - R}{r + \lambda} - T - C + H\right) = \frac{c}{q(\theta)}. \tag{2.23}$$

In (2.22), the reservation product, R, plus the option value of continuing the match attributable to the possibility that match product will increase in the future (the lefthand side of the equation), equals the match continuation opportunity cost flow (the righthand side). Higher market tightness increases the reservation productivity because the worker's outside options improve with θ. For given market tightness, both the firing tax and the employment and wage tax increase the reservation productivity and consequently reduce the surplus value of a continuing match.

In (2.23), the lefthand side is the firm's share of the expected net surplus attributable to a newly created job. The righthand side is the expected recruiting cost. Higher reservation productivity implies a shorter expected life of a new job, and so desired job creation falls and with it market tightness. For given reservation productivity, higher job creation or job destruction costs reduce desired job creation as well.

Now, (2.22) and (2.23) can be represented by two curves in $R \times \theta$ space, the former sloping up and the latter sloping down, for reasons just explained. This is shown in figure 2.1. Hence there is an equilibrium pair (R^*, θ^*) for each p that is unique. Of course, the ratio of vacancies to unemployment must be strictly positive ($\theta > 0$) in any meaningful equilibrium. Indeed, the following conditions are necessary but not generally sufficient:

$$1 > (r + \lambda)(C - H + T) \tag{2.24}$$

$$p(1 + rT) > a + (1 + t)(b + \rho\bar{w}).$$

Satisfaction of these two conditions restricts the magnitude of hiring and firing costs and the income while unemployed relative to the level of average productivity.

Outcome variables of interest include the unemployment rate, the average wage and aggregate income per participant. Given the equilibrium pair (R^*, θ^*), the associated unemployment rate, u, is determined by the Beveridge equation (2.3).

For given θ, the wage equations (2.16) and (2.17) define the equilibrium wage schedules in new and continuing jobs, respectively. As the steady-state fraction of newly created jobs is $F(R)$ and the fraction of continuing jobs with idiosyncratic productivity x or less is $F(x) - F(R)$, the average wage is simply

$$\bar{w} = w_0 F(R) + \int_R^1 w(x) dF(x). \tag{2.25}$$

After rearranging terms and substituting from (2.16) and (2.17) into (2.25), one obtains

$$\bar{w} = w_0 F(R) + (1 - F(R))w(R) + \frac{\beta p}{1 + t}\int_R^1 (x - R) dF(x)$$

$$= (1 - \beta)(b + \rho\bar{w}) + \frac{\beta}{1 + t}$$
$$\times \left[\begin{array}{l} p\left((1 - R) - (r + \lambda)(C - H + T)\right) F(R) \\ + p(R + rT) - a + pc\theta + \int_R^1 (x - R) dF(x) \end{array} \right].$$

Therefore, the equilibrium conditions (2.22) and (2.23) imply

$$\bar{w} = b + \rho\bar{w} + \frac{p\beta}{(1 + t)(1 - \beta)} \left[\begin{array}{l} \frac{c}{q(\theta)}((r + \lambda)F(R) + \theta q(\theta)) \\ + \frac{r(1 - \beta)}{r + \lambda}\int_R^1 (x - R) dF(x) \end{array} \right]. \tag{2.26}$$

Finally, aggregate income per participant, the sum of market output net of recruiting and job creation costs plus unemployment output, can be written as

$$y = p \left[F(R) + \int_R^1 x dF(x) \right] (1 - u) + bu - pcv - pCm(v, u)$$

$$= p \left[F(R) + \int_R^1 x dF(x) \right] (1 - u) + (b - pc\theta - pC\theta q(\theta))u. \tag{2.27}$$

Given unemployment, income increases with the reservation product and decreases with market tightness.

The differences between the equilibrium employment-wage combinations of skilled and unskilled workers can be seen with the help of figure 2.1. Inspection of the equations for the two curves, (2.22) and (2.23), shows that differences in the skill parameter p are reflected in differences in the location of the job destruction curve (2.22). Higher p implies that the job destruction curve lies at a lower position than it does with lower p. So skilled workers, who have the higher p, experience equilibrium outcomes with lower R and higher θ, i.e., for given unemployment, lower job destruction rate and higher job creation rate. The Beveridge curve then implies that the unemployment rate for skilled workers is lower in equilibrium. The wage equations also imply that the wage rate for skilled workers is higher, partly because of their higher productivity but also because of the tighter skilled markets.

Equation (2.22) makes clear why there are differences between the equilibrium combinations of the two skill groups. In the absence of policy, both skilled and unskilled workers have the same imputed value of leisure but different market returns. So the more-skilled workers gain more from employment, relative to their home returns, giving rise to their higher employment rates. With policy, the gain is affected by the employment subsidy and the tax rate (but not by the unemployment benefit, which is proportional to wages), both of which are independent of skill.

3.2   Comparative static results

The tax parameters a and t, as well as the supply price of labor, b, and unemployment compensation, $\rho\bar{w}$, all shift the job destruction curve up but have no direct effect on the job creation curve. As a consequence, the equilibrium value of the reservation threshold increases and the equilibrium value of market tightness falls. Hence, steady-state unemployment increases because unemployment duration and incidence both increase in response. Wages, however, increase in b and $\rho\bar{w}$ but fall in the tax instruments. It follows that, if we interpret a fall in a financed by a lump-sum consumption tax as an employment subsidy, both employment and wages rise in response. A fall in t has similar effects.

Now, because the effect of both a and t on employment is inversely proportional to p, the general productivity of a skill group, the effect of taxing or subsidizing employment by a given amount is larger for low-skill groups. Of course, if employment subsidies were proportional to the average skill level in each case, the differential effect of employment subsidies would disappear. But then the authorities would be spending a lot more on subsidizing skilled employment than unskilled. Also, the differential effects of the tax rate would remain. The reason for the differential effects of tax rates, if we ignore employment subsidies, is that leisure activities are not taxed. Therefore, the effect of the tax is the same as the effect of a subsidy on home activities. Because low-skill groups have higher imputed income from home production, a given percentage subsidy has a bigger impact on behavior. If home production were taxed, or if it depended on wealth that was taxed, directly or indirectly, the effect would disappear in the long run.

With flat-rate subsidies and untaxed home production, it would be beneficial in terms of overall employment to tax high-skill groups and use the revenue to subsidize low-skill groups. The employment benefit at the lower end of the skill distribution outweighs the loss at the top end. In the wage equations, the effect of different a on wages is the same across all occupational groups. But the effect of different t is higher for higher-skill groups than for lower ones. So a uniform tax should reduce wage inequality. Of course, taxing high-skill groups and subsidizing low-skill groups should also reduce inequality.

An increase in the hiring subsidy, H, inflates demand and consequently shifts the job creation curve up in figure 2.1. Both the equilibrium reservation threshold and market tightness rise in response, inducing respectively a decrease in unemployment duration and an increase in unemployment incidence. Hence, the net effect on steady-state unemployment is qualitatively indeterminate. Initial wages also increase with H, but wages in continuing jobs are not directly affected, except to the extent that the rise in tightness increases them. It follows that, if the government subsidizes job creation, it reduces unemployment duration but increases unemployment incidence. It also increases wages, especially those of newly hired workers.

Changes in the firing tax, T, have more complicated effects on unemployment duration and incidence. An increase in T shifts both the job destruction curve and the job creation curve down. Although the effect on market tightness appears ambiguous, a formal differentiation of the equilibrium conditions yields a negative net effect on both R and θ. Still, because of the negative effect of firing costs on job creation, the qualitative effect on steady-state unemployment is indeterminate. Initial wages fall with T but wages in continuing jobs rise, thus making the wage-tenure profile steeper.

4   Computation experiments

In this section, we present computed solutions to the model that provide some numerical feel for its policy implications. Parsimonious functional forms are assumed. Some of the parameters are set at reasonable values

Table 2.1 *Baseline parameter values*

Parameter	Case 1: US policy	Case 2: EU policy
Match product, p	1	1
Interest rate, r	0.02	0.02
Shock arrival rate, λ	0.1	0.1
Lower shock support, γ	0.646	0.646
Duration elasticity, η	0.5	0.5
Recruiting cost, c	0.3	0.3
Creation cost, C	0.3	0.3
Value of leisure, b	0.349	0.349
Payroll tax rate, τ	0.2	0.2
Firing tax, T	0	0.78
UI replacement ratio, ρ	0.2	0.34

and others are chosen to match unemployment spell durations and incidences typically experienced by workers in the US economy. Two different initial labor policy configurations are considered, one in which the unemployment benefit replacement ratio is moderate and unemployment protection legislation is weak, as in the United States, and another in which both the level of unemployment compensation and the extent of employment protection are relatively high, as in Europe. The simulated numerical effects of employment and hiring subsidies are reported for each case for both "high" and "low" skill workers.

4.1   *Functional forms and baseline parameters*

The matching function is log-linear. Formally,

$$q(\theta) = \theta^{-\eta}, \tag{2.28}$$

where, without loss of generality, the scale parameter is normalized to one (this assumption simply determines the units in which v, and so θ, are measured) and η is the constant elasticity of the matching function with respect to unemployment. The distribution of the idiosyncratic shock to match productivity is uniform over the interval $[\gamma, 1]$, i.e.

$$F(x) = \frac{x - \gamma}{1 - \gamma}. \tag{2.29}$$

The baseline parameters used for the two policy cases under study are presented in table 2.1. The normalized skill parameter value $p = 1$ is interpreted as the initial match product of a worker of average ability. The difference between the two policy scenarios involves the values of the policy parameters ρ and T. In case 1, the replacement ratio is set equal to 0.2 and there is no employment protection policy, a specification consistent with the OECD characterization of US policy (see OECD, 1994).

The numerical analysis abstracts from the possible effects of search externalities by considering only the case of an efficient equilibrium solution to the model, which is obtained by imposing the condition $\beta = \eta$. As is well known, this condition internalizes the effects of the search externalities on the equilibrium outcome (Hosios, 1990; Pissarides, 1990). In the initial calibration exercise, the wage tax, t, is set equal to a typical payroll tax rate of $\tau = 0.2$. This payroll tax, used in virtually all countries to finance social security expenditures, is possibly a bit high in a US context and definitely too low for the typical European country.

After setting all the other parameter values as in Mortensen (1994), unemployment output, b, and the lower shock bound, γ, are chosen so that the steady-state unemployment rate, u, equals 6.5 percent and the average duration of an unemployment spell, $1/\theta q(\theta)$, is one-quarter, values that reflect US experience in the past twenty years. In case 2, the policy parameters are set to obtain the same steady-state unemployment rate but an average unemployment duration twice as long, about six months. This case, in which unemployment spells are longer but less frequent, reflects European experience (see OECD, 1994), at least until the recent runup in long-term unemployment. These assumptions, the other parameter values and the model imply a case 2 replacement ratio consistent with those observed in Europe, $\rho = 0.34$, and an implicit firing cost, $T = 0.78$, which is roughly equal to the average quarterly wage in the benchmark model.

4.2   Outcomes

Outcome variables include the steady-state unemployment rate, the average wage and aggregate income. After solving for the equilibrium (R, θ) pair, unemployment is computed using the Beveridge equation (2.3). Equations (2.26) and (2.27) are used to calculate the average wage and aggregate income per participant, respectively.

In tables 2.2 and 2.3, outcome variable values are reported for both policy scenarios and two levels of worker "skill." For each outcome variable, case and work skill type, both the actual simulated value and the "first-best" value are reported, along with an employment subsidy and hiring subsidy that will implement first-best. First-best is defined as the equilibrium where the effect of all policy instruments combined on the (R, θ) pair is zero. From (2.22) and (2.23), given that $\beta = \eta$, first-best

Table 2.2 *Outcomes: high skill (*p = *1.4)*

	Case 1: $(\rho, T) = (0.2, 0)$		Case 2: $(\rho, T) = (0.34, 0.78)$	
	Actual	First-best	Actual	First-best
Unemployment rate, u	5.3	4.2	4.5	4.2
Average wage, $\overline{w}$	1.08	1.41	1.03	1.71
Aggregate income, y	1.25	1.26	1.25	1.26
Replacement ratio, ρ	0.2	0.2	0.34	0.34
Firing cost, T	0.0	0.0	0.78	0.78
Wage tax, t	0.2	0.2	0.2	0.2
Employment subsidy, $-a$	0.0	0.41	0.0	0.75
Hiring subsidy, H	0.0	0.0	0.0	0.78

Table 2.3 *Outcomes: low skill (*p = *0.75)*

	Case 1: $(\rho, T) = (0.2, 0)$		Case 2: $(\rho, T) = (0.34, 0.78)$	
	Actual	First-best	Actual	First-best
Unemployment rate, u	9.0	5.2	16.2	5.2
Average wage, $\overline{w}$	0.588	0.796	0.563	0.965
Aggregate income, y	0.679	0.684	0.651	0.684
Replacement ratio, ρ	0.2	0.2	0.34	0.34
Firing cost, T	0.0	0.0	0.78	0.78
Wage tax, t	0.2	0.2	0.2	0.2
Employment subsidy, $-a$	0.0	0.261	0.0	0.452
Hiring subsidy, H	0.0	0.0	0.0	0.78

is a configuration of the policy instruments that satisfies

$$a + (1 + t)(b + \rho\overline{w}) - rpT = b \tag{2.30}$$

and

$$H = T. \tag{2.31}$$

In working out the simulated first-best solution, we treat T, ρ and t as parameters and H and a as the "unknowns" of the simultaneous solution of (2.30) and (2.31); that is, we look for a hiring subsidy and an employment subsidy that will offset the effects of the tax, firing restrictions and unemployment benefit on the equilibrium outcome. "High-skill" workers are assigned a productivity parameter of $p = 1.4$ whereas low-skill workers are assigned $p = 0.75$. Given the normalization $p = 1$ for the productivity parameter of an average worker, these are the average calibrated values derived in Millard and Mortensen (1996) using 1990 aggregate US earnings data by educational attainment if one defines "low skill" as those with a high-school diploma or less and "high skill" as those with more than a high-school education.

For high-skill workers in the "US" policy scenario, the first-best unemployment rate is only 1 percentage point less than the actual rate in policy case 1 and $3/10$ of a point in policy case 2, and there is little overall welfare loss attributable to passive labor market policies as measured by aggregate income per participant in either case. However, the average wage after first-best is attained by subsidizing employment is much larger than the actual in both cases.

There are two interrelated reasons for such a large response in the wage to an employment subsidy. First, a higher subsidy has a direct positive effect on wages but also increases unemployment compensation given a fixed replacement ratio, which in turn induces a second-round increase in the wage (see equations (2.16) and (2.17)). Second, the induced increase in unemployment compensation increases the distortion further, which causes a need for a second-round increase in the subsidy to achieve first-best. As a consequence of these multiplier processes, the wage increases by almost the amount of the subsidy, 0.41, in spite of the fact that the workers' share of the direct subsidy is only equal to $\beta = 0.5$.

For "low-skill" workers, the employment and efficiency gains are large. Even in the "US" policy scenario, actual unemployment is twice first-best and aggregate output per participant is almost 2 percent less than potential. In policy case 2, characterized by high unemployment compensation and strict employment protection, the actual unemployment rate is three times first-best and first-best output is over 3 percent larger than actual. In both cases, the wage is again augmented by almost the size of the subsidy.

4.3   Marginal effects of an employment subsidy

An employment subsidy is an employment-contingent flow paid throughout the duration of a job–worker match. This contrasts with a wage subsidy, which can be regarded as a reduction in the payroll tax. We report results with wage subsidies normalized by the average wage; that is, if a is the flat employment subsidy, we report results for a range of s values, where s is defined by

$$s = -a/\bar{w}. \qquad (2.32)$$

The normalization in (2.32) helps in the comparison with a wage subsidy in the following sense. Define a wage subsidy by a reduction in the tax rate, t. The cost to the government of this reduction is $t\bar{w}$, so a reduction of the tax by an amount s is comparable to an employment subsidy of s as defined in (2.32), in the sense that to finance either requires the same consumption tax. Now, from (2.22) and (2.23), if an employment subsidy, s, were enacted, its effect on equilibrium would be a displacement of (2.22) by an amount $s\bar{w}/p$. If a wage subsidy of s were offered, its effect would be a displacement of the same condition by an amount $s(b + \rho\bar{w})/p$. Because a meaningful equilibrium requires that unemployment income be less than income from work, i.e. $b + \rho\bar{w} < \bar{w}$, the effect of an employment subsidy per dollar of consumption tax dominates that of a wage subsidy (holding $\rho\bar{w}$ constant). Thus, it is cheaper to use an employment subsidy to achieve whatever effect on the employment outcome is desired than to use a wage subsidy. But the effects of the two policies on wages are different, as the wage equations (2.16) and (2.17) make clear. A reduction of t by an amount s and a reduction of a by an amount $s\bar{w}$ both increase wages at all productivity levels, but, because mean wages have to be less than productivity in a meaningful equilibrium, a wage subsidy has a bigger effect on wages than an employment subsidy of the same value.

In what follows we consider only the marginal effects of an employment subsidy, s, as defined in (2.32). The values considered in the simulations range from 0 to 20 percent of the average wage. The upper bound is equal to the size of the underlying payroll tax assumed in the experiment, and in all cases is less than the level required to attain first-best (see tables 2.2 and 2.3). In all likelihood, it also exceeds the magnitude of any politically feasible subsidy.

The computed numerical effects of the employment subsidy on the unemployment rate and the other two outcome variables – the average wage and aggregate income per participant – for both policy scenarios and skill levels are reported in table 2.4. The subsidy is expressed as a percentage of the initial average wage, and the wage and income effects are stated as percentage changes relative to their initial values to facilitate comparison.

Table 2.4 sends a clear message. Although an employment subsidy reduces unemployment in all cases, the effect is virtually non-existent for a worker of high skill ($p = 1.4$) under either policy scenario. However, the low-skill unemployment rate falls substantially with the employment subsidy, although much more so under a "European" policy regime (case 2) than under a "US" policy regime (case 1). For a worker of high skill there is virtually no efficiency gain to be realized over the employment subsidy range under consideration, despite the unemployment fall, but the average worker's wage does increase, at the rate of 80 cents on a dollar of subsidy.

Table 2.4 *Effects of an employment subsidy*

	Case 1: $(\rho, T) = (0.2, 0)$			Case 2: $(\rho, T) = (0.34, 0.78)$		
Subsidy 100s	Unemployment rate u	Income $\Delta y/y$	Wage $\Delta \overline{w}/\overline{w}$	Unemployment rate u	Income $\Delta y/y$	Wage $\Delta \overline{w}/\overline{w}$
High Skill: $p = 1.4$						
0	5.4	0.0	0.0	4.5	0.0	0.0
4	5.1	0.0	3.2	4.3	0.0	3.2
8	5.0	0.1	6.4	4.1	0.0	6.5
12	4.8	0.1	9.6	3.9	0.0	9.7
16	4.7	0.1	12.9	3.8	0.0	13.1
20	4.5	0.1	16.1	3.6	0.0	16.2
Low skill: $p = 0.75$						
0	9.0	0.0	0.0	16.2	0.0	0.0
4	8.4	0.2	3.2	12.8	1.6	3.1
8	7.9	0.3	6.3	10.8	2.4	6.2
12	7.4	0.4	9.5	9.4	2.9	9.4
16	7.0	0.5	12.7	8.4	3.2	12.6
20	6.7	0.5	15.0	7.6	3.4	15.8

Table 2.5 *Effects of a hiring subsidy*

	Case 1: $(\rho, T) = (0.2, 0)$			Case 2: $(\rho, T) = (0.34, 0.78)$		
Subsidy 100s	Unemployment rate u	Income $\Delta y/y$	Wage $\Delta \overline{w}/\overline{w}$	Unemployment rate u	Income $\Delta y/y$	Wage $\Delta \overline{w}/\overline{w}$
High Skill: $p = 1.4$						
0	5.3	0.0	0.0	4.5	0.0	0.0
4	6.2	−0.4	5.1	6.2	0.8	6.0
8	7.0	−1.5	11.1	7.7	−0.1	13.8
12	7.7	−3.4	17.9	8.8	−2.1	23.3
16	8.3	−6.1	25.4	9.8	−5.9	34.4
20	8.9	−9.5	33.8	10.5	−11.2	47.3
Low skill: $p = 0.75$						
0	9.0	0.0	0.0	16.2	0.0	0.0
4	9.6	−0.3	4.6	15.0	1.7	4.6
8	10.2	−1.2	9.9	14.8	2.1	10.3
12	10.6	−2.7	15.8	14.5	1.3	17.0
16	11.0	−4.8	22.3	14.5	−0.0	24.7
20	11.3	−7.4	29.4	14.5	−3.1	33.5

In the low-skill worker case, the allocation effects are dramatic, particularly under the case 2 policy scenario. Even when policy is of the "US" variety (case 1), the unemployment rate falls from 9.0 to 6.7 percent as the subsidy increases from zero to 20 percent of wages. When employment protection policy restricts reallocation and unemployment compensation is high, as in Europe (case 2), the model suggests that efficiency gains are substantial as well. For example, a 20 percent subsidy induces a 3.4 percent increase in income. Furthermore, unemployment falls from 16.2 percent to less than 8 percent, and again wages increase with the subsidy at a rate of roughly 80 cents on the dollar in both cases.

In conclusion, an employment subsidy financed with a non-distortionary consumption tax has large positive effects on both the employment level and the wage earned. This conclusion is particularly true of low-skill workers in a regime of high unemployment compensation and employment protection. Furthermore, the subsidy offsets efficiency distortions induced by the payroll tax used to finance social security programs, by unemployment compensation and by employment protection policy.

4.4   *Marginal effects of a hiring subsidy*

In this section, the simulated effects of a job creation subsidy are reported. A hiring subsidy is a payment that can be either a direct transfer to the employer or a tax rebate made to offset job creation costs. As pH is the subsidy per worker hired and the gross hiring rate is the product of the unemployment hazard and the unemployment rate, a comparable measure is the total hiring subsidy flow divided by the total wage bill, i.e.

$$s = \frac{pH\theta q(\theta)u}{\bar{w}(1-u)}. \tag{2.33}$$

This measure is expressed in the same units as a wage subsidy and an employment subsidy normalized by wage.

The unemployment effects of a hiring subsidy for both policy cases and both worker skill groups are reported in table 2.5. As reflected in equation (2.33), the gross subsidy flow is expressed as a percentage of the total wage bill for comparison with the results for an employment subsidy reported in table 2.4. Wage and income effects too are stated as percentage changes relative to their initial values, also to facilitate comparison.

The algebraic effect of the hiring subsidy on unemployment is positive in three of the four cases but negative for "low-skill" workers in policy scenario case 2. Recall, the qualitative effect of a hiring subsidy is theoretically ambiguous for the following reason. By making the cost of job creation less expensive, job creation is stimulated. However, a tighter market induces more job destruction as well because the opportunity cost of a match rises with θ. Unemployment increases when the positive effect on unemployment incidence exceeds the negative effect on unemployment duration.

When unemployment compensation is low and there is no employment protection policy (the "US" policy, case 1), unemployment increases with the hiring subsidy for both high- and low-skill workers. However, the reverse is true for low-skill workers in the "EU" policy (case 2) characterized by high unemployment compensation and stringent employment protection. Furthermore, the subsidy decreases aggregate income by a substantial amount in case 1 for workers of both skill levels but can generate increases in case 2. The reason for this difference would seem to be the implicit firing cost of employment protection present in case 2. The hiring subsidy offsets the negative effect of the firing cost on job creation and on aggregate income. That wages are bid up by a hiring subsidy in all cases is confirmed. Indeed, the wage is much more responsive to a hiring subsidy than to an employment subsidy increase of comparable size.

The lessons learned from this computational experiment are also clear. A hiring subsidy can *decrease both employment and efficiency*, essentially by encouraging too much replacement of old jobs by new through creative destruction. Indeed, a hiring subsidy is welfare improving only to the extent that it offsets the negative effects of firing costs on job creation, as the earlier first-best analysis indicated.

4.5   A self-financing employment subsidy and wage tax

Because a non-distortionary consumption or lump-sum tax is not a practical possibility in fact, the results reported above overstate the net effects of employment and hiring subsidies by an amount equal to the deadweight loss of some alternative form of taxation. Furthermore, the only alternative in this environment, an income tax, is equivalent to a wage tax if employers can fully expense recruiting and training costs, as is the case under the US tax code. Hence, any employment subsidy must ultimately be financed by an offsetting increase in tax on labor earnings.

Because the distortion caused by a dollar collected from a wage tax is less than the offsetting effect on the same worker of using that dollar to subsidize employment, a fact noted above, employment, wage and welfare improvements could be achieved in principle by increasing the wage tax and using the proceeds to subsidize employment even if there were only one worker type. However, the computed consequences of this

Table 2.6 *Effects of a "low-skill" subsidy and "high-skill" surtax*

Subsidy 100s	Low skill ($p = 0.75$)		High skill ($p = 1.0$)		Income	Surtax
	u_1	$\Delta \bar{w}_1 / \bar{w}_1$	u_2	$\Delta \bar{w}_2 / \bar{w}_2$	$\Delta y / y$	$100(t - \tau)$
Policy case 1: $(\rho, T) = (0.2, 0)$						
0	9.0	0.0	5.3	0.0	0.0	0.0
4	8.4	3.2	5.4	−1.7	0.1	2.1
8	7.9	6.3	5.4	−3.5	0.1	4.4
12	7.4	9.5	5.5	−5.2	0.1	6.7
16	7.0	12.7	5.5	−7.0	0.1	9.2
20	6.7	15.9	5.6	−8.8	0.1	11.8
Policy case 2: $(\rho, T) = (0.34, 0.78)$						
0	16.2	0.0	4.5	0.0	0.0	0.0
4	12.8	3.1	4.6	−1.6	0.5	2.0
8	10.8	6.2	4.6	−3.3	0.8	4.2
12	9.4	9.4	4.7	−5.1	1.0	6.6
16	8.4	12.6	4.8	−6.9	1.1	9.0
20	7.6	15.8	4.9	−8.7	1.1	11.6

policy (not reported here) are quite small, as one might expect, over a reasonable range of the subsidy and associated required tax.

Suppose instead one were to levy a surtax on high-skill workers and use the proceeds to target an employment subsidy to low-skill workers. To the extent that our previous results show that the impacts of the policy parameters are much larger for low-skill workers, this form of cross-subsidization is likely to increase both the wage and the employment of low-wage workers significantly, with only a small negative effect on the wage and employment of high-wage workers.

The results of a computational experiment along these lines are reported in table 2.6. These numbers are obtained by calculating the market equilibrium for "low" and "high" skill workers simultaneously when the two markets are interconnected by a government budget constraint. Because the wage surtax above and beyond the baseline payroll tax, $t - \tau$, levied on the "high-skill" workers must cover the cost of a "low-skill" employment subsidy $-a = s\bar{w}_1$, the constraint can be written as

$$(t - \tau)\bar{w}_2(1 - u_2)\ell_2 = s\bar{w}_1(1 - u_1)\ell_1, \qquad (2.34)$$

where $(1 - u_i)\ell_i$ is the equilibrium level of employment, ℓ_i is the fraction in the labor force, and $\bar{w}_i$ is the average wage of workers in skill group i respectively, given that $i = 1(2)$ denotes the low (high) skill type. Reflecting the fact that about half of the US labor force had more than a high-school education in the 1990s, the computations in table 2.6 reflect the assumption that $\ell_1 = \ell_2 = 0.5$.

The results reported in table 2.6 are quite encouraging. Over the rather reasonable low-skill employment subsidy range equal to 0 to 20 percent of earnings, the low-skill unemployment rate falls by over 2 points under the "US" style policy and by more than half (from 16 percent to less than 8 percent) in the "European" policy regime, with very little impact on the level of unemployment of the high-skill workers in either case. Although the surtax on high-skill worker earnings lowers the wage of high-skill workers, the low-skill wage increases by twice as much in percentage terms. Furthermore, the low-skill wage increases by between 77 and 80 cents on the dollar of employment subsidy over the range studied in both policy cases. Hence, the combined subsidy–tax policy promotes considerable wage equality. At the same time, the level of aggregate income increases in response to the subsidy, particularly when unemployment compensation is high and employment protection is stringent.

Note that the combined wage tax and employment subsidization policy studied in this section is a reallocation scheme similar to the Earned Income Tax Credit that is part of the US income tax code. Like the credit in combination with a progressive income tax, those who earn more pay a higher marginal tax rate while those with low earnings receive an employment-contingent income supplement. Indeed, in the environment under study the two schemes are formally equivalent because an employment subsidy has the same effects as an employment-contingent payment made to the worker and the incidence of a wage tax is independent of whether it is the employer or the worker who actually pays it.

5   Conclusions and a future research agenda

In this chapter we have derived the effects of wage, employment and hiring subsidies on job creation, job destruction, employment and wages implied by an extended version of the Mortensen–Pissarides (1994) model of labor market equilibrium. Qualitative analytical results show that wage and employment subsidies increase employment, especially of low-skill workers, and also increase wages. A job creation or hiring subsidy reduces unemployment duration but increases incidence, with an ambiguous effect on overall employment. A firing tax has the reverse effects and also has an indeterminate employment effect.

Because a pure consumption tax has no effect on resource allocation decisions in the environment modeled, a first-best tax and subsidy configuration always exists even when an unemployment compensation scheme and an employment protection policy are in place and when search externalities are present. One configuration includes the case of no wage tax, an employment subsidy set to offset the distortions of unemployment compensation and employment protection on the job destruction decision, and a hiring subsidy that corrects any job creation distortion imposed by employment protection and search externalities.

Computational experiments confirm that this ideal also determines the direction in which significant marginal improvements in both efficiency and equity can be made. However, simulation results also suggest that a hiring subsidy larger than that required to offset the effects of employment protection typically reduces employment and income by encouraging the replacement of old jobs with new too frequently. Finally, an employment subsidy targeted at low-skill workers but financed by a wage tax on high-wage workers, a policy equivalent to an "earned income tax credit" in our framework, can induce significant increases in the employment and wage of low-skill workers with little increase in the unemployment rate of high-wage workers.

There are many caveats to add concerning the limitations of the model used to draw these conclusions, and qualifications that identify needs for future research. Important among these is our assumption that the opportunity cost of employment as reflected in unemployment-contingent income, or the value of leisure (b in our notation), is independent of worker skill. This assumption is critical to the theoretical and computational outcomes reviewed above. To a first approximation, the quantitative importance of outcomes is proportional to the ratio of productivity to b. Empirical testing of this condition is, therefore, an important topic for future research.

Other research topics are suggested by the need to consider alternative specifications to those used here. For example, much has been made of worker "hold-up" possibilities that arise because match-specific investments made by employers in hiring, training and equipping a worker more generally are irreversible ex post. In this environment, workers have an incentive to renege on any initial agreement to share these costs through a lower wage. One parsimonious way to capture the effects of this time consistency problem is to assume that the initial wage is determined "as if" the match-specific investments were made prior to the initial wage bargaining game. The result would be an initial wage equal to the continuing wage at the initial value of the match-specific component of productivity, i.e. $w_0 = w(1)$ in the notation of the chapter. As the employer incentives to create job vacancies are lower under this "insider-wage" contract, a hiring subsidy might be expected to perform somewhat better than under the investment-sharing contract assumed in the chapter. The effects given alternative methods of wage determination, particularly those associated with the "efficiency wage" hypothesis, might also be studied.

In their analysis of wage subsidies using a similar model to ours, Davidson and Woodbury (1995) allow for endogenous worker search intensity. This generalization adds nothing to this analysis from a purely theoretical point of view but does introduce a new channel of influence for policy, skill and bargaining power. Suppose the matching function takes the form $m(v, eu)$, where here e represents the search effort of the typical unemployed worker. Given the assumption that effort reduces net value of leisure, say it is equal to $b(1 - (e^{1/\gamma}/\gamma))$ where $\gamma \in (0, 1)$, then one can show that optimal effort is a function of the market tightness. Formally,

$$be^{\frac{1}{\gamma}-1} = \frac{m(v, eu)}{eu}(W_0 - U) = \frac{m(v, eu)}{eu}\frac{\beta(\mathcal{J}_0 - C + H)}{(1+t)(1-\beta)}$$

$$= \left(\frac{v}{eu}\right)\frac{\beta pc}{(1+t)(1-\beta)},$$

where the first equality is the first-order condition for an individual's optimal choice of effort, the second is an implication of the bargaining outcome rule and the third is implied by the free entry condition. As a result, one can simply substitute appropriately to derive the reduced-form matching function

$$M(v, u) = m\left(v, \left(\frac{\beta pc(v/u)}{b(1+t)(1-\beta)}\right)^\gamma u\right).$$

Given m concave and linearly homogeneous, so is M, so the basic theory applies.

However, now the wage tax, the skill productivity parameter and the "market power" parameter have added direct effects on the matching process given market tightness $\theta = v/u$ and indirect effects on the job creation and job destruction conditions. The reduced-form vacancy hazard is now

$$q(\theta) = \frac{M(v, u)}{v} = m\left(1, \left(\frac{\beta pc}{b(1+t)(1-\beta)}\right)^\gamma \theta^{\gamma-1}\right). \qquad (2.35)$$

Otherwise, the job creation condition (2.23) holds as stated. Substituting $b(1 - \gamma e^{1/\gamma})$ for unemployment-contingent income b on the righthand side of (2.22), we obtain the following modified opportunity cost of employment:

$$\frac{a + (1+t)(b(1 - \gamma e^{1/\gamma}) + \rho\bar{w})}{p} + \frac{\beta(1 - \gamma)}{1 - \beta}c\theta - rT. \qquad (2.36)$$

The principal qualitative changes are reductions in the sensitivity of the vacancy hazard and the opportunity cost of a match to the vacancy–unemployment ratio. In addition, a wage tax now discourages search effort, which in turn reduces the equilibrium employer incentive to create jobs, given the complementarity of vacancies and search effort in the matching function.

The Davidson and Woodbury specification also differs from ours by assuming that the total number of jobs available is fixed rather than endogenously determined by a free entry condition. Not surprisingly, they conclude that a targeted subsidy will have a large displacement effect. Still, their result illustrates that our specification assumes a large part of the crowding-out problem away. One way to introduce a middle ground would be to assume that worker productivity depends on employment levels. For example, let $p_i = f_i(n_1, n_2)$, where $n_i = (1 - u_i)\ell_i$ represents the employment level of skill group i and where $f_i(.)$, the marginal product of skill i workers, allows for diminishing returns and substitution between the two worker types.

References

Binmore, K.G., A. Rubinstein and A. Wolinsky (1986). "The Nash Bargaining Solution in Economic Modelling," *Rand Journal of Economics* 17: 176–188.

Burda, M.C. (1992). "A Note on Firing Costs and Severance Benefits in Equilibrium Unemployment," *Scandinavian Journal of Economics* 39: 479–489.

Davidson, K. and S.A. Woodbury (1995). "Wage Subsidies for Dislocated Workers," Upjohn Institute Staff Working Paper 95-31.

Davis, S.J., J. Haltiwanger and S. Schuh (1996). *Job Creation and Destruction*. Cambridge, MA: MIT Press.

Diamond, P.A. (1981). "Mobility Costs, Frictional Unemployment, and Efficiency," *Journal of Political Economy* 89: 798–812.

——— (1982a). "Aggregate Demand Management in Search Equilibrium," *Journal of Political Economy* 90: 881–894.

——— (1982b). "Wage Determination and Efficiency in Search Equilibrium," *Review of Economic Studies* 49: 217–227.

Friedman, M. (1968). "The Role of Monetary Policy," *American Economic Review* 58: 1–17.

Hosios, A.J. (1990). "On the Efficiency of Matching and Related Models of Search and Unemployment," *Review of Economic Studies* 57: 279–298.

Lazear, E. (1990). "Job Security Provisions and Employment," *Quarterly Journal of Economics* 105: 699–726.

MacLeod, W.B. and J. Malcomson (1993). "Investments, Holdup, and the Form of Market Contracts," *American Economic Review* 83: 811–837.

Millard, S.P. and D.T. Mortensen (1996). "The Unemployment and Welfare Effects of Labour Market Policy: A Comparison of the US and UK," in

D. Snower and G. de la Dehesa (eds.), *Unemployment Policy: How Should Governments Respond to Unemployment?* Oxford: Oxford University Press.

Mortensen, D.T. (1978). "Specific Capital and Labor Turnover," *Bell Journal of Economics* 9(2): 572–586.

(1982). "The Matching Process as a Noncooperative/Bargaining Game," in J.J. McCall (ed.), *The Economics of Information and Uncertainty*, 233–254. Chicago: University of Chicago Press.

(1994). "Reducing Supply Side Disincentives to Job Creation," in *Reducing Unemployment: Current Issues and Policy Options.* Kansas City: Federal Research Bank of Kansas City.

Mortensen, D.T. and C.A. Pissarides (1994). "Job Creation and Job Destruction in the Theory of Unemployment," *Review of Economic Studies* 61: 397–415.

OECD (Organisation for Economic Co-operation and Development) (1994). *Jobs Study.* Paris: OECD.

Petrongolo, B. and C.A. Pissarides (2001). "Looking into the Black Box: A Survey of the Matching Function," *Journal of Economic Literature* June.

Phelps, E.S. (1968). "Money-Wage Dynamics and Labor Market Equilibrium," *Journal of Political Economy* 76: 254–281.

(1997). *Rewarding Work.* Cambridge, MA: Harvard University Press.

Phelps, E.S. et. al. (1970). *Microeconomic Foundations of Employment and Inflation Theory.* New York: W.W. Norton.

Pissarides, C.A. (1985). "Short-Run Equilibrium Dynamics of Unemployment, Vacancies and Real Wages," *American Economic Review* 75: 676–690.

(1986). "Unemployment and Vacancies in Britain," *Economic Policy* 3: 499–559.

(1990). *Equilibrium Unemployment Theory.* Oxford: Basil Blackwell.

Rubinstein, A. and A. Wolinsky (1985). "Equilibrium in a Market with Sequential Bargaining," *Econometrica* 53: 1133–1150.

Stigler, G.J. (1961). "The Economics of Information," *Journal of Political Economy* 69: 213–225.

Wolinsky, A. (1987). "Matching, Search, and Bargaining," *Journal of Economic Theory* 42: 311–333.

3   Learning-by-doing versus on-the-job
     training: using variation induced by
     the EITC to distinguish between models
     of skill formation

James J. Heckman, Lance Lochner and Ricardo Cossa

1   Introduction

Recent calls for wage subsidies have emphasized their value for attaching
low-skill persons to the workplace, attracting them away from lives of
idleness or crime (Phelps, 1997; Heckman, Lochner, Smith and Taber,
1997; and Lochner, 1998). Previous empirical research on wage subsidies
has focused exclusively on their effects on employment and labor supply.
This chapter examines the impact of wage subsidies on skill formation.

By promoting work among those who would not otherwise work, wage
subsidies create incentives for workers to invest in skills that are useful in
the workplace. The skill formation effects of wage subsidies on persons
who would work without the subsidy are more subtle. If skills are acquired as a by-product of work (learning-by-doing), wage subsidies will
encourage skill acquisition to the extent that workers increase their labor
supply in response to the subsidy. However, if learning is rivalrous with
working, as in Becker (1964) or Ben Porath (1967), wage subsidies can
discourage investment in skills.

There are even more subtle effects of wage subsidies on skill formation arising from the non-linearity in the return to work created by many
proposed schemes. These non-linearities arise from the targeted nature
of most programs. Specifically, consider the Earned Income Tax Credit
(EITC) in the United States, which supplements annual labor earnings

This research was sponsored by NSF-97-09-873 and NSF-SES-0079195 and a grant from
the American Bar Foundation. This chapter was originally presented at a conference on
wage subsidies sponsored by the Russell Sage Foundation, New York, December 1997, at
the IRP conference at the University of Wisconsin, June 1998, at the Western Economics
Association Meeting, July 1998, at the University of Rochester, November 1998, and at a
Public Sector Workshop at the University of Chicago, May 1999. We thank Alejandra Cox
Edwards, Nada Eissa, Larry Summers, Edmund Phelps and especially Casey Mulligan and
Yona Rubinstein for comments on this paper.

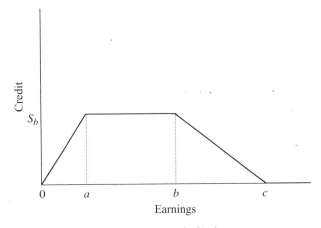

Figure 3.1 *Earned Income Tax Credit*

for those who work, as shown in figure 3.1.[1] (For analytical simplicity, we abstract from all other tax and transfer programs implicitly assuming that they generate proportional schedules that preserve figure 3.1 as a key feature of the budget set facing workers. Whether or not this is true is an open empirical question.) In the first region of figure 3.1, [0, a), the hourly wage is subsidized. In the second region, [a, b), the hourly wage is the pre-subsidy wage, but the worker's total income is increased by the amount of the annual subsidy, S_b. In the third region, [b, c), the subsidy is phased out and the effective marginal hourly wage is *below* the pre-subsidy wage level, because each hour worked eliminates part of the subsidy. When earnings are sufficiently high, at or above c, the effective wage again equals the pre-subsidy wage. In this chapter, we consider the effect of this subsidy on skill formation.

In the standard Becker–Ben Porath economic model of skill formation, the major cost of skill investment is forgone earnings. Assume, for simplicity, that these are the only costs and ignore forgone leisure. Time is devoted either to work or to investment and people seek to maximize the present value of their earnings. (We temporarily abstract from the labor–leisure decision in order to focus on the main impact of the program on skill investment without worrying about wealth effects on labor supply.)

If skills do not depreciate, wages always rise (or remain constant) over the life cycle as skill investments are made. For a person starting life on

---

[1] Strictly speaking, the EITC subsidizes wage earnings rather than wage rates. For a given pre-subsidy wage, the EITC alters the post-subsidy wage received for each hour worked and is in effect a wage subsidy.

the first segment of the EITC schedule, the opportunity cost of time investing in skill is raised compared with what it would be in the absence of the program. If the investment produces sufficient earnings growth that persons eventually leave the first segment as their skills are enhanced, the effect of the subsidy is to *reduce* skill formation, because the opportunity cost of time spent investing is increased during the years when investment is made but the wage payment per hour of work is not increased during the payoff years. Only if a person stays on the first segment throughout his or her working lifetime will the effect of the subsidy be neutral on skill formation. In this case, marginal returns and costs rise in the same proportion and there is no effect on skill investment.

For a person who starts life on the flat segment of the subsidy schedule, the effects of the subsidy on investment are ambiguous. First, if a person has annual earnings that never leave the flat segment, there is no effect of the subsidy on skill formation, since there is no marginal effect of the program on either returns or costs.[2] Second, if earnings rise so that the person spends part of his or her career on the declining segment, skill formation is retarded, because the payoff to investment in human capital is reduced as the subsidy is withdrawn. If a person jumps from the flat segment to a post-program earnings level above c, there again would be no effect of the program on skill formation, although the continuous nature of the skill formation process makes this case an empirically unlikely one.

Finally, consider a person who begins life with initial earnings in the phase-out segment. In this case, the implicit tax on earnings makes investment *less costly* compared with a no-program world, since earnings forgone are reduced by the subsidy. If investment eventually causes the person to leave the third segment, the tax on earnings is eventually removed and, hence, the relative payoff to investment is increased by the subsidy. This case *promotes* skill formation.

The overall effect of the program on the skill formation of workers affected by the program is ambiguous even in this simple model. It depends on where workers' earnings place them in the schedule and this can be determined only by an empirical analysis. Adding the labor–leisure choice further complicates matters. The wealth effects of the subsidy serve to reduce labor supply and, hence, the incentive to acquire skills. For workers spending their entire careers on the plateau or in the phase-out region, wealth effects created by the EITC cause labor supply and investment to decline. Effects on wage growth are ambiguous, depending on the relative strengths of income and substitution effects. When substitution effects dominate, the EITC encourages skill investment for individuals

---

[2] Recall that we assume that there are no wealth effects.

who spend their entire careers in the phase-in region or for those who move from the phase-out region off the schedule. Finally, the benefits received from the EITC may attract people into the workplace. This will increase their hours of work and will increase their incentive to invest in work-related skills.

Next, consider the case when skills are acquired through work experience rather than through a separate learning activity, as in the Becker–Ben Porath model. In the conventional learning-by-doing model, investment time and work are the same, and the activity of investment is not rivalrous with work. In this framework, the effects of the EITC on skills accumulated through learning-by-doing are much different. For those who would work even in the program's absence, skill accumulation depends only on labor supply. So, for workers induced to work more hours, the EITC raises skills. Those induced to work less by the program accumulate fewer skills. The EITC raises hours worked only among workers whose earnings lie in the phase-in region of the schedule, assuming substitution effects dominate income effects in determining labor supply. For all other workers, the EITC reduces hours worked and, therefore, the skills acquired through learning-by-doing. The contrast between the effects of wage subsidies on skill formation in a learning-by-doing model and in a Becker–Ben Porath model is a major finding of this chapter. In both models, the inducement to enter the workforce raises skills by increasing the reward to them.

In order to clarify the essential features of the program, we initially simplify the analysis. In section 2, we use a two-period model of skill formation to analyze the effects of *age-specific* proportional wage subsidies or wage taxes on skill acquisition for several types of subsidy programs using the two competing models of skill formation. At any age, we assume that tax or subsidy rates are the same irrespective of earnings levels. Thus, we initially abstract from the endogenously determined tax/subsidy rates of the EITC to avoid non-concavity of the criterion and non-uniqueness in investment.

We establish that the two main models of skill formation widely used in the literature, the Becker–Ben Porath on-the-job training (OJT) model and a learning-by-doing (LBD) model, have different implications for the effect of wage subsidies on skill formation. When the conventional LBD model is carefully examined, it contains an apparent "free lunch" feature – persons who work also acquire skill. The more they work, the more skills they acquire, so no earnings are forgone. Forgone leisure is the sole cost of investment in this model. When a market for jobs with different learning content is introduced, following Rosen (1972), earnings forgone are added as a cost of acquiring skills in a learning-by-doing model and the two models become much more similar. In a very special case, which we establish below, the two models are equivalent if leisure is added to the Becker–Ben Porath framework and if learning-by-doing opportunities are priced appropriately.

In section 3, we discuss specific features of the EITC program. We go beyond the simple analysis of age-specific wage subsidies to consider the actual wage subsidies implicit in the EITC program, which depend on the level of earnings. We discuss the resulting non-differentiability and non-concavity of the criterion function as well as the need to account for a multiplicity of local optima in estimating the impact of the EITC program and simulating its impact.

We present an analysis of the distribution of female workers with low education over the four segments of figure 3.1. The least educated typically begin their careers in the phase-in region, $[0, a)$, and move to either the plateau region, $[a, b)$, or the phase-out region, $[b, c)$. Thus, investment is initially discouraged in the OJT framework, whereas work (and learning) are encouraged in the LBD framework. Wealth effects of the EITC typically reduce skill acquisition in both models of skill formation for women receiving substantial credit amounts.

Section 4 extends the analysis of section 3 to a multi-period setting. The intuition developed in the simple two-period models applies more generally. Section 5 presents estimates of two canonical models of skill formation using data from the Current Population Survey on wages and hours worked for women with low levels of education.

Section 6 uses those estimates to explore the impacts of the EITC program on earnings and wage growth in the two different models of skill formation. Both models produce similar estimates of EITC-induced entry into the workforce and its associated human capital accumulation. The models differ greatly in their prediction of the quantitative impact of the EITC program on the wage growth of those who would work even in the absence of the program. Qualitatively, the models agree. Both predict declines in potential skill levels among the women we study. But the predicted declines are quantitatively greater in the OJT model than in the LBD model. The LBD model predicts substantially larger negative impacts of the EITC on hours worked. It also predicts larger declines in earnings than the OJT model. If the entry effects of the EITC are small, the reductions in average earnings among all uneducated women can be as large as 18 percent of the average skill level supplied to the market. Although the aggregate effects of the EITC on skills are similar in the two models, the predicted impacts on specific groups of workers are often quite different depending on which region of the schedule workers spends most of their time in.[3] Average measures of the impact of the EITC on skills mask considerable heterogeneity in individual responses. These findings highlight the importance of determining the appropriate model of skill formation in assessing the impact of the EITC program on the skills and earnings of workers.

Section 7 briefly discusses other empirical evidence about the process of skill formation, and section 8 summarizes and concludes.

2   Models of wage subsidies and skill formation

This section analyzes several two-period models of skill accumulation to investigate the effect of period-specific proportional wage subsidies on skill formation. The EITC is not a period-specific proportional wage subsidy. But the intuition obtained from an analysis of the simple period-specific proportional subsidy and tax case carries over to the more general EITC structure. We consider both income-maximizing models and models with labor supply assuming perfect credit markets.[4] Throughout this chapter, we ignore the practically important issues of fraud and enforcement in the administration of wage subsidy programs that are discussed by Phelps (1997).

Central to our investigation is the specification of the skill formation process. The conventional Becker–Ben Porath model features earnings forgone as the main cost of skill formation. In this model, a wage subsidy in the first period of a two-period model tends to divert workers away from investment and toward market work. On the other hand, second-period wage subsidies encourage first-period investment.

A model of learning-by-doing (as developed by Heckman, 1971; Weiss, 1972; Killingsworth, 1982; Shaw, 1989; and Altug and Miller, 1990, 1998) produces completely different predictions. In this model, an hour of work at any job produces general skills that have the same value in all sectors of the economy. A wage subsidy that promotes work in the first period *promotes* skill formation. The cost of work and skill acquisition in this model is leisure forgone. .

This second model of skill formation appears to have a free lunch aspect to it. People who work more earn more in that period and in the future.

---

[3] Even greater heterogeneity is observed when the impacts of the EITC on male earnings and more educated workers are considered. See Heckman, Lochner and Cossa (1999).

[4] In Heckman, Lochner and Cossa (1999) we consider versions of our labor supply models with borrowing constraints. Analytically, the qualitative features are quite similar to those presented here; even the quantitative results from our simulations in section 6 do not change much when borrowing constraints are imposed.

There is no tradeoff between skill formation and earnings from work as in the Becker–Ben Porath model. Yet learning is not entirely free, since a tradeoff between leisure and acquiring skills through work still exists.

What produces the apparent free lunch is the implicit assumption that, for any worker, an hour of work in any job is equally effective in producing skill. If jobs differ in the rate at which an hour of work produces skill, a market for jobs arises that is usually ignored in analyses of learning-by-doing models. All current workers who plan to work in the future will cluster in jobs with the highest learning content unless those jobs command higher prices. Higher prices for jobs with more training content mean lower first-period wages for such jobs if workers of the same skill level and tastes have choices among otherwise equal jobs with different training content.[5] With the addition of heterogeneity in learning opportunities, and prices of those opportunities, a tradeoff between first-period investment and earnings from work re-emerges.

2.1   Specifications of skill formation equations

The most commonly used specification of the human capital accumulation process is due to Ben Porath (1967). Human capital in period 1, H_1, is produced by time investment, I. (We assume there is no depreciation, so human capital is non-decreasing.) Thus, we write

$$H_1 - H_0 = F(I), \tag{3.1}$$

with $F' > 0$, $F'' < 0$, $0 \leq I \leq 1$, where I is the proportion of time spent investing and H_0 is the initial stock of human capital.

Assuming a perfect capital market with interest rate r and an efficiency units model of labor services with price R per efficiency unit of human capital, and period 0 and 1 tax-subsidy rates of τ_0 and τ_1, respectively, agents choose I to maximize

$$(1 + \tau_0)RH_0(1 - I) + \frac{(1 + \tau_1)R}{1 + r}H_1,$$

subject to equation (3.1). Investment is rivalrous with earnings. This formulation recognizes that there will be no investment in the second (and final) period of life.[6]

Optimality requires that

$$(1 + \tau_0)RH_0 \leq \frac{(1 + \tau_1)R}{1 + r}F'(I).$$

[5] Rosen (1972) introduced the notion of a market for jobs with different training/learning content. However, our analysis differs in important details from his, as we note below.

[6] In this chapter, we consider only the individual's problem, ignoring the general equilibrium effects of policy on factor prices.

Changes in R do not affect skill investment. At an interior solution $(0 < I < 1)$, increases in r and H_0 decrease investment. The higher the first-period opportunity wage or the lower the discounted return from investment, the less time is spent investing.[7]

A common wage subsidy or tax across periods ($\tau_0 = \tau_1$) clearly does not affect investment. Both marginal returns and marginal costs are affected equally. However, if $\tau_0 > \tau_1$, investment is reduced compared with the case where $\tau_0 = \tau_1$; if $\tau_0 < \tau_1$, then investment is increased. We return to this model and analyze it more thoroughly after we develop a comparison model of learning-by-doing.

In the LBD model, skills are produced by work. Let L_t be leisure in period t. There is no investment time, so hours of work in period t are given by $1 - L_t$. In this scheme,

$$H_1 - H_0 = \varphi(1 - L_0), \tag{3.2}$$

with $\varphi' > 0$, $\varphi'' < 0$. In principle, work in the second period also produces human capital, but that output is not valued since there is no third period. The cost of work and acquiring new skills is leisure forgone. To introduce such costs, it is necessary to introduce a utility function that values leisure. Then, individuals choose consumption and leisure to

$$\text{Max } U(C_0, L_0) + \frac{1}{1 + \rho} U(C_1, L_1), \tag{3.3}$$

where U is strictly concave in its arguments and ρ is a time discount factor, subject to the lifetime budget constraint

$$RH_0[1 - L_0](1 + \tau_0) + \frac{R}{1 + r} H_1[1 - L_1](1 + \tau_1) + A_0$$

$$= C_0 + \frac{C_1}{1 + r} \tag{3.4}$$

and (3.2), where A_0 represents initial assets. Throughout this chapter, we assume that goods and leisure are normal. Let λ denote the Lagrange multiplier associated with (3.4). Assuming an interior solution, we obtain the following first-order conditions:

$$U_1(C_0, L_0) = \lambda \tag{3.5a}$$

$$U_1(C_1, L_1) = \lambda \left(\frac{1 + \rho}{1 + r} \right) \tag{3.5b}$$

---

[7] At the $I = 1$ boundary, we obtain the stated results as "tendencies," i.e. predicted increases in investment become predicted non-decreases.

$$U_2(C_0, L_0) = \lambda R \left(H_0(1 + \tau_0) + \frac{\varphi'(1 - L_0)[1 - L_1](1 + \tau_1)}{1 + r} \right)$$

$$(3.6a)$$

$$U_2(C_1, L_1) = \lambda \left(\frac{1 + \rho}{1 + r} \right) R(H_0 + \varphi(1 - L_0))(1 + \tau_1). \qquad (3.6b)$$

The price of time in the first period includes potential earnings $(RH_0(1 + \tau_0))$ plus the effect of an extra unit of work on discounted future earnings. As first noted by Heckman (1971), even when $\rho = r$, it is possible that wages grow between periods 0 and 1 but labor supply remains the same. This occurs if the total opportunity cost of leisure

$$RH_0(1 + \tau_0) + \frac{R\varphi'(1 - L_0)[1 - L_1](1 + \tau_1)}{1 + r}$$

in period 0 equals the realized wage in period 1

$$[RH_0 + R\varphi(1 - L_0)](1 + \tau_1).$$

In this model, an increase in R produces income and substitution effects. Compensating to eliminate income effects (holding λ constant), an increase in R promotes skill formation and labor supply. There is no tradeoff between investment and work, because work is investment. If wages are subsidized ($\tau_0 > 0$) in period 0 and taxed ($\tau_1 < 0$) in period 1, the effects on skill formation are ambiguous. The first-period wage, $RH_0(1 + \tau_0)$, is increased but the future return,

$$\frac{R\varphi'(1 - L_0)[1 - L_1]}{1 + r}(1 + \tau_1),$$

is diminished.

In contrast to the OJT model of skill investment, a compensated wage subsidy in period 0 that is changed to a wage tax in period 1 has ambiguous effects. It may *increase* skills if the positive effects on current returns more than offset the negative effects on future returns. Similarly, a compensated wage tax applied in period 0 followed by a wage subsidy in period 1 also has ambiguous effects on skills. The resulting increase in the return on future work may promote work (and, hence, learning) in the initial period. If $\tau_1 = 0$, a wage subsidy in period 0 ($\tau_0 > 0$) promotes skill formation, whereas a wage tax ($\tau_0 < 0$) lowers skills – exactly the opposite of what is predicted in the Becker–Ben Porath investment framework.

2.2   Reconciling the two models of skill formation

The two models just considered have different predictions about the effects of simple tax and subsidy schemes on skill formation. What is the source of this difference? We now show that adding leisure to the OJT model does not change the qualitative predictions derived from it, provided that we compensate for income effects and that solutions are interior. Allowing different jobs to have different training content and pricing out the training moves the two models together.

To augment the first model, the utility function described by (3.3) is maximized with respect to consumption, leisure and investment, subject to the lifetime budget constraint:

$$RH_0[1 - I - L_0](1 + \tau_0) + \frac{R}{1+r}[F(I) + H_0][1 - L_1](1 + \tau_1)$$

$$+ A_0 = C_0 + \frac{C_1}{1+r}.$$

(This expression incorporates the observation that there is no investment, I, in the final period.) The interior first-order conditions for leisure and investment become

$$U_2(C_0, L_0) = \lambda RH_0(1 + \tau_0) \tag{3.7a}$$

$$U_2(C_1, L_1) = \lambda R[H_0 + F(I)]\left(\frac{1+\rho}{1+r}\right)(1 + \tau_1) \tag{3.7b}$$

$$\frac{R}{1+r}F'(I)[1 - L_1](1 + \tau_1) = RH_0(1 + \tau_0). \tag{3.7c}$$

In this extended Becker–Ben Porath OJT model, changes in R are no longer neutral. Holding wealth effects (λ) constant, an increase in R *increases* skill formation by encouraging labor supply in period 1. The qualitative effects of changes in taxes and subsidies in periods 0 and 1 are the same as in the income-maximizing version of this model. If $\tau_0 < 0$ and $\tau_1 > 0$, skill accumulation is fostered, compared with the case where $\tau_0 = \tau_1 = 0$. If $\tau_0 > 0$ and $\tau_1 < 0$, skill accumulation is dampened. Adding leisure but compensating for wealth effects, we obtain the same predictions about the impact of period-specific wage subsidies on investment as those produced in the original Becker–Ben Porath model. The crucial economic difference between the OJT and LBD models of skill formation is not that one model excludes leisure whereas the other includes it. Rather, the major source of the difference derives from the fact that investment and labor supply compete for the agent's time in the OJT model, whereas they do not in the LBD model.

Now consider another case where firms differ in the rate at which workers learn from an hour of work. All workers who plan to work in period 1 would flock to the firms offering the highest total earnings package (inclusive of future earnings). If firms pay the same spot wage, R, for H_0, the firm with the higher learning potential would attract all the workers if it did not charge for its learning opportunities. Only workers who did not plan to work in period 1 would ignore the training potential of a prospective job. Those who plan to work a lot would value its contribution to earnings growth.

To investigate this model more systematically, let θ index the investment content of a job, so we write the learning-by-doing function as $\varphi(1 - L_0; \theta)$. Assume

$$\frac{\partial^2 \varphi}{\partial \theta \partial (1 - L_0)} > 0,$$

so opportunities with higher θ produce greater learning-by-doing per hour of work. Assume further that $\varphi(0; \theta) = 0$, for all θ, so that a person must work in order to harvest the benefit of θ. For the same wage, RH_0, young workers would prefer to work in firms with higher θ. Only persons who choose not to work in the future are unconcerned about the θ content of their job. Implicit in the learning-by-doing specifications used in the literature is the assumption that all firms provide the same learning opportunities; that is, θ is identical across firms.

If it is not, and if there is a distribution of θ across firms, say with an upper limit $\overline{\theta}$ and a lower limit $\underline{\theta}$ on its support, and if, for whatever reason, there are two or more θ-types of firms in the market at any time, then a market price for training, $P(\theta)$, will emerge. The exact specification of the pricing function critically affects the analysis and depends on both supply and demand factors for labor and learning. In this revised LBD model, the agent's problem is to choose θ along with C_0, C_1, L_0 and L_1 subject to the revised budget constraint. Consider two firms that differ in their training effectiveness. Firm 1 offers less learning, so $\theta_1 < \theta_2$. For the same hours of work in period 0, an hour of work at firm 2 produces greater earnings in period 1. The more hours spent working in period 1, the greater the gain from working at firm 2 in period 0. If there were an unlimited supply of training opportunities at $\theta = \overline{\theta}$, all young workers would congregate at firms with such opportunities if they plan to work in the second period. If the supply of training jobs is limited for some reason, workers will sort to firms with different θ-types. A market for training options will emerge. *Ceteris paribus*, workers who will work more in the second period will place greater value on high-θ jobs and will be willing to pay more for them.

For analytical simplicity, assume that a continuum of θ-type firms co-exist in the market, where $\theta \in [\underline{\theta}, \overline{\theta}]$. Young workers who do not plan to work in period 1 will sort into low-θ firms. So will old workers. We assume that the price for a job of type θ exists and the pricing function, $P(\theta)$, is differentiable in θ.[8] In this specification, we think of the firm as providing a learning environment common for all workers irrespective of the hours they work. Persons who work more will derive more learning from their jobs. A fixed charge $P(\theta)$ is paid by all workers in the firm. Assuming that firms use H in production and that only efficiency units matter in producing final output, the gross payment to human capital is RH for a person with human capital bundle H.

The pre-subsidy period 0 earnings for a person who chooses a job θ and has human capital H_0 is

$$W(H_0, \theta) = RH_0(1 - L_0) - P(\theta).$$

The pre-subsidy hourly wage rate is

$$w(H_0, \theta) = W(H_0, \theta)/(1 - L_0).$$

The pre-subsidy hourly wage understates the potential wage rate, RH_0, as long as $P(\theta) > 0$. The understatement is greater, the greater the learning content of the job.[9]

The budget constraint for the extended learning-by-doing model is

$$[RH_0[1 - L_0] - P(\theta)](1 + \tau_0) + \frac{RH_1[1 - L_1](1 + \tau_1)}{1 + r} + A_0$$
$$= C_0 + \frac{C_1}{1 + r}, \tag{3.4'}$$

and the revised skill accumulation equation is

$$H_1 - H_0 = \varphi(1 - L_0; \theta). \tag{3.2'}$$

---

[8] Rosen (1972) introduced the notion of a market for jobs with different learning content. He reinterprets the Ben Porath model to let I play the role of the index θ in our notation. Different firms may offer jobs with different investment/learning content, I, and firms producing more learning for workers produce less output of the consumption good. This generates an implicit market whereby firms charge workers an amount RHI for their learning. It also produces mobility across jobs as workers reduce I over the life cycle. Rosen does not consider the learning-by-doing model analyzed in this chapter, in which hours of work at a firm produce skill.

[9] This observation has substantial implications for econometric estimates of learning-by-doing models as estimated in Altug and Miller (1990, 1998). They implicitly assume that all firms offer the same training opportunities and that these are free. If training is costly, they understate the first-period wage, and the understatement is greater for firms with workers making more investment.

With obvious notational changes to reflect the introduction of θ, the first-order conditions (3.5a, b) and (3.6a, b) are the same. The new first-order condition arising from the choice of θ is

$$(1 + \tau_0)P'(\theta) = (1 + \tau_1)\left(\frac{R}{1+r}\right)[1 - L_1]\frac{\partial\varphi(1 - L_0; \theta)}{\partial\theta}.^{10}$$

(3.8)

This equation makes clear that individuals who intend to work more in period 1 (for example, if they have high skill levels or few assets) will sort into high-θ jobs. In the second and final period, workers will cash out their investment and choose jobs with low training content.

In this amended learning-by-doing model, a compensated wage subsidy in period 0 ($\tau_0 > 0$) raises the cost of θ and causes agents to reduce the learning content of their work compared with the non-subsidized case ($\tau_0 = 0$). The net effect on skill formation is ambiguous. Labor supply $(1 - L_0)$ increases and θ decreases. Thus,

$$\left.\frac{\partial(H_1 - H_0)}{\partial\tau_0}\right|_{\text{utility constant}} = \varphi_1 \left.\frac{\partial(1 - L_0)}{\partial\tau_0}\right|_{\text{utility constant}}$$

$$+ \varphi_2 \left.\frac{\partial\theta}{\partial\tau_0}\right|_{\text{utility constant}}.$$

The first term on the righthand side is positive and the second term is negative, making the overall impact of the subsidy on skill formation ambiguous. A wage subsidy in the second period ($\tau_1 > 0$) promotes investment. A similar decomposition and ambiguity plagues the λ-constant function.

If there are implicit prices for jobs with different training content, then a period 0 wage subsidy in an LBD model *may* retard skill formation, just as it does in a Becker–Ben Porath OJT model. In general, the extended LBD model considered here produces two offsetting effects. Compensating for income effects, a higher wage subsidy will induce more hours of work and will produce more skills. At the same time, subsidized agents shift to lower-θ jobs, so the investment content of learning is diminished. The net effect on skill formation is ambiguous. Adding back income effects tends to reduce incentives to acquire skills.

Notice the similarity in the first-order condition for θ (equation (3.8)) and the first-order condition for investment, I, in the Becker–Ben Porath model (equation (3.7c)). Conditions governing consumption are

---

[10] To guarantee an interior solution for θ, it is sufficient that $P''(\theta) > 0$ and $\partial^2\varphi/\partial\theta^2 < 0$. More generally we just require that standard second-order conditions hold.

identical. The greatest difference between the models arises in the first-order conditions for leisure (compare the conditions in (3.6a, b) with those of (3.7b)). If learning opportunities in a firm can be tailored to the individual worker and it is possible to appropriately price out each hour of learning for a fixed θ, then the LBD model and the Becker–Ben Porath OJT model are analytically equivalent. However, this requires firms to be able to price θ differently for persons who work different hours in periods 0 and 1. The simple pricing scheme $P(\theta)$ is not enough.

To see this, consider a more general pricing scheme for learning opportunities, θ:

$$P(\theta, 1 - L_0) = f(\theta) + \omega(\theta)[1 - L_0],$$

where $f(\theta)$ is a fixed charge for training opportunity θ and $\omega(\theta)$ is the marginal cost of an hour of training in a firm with learning parameter θ.

Replacing $P(\theta)$ with the more general $P(\theta, 1 - L_0)$ yields the revised first-order condition for first-period leisure:

$$U_2(C_0, L_0) = \lambda \left(RH_0(1 + \tau_0) - \omega(\theta)(1 + \tau_0) \right.$$

$$\left. + R \frac{\partial \varphi}{\partial (1 - L_0)} \frac{[1 - L_1](1 + \tau_1)}{1 + r} \right). \qquad (3.6a')$$

The new first-order condition for θ now becomes

$$(1 + \tau_0)(f'(\theta) + \omega'(\theta)[1 - L_0]) = (1 + \tau_1) \frac{R[1 - L_1]}{1 + r} \frac{\partial \varphi}{\partial \theta}. \qquad (3.8')$$

Under certain conditions, the OJT model and the extended LBD model are analytically equivalent. To establish this equivalence, observe that θ in the LBD model plays a role similar to I in the OJT model with leisure. The marginal cost of $\theta((1 + \tau_0)\partial P/\partial \theta)$ plays the role of the marginal cost of I ($RH_0(1 + \tau_0)$). $\partial \varphi/\partial \theta$ and $F'(I)$ play comparable roles in terms of investment productivity. The price of leisure, L_0, is the same in both models if the firm is able to set the marginal price of θ as

$$\omega(\theta) = \frac{\partial \varphi}{\partial (1 - L_0)} \frac{R[1 - L_1]}{1 + r} \left(\frac{1 + \tau_1}{1 + \tau_0} \right).$$

If this condition is satisfied, the marginal price of L_0 in both models is $RH_0(1 + \tau_0)$. Qualitative predictions about the effects of taxes and subsidies on human capital and wage growth are identical in both models when θ is priced in this fashion. They can be made quantitatively identical with a suitable choice of F and φ and the parameters of the model.

For this equivalence to arise, firms must be able to price discriminate based on the current *and future* number of hours a worker wants to work. That is, firms must be able to marginally charge workers based on the total return they receive from learning at their θ firm. The marginal relative return to providing additional θ (scaled by its price) must match the marginal relative return to investment in the Becker–Ben Porath model.

In equilibrium, the pricing scheme for θ will depend not only on the technology of learning but also on the supply of learning capabilities (θ) at existing firms. Recall that the prices for θ arise from a market equilibrium between buyers and sellers of labor and learning opportunities. From these conditions, a hedonic pricing scheme for work/learning will arise. We would not expect the fine price discrimination required to equate the two models to arise in general. Furthermore, it seems extremely unlikely that firms can accurately predict the number of hours a worker plans to work in the future, even if they could perfectly price their learning/work package. Thus, the two models are quite distinct and require separate analyses.

2.3   Employment and skill formation

For all of the models of skill formation we have discussed, subsidies that promote work compared with non-employment will promote the acquisition of skills. In the LBD model, subsidies in any period encourage employment in all periods. Wage subsidies in the first period promote first-period employment, thereby generating new skills. Those new skills create additional incentives to work in the second period. On the other hand, second-period wage subsidies that create employment in the second period also raise the return to work in the initial period. In the Becker–Ben Porath OJT model, only subsidies that generate employment in the *second period* promote skill formation, because they raise the value of investment in the initial period. However, first-period wage subsidies actually discourage skill formation, since investment is rivalrous with work.

2.4   Schooling

Schooling is defined as the case where $I = 1$ in the Becker–Ben Porath model. Wage subsidies during the schooling years divert persons away from investment (in schooling or job training) and toward work. However, wage subsidies during the post-schooling years raise the payoff to work and, hence, promote schooling earlier on.

The learning-by-doing model must be extended to accommodate schooling. If schooling is modeled as an activity that is rivalrous with work, we obtain the same predictions from this model as from a Becker–Ben

Porath model: Wage subsidies during the schooling years reduce school-ing. However, the reductions in overall skill formation are partially offset by increases in skill acquired through work experience.

We now adapt the framework of this section to analyze the EITC program in the United States.

3   The EITC program and its recipients

3.1   *A description of the EITC program*

Beginning in 1975, the EITC program has provided a subsidy (or tax credit) to low-income workers. The amount of the subsidy depends on total labor income as well as the number of children living with (and supported by) the worker.[11] For wage income W, the EITC schedule (for any given number of children) can be described as follows:

$$S(W) = \begin{cases} S_a W & W < a & \text{``phase-in''} \\ S_b & a \leq W < b & \text{``plateau''} \\ S_b - S_c(W - b) & b \leq W < c & \text{``phase-out''} \\ 0 & W \geq c \end{cases}$$

where $S_a = S_b/a$ and $S_c = S_b/(c - b)$. Figure 3.1 graphs the EITC schedule as a function of pre-subsidy earnings. In terms of the notation of the previous section, S_a plays the role of $(1 + \tau)$, $\tau > 0$, for a person with wages $w = W/(1 - L)$ provided $W < a$; S_b corresponds to $\tau = 0$ with A_0 enhanced by S_b; and phase three corresponds to $S_c = 1 + \tau$ with $\tau < 0$ and asset income adjusted by $S_b + S_c b$. In the case of the EITC however, the subsidy level depends on earnings levels, which depend on individual work and investment choices. The EITC program generates non-differentiable constraints with non-convex regions so that some care must be taken in analyzing it.

If agents are uncertain about the exact location of the budget set, and we account for the effects of all other programs on the effective tax-subsidy schedule facing workers, the problem of non-convexity may diminish. In this chapter we focus on the EITC program in isolation from other programs, assuming that persons know their non-convex budget set.

Table 3.1 shows the EITC schedule for tax year 1994 as an example. Families with two or more children receive the greatest credit for any given income level, with a maximum credit of US$2,528. Families with

---

[11] The current law states that only children under 19 (or under 24 if a full-time student) living in the taxpayer's household for more than half of the calendar year qualify.

Table 3.1 *Earned Income Tax Credit for 1994*

	Families with one child	Families with two or more children	Childless adults
Phase-in			
Income range (US$)	1–7,749	1–8,424	1–3,999
Phase-in rate (percent)	26.30	30.00	7.64
Plateau			
Income range (US$)	7,750–10,999	8,425–10,999	4,000–4,999
Maximum credit (US$)	2,038	2,528	306
Phase-out			
Income range (US$)	11,000–23,754	11,000–25,295	5,000–8,999
Phase-out rate (percent)	15.98	17.68	7.65

one dependent child can receive up to US$2,038, whereas adults with no children can receive at most US$306. Although the amount of the subsidy has risen substantially since the early 1980s (with major expansions in 1986, 1990 and 1993), the basic structure has not changed. Only modest changes have taken place since 1994.

3.2   The qualifying population

Since nearly one-quarter of all families with two or more children who qualify for the EITC are headed by a single mother and more than one-third of qualifying families with one child (or no children) are single women (see table 3.2), we focus our empirical analysis on women. Furthermore, the EITC aims to supplement the incomes of less educated women. As a result, more than half of qualifying women have no college experience. We therefore further concentrate our efforts on understanding the role of the EITC in decisions among women with a high-school education or less. Using the 1994 March Current Population Survey (CPS), we study the distribution of women qualifying for the EITC by age, race and educational background.

We divide family income into seven distinct regions, including the phase-in, plateau and phase-out zones, as well as regions around the kinks at a, b and c.[12] The values of a, b, and c depend on the number of qualifying children and are based on the 1994 EITC schedule shown in table 3.1.

Since it is necessary to identify qualifying children, we limit our sample of potential female recipients to heads of household. The EITC

---

[12] See table 3A.1 in appendix 3A for a more detailed description of the seven regions.

Table 3.2 *Distribution of households qualifying for the EITC*

		Percentage by education level			
	<10 years	11–12 years	High-school graduate	Some college	College graduate
No qualifying children					
Single women (36.1 percent)	9.40	6.98	33.97	33.16	16.48
Single men (29.8 percent)	10.05	8.21	32.23	31.25	18.26
Married (34.1 percent)	18.76	9.11	37.19	18.33	16.61
One qualifying child					
Single women (36.4 percent)	5.74	8.38	42.09	36.72	7.06
Single men (8.2 percent)	9.21	10.04	47.70	26.36	6.69
Married (55.4 percent)	15.21	10.20	39.95	22.94	11.69
Two or more qualifying children					
Single women (23.3 percent)	8.06	11.65	38.25	33.69	8.35
Single men (3.5 percent)	11.54	12.82	42.31	25.00	8.33
Married (73.1 percent)	17.79	9.14	38.02	23.77	11.28

amount is based on family earnings, so we add a spouse's earnings, if present, to those of the household head. (We do not model joint labor supply decisions.) Earnings include wage income, farm self-employment income and business self-employment income. We also limit our sample to women ages 18–65. When determining the number of qualifying children for a household, we include all of the household head's natural or adopted children, grandchildren, stepchildren and foster children under 19 (or under 24 if the child is currently enrolled in school full time).

Table 3.3 shows the distribution of working female high-school dropouts with one or two children with respect to their position within the EITC schedule. Overall, about 35–43 percent of them have earnings low enough to place them in the phase-in region of the schedule, and around 30 percent lie in the phase-out region. Among single mothers with less than a high-school education, around 50 percent have earnings in the phase-in region. Disaggregating by age, approximately 50 percent of all young female high-school dropouts with children have earnings in the phase-in region. That number drops about ten percentage points for each ten years of age for women with one child, owing to rising income profiles over the life cycle. The fraction of women with two or more children and earnings in the phase-in region declines only as they move from their twenties to their thirties. The fraction of working dropouts in the phase-out region moves in the opposite direction from the fraction in

Table 3.3 *Distribution of earnings for working female high-school dropouts over the EITC schedule (household heads with children)*

	Percentage in EITC region							No. of observations
	I	II	III	IV	V	VI	VII	
One child								
All	35.50	4.30	8.70	4.00	31.10	2.00	14.40	299
Age <30	50.00	2.56	7.69	1.28	21.79	0.00	16.67	78
Ages 30–40	39.13	2.90	7.25	5.80	31.88	4.35	8.70	69
Ages 40–50	29.67	4.40	10.99	3.30	34.07	2.20	15.38	91
Age >50	21.31	8.20	8.20	6.56	37.70	1.64	16.39	61
Single women	42.50	5.63	8.13	5.63	31.25	0.63	6.25	160
Married women	27.34	2.88	9.35	2.16	30.94	3.60	23.74	139
Two children								
All	42.70	1.20	10.90	3.90	27.60	2.80	10.90	431
Age <30	47.50	0.83	9.17	5.00	22.50	1.67	13.33	120
Ages 30–40	39.59	1.52	11.17	1.52	31.98	4.57	9.64	197
Ages 40–50	41.77	0.00	13.92	7.59	22.78	1.27	12.66	79
Age >50	45.71	2.86	8.57	5.71	31.43	0.00	5.71	35
Single women	56.94	1.44	11.96	2.39	23.44	0.96	2.87	209
Married women	29.28	0.90	9.91	5.41	31.53	4.50	18.47	222

Note: EITC regions correspond to: (I) phase-in region, (II) kink between the phase-in and plateau region, (III) plateau region, (IV) kink between plateau and phase-out region, (V) phase-out region, (VI) maximum allowable earnings, and (VII) above the maximum allowable earnings limit. See appendix table 3A.1 for a precise definition of these regions.

the phase-in region. The fraction of working dropouts with one or two children who earn more than the maximum cutoff for the EITC is quite small, ranging from 5 to 17 percent. Single women with little schooling are almost twice as likely to have earnings in the phase-in region as are married women who are the heads of their households. Single mothers earning more than the maximum allowable amount are quite rare.

As seen in table 3.4, a somewhat similar story can be told for high-school graduates (without any college), except that their earnings distribution is shifted to the right. About 20 percent of graduate mothers with one child and 27 percent with two or more children – most of them under age 30 – have earnings in the phase-in region. By age 30, a large majority of graduates have earnings in the phase-out region or higher. By age 40, about 40 percent of female high-school graduates with children have earnings too high to qualify for the EITC.

In summary, dropout mothers typically earn incomes placing them in the phase-in region of the EITC schedule, whereas mothers with a high-school diploma are more likely to have earnings in the phase-out

Table 3.4 *Distribution of earnings for working female high-school graduates over the EITC schedule (household heads with children)*

	Percentage in EITC region							No. of observations
	I	II	III	IV	V	VI	VII	
One child								
All	21.40	1.90	6.90	2.10	31.60	3.90	32.10	893
Age <30	32.02	2.19	9.65	3.51	32.02	3.51	17.11	228
Ages 30–40	20.07	2.08	6.92	1.73	31.83	3.81	33.56	289
Ages 40–50	16.67	1.19	5.16	1.59	30.56	3.57	41.27	252
Age >50	14.52	2.42	5.65	1.61	32.26	5.65	37.90	124
Single women	25.64	2.91	8.55	2.55	37.45	4.18	18.73	550
Married women	14.58	0.29	4.37	1.46	22.16	3.50	53.64	343
Two children								
All	27.00	1.20	6.30	3.20	28.80	4.00	29.40	966
Age <30	40.85	0.47	7.51	4.69	29.58	0.94	15.96	213
Ages 30–40	25.56	2.03	6.29	2.84	29.21	4.87	29.21	493
Ages 40–50	17.14	0.48	3.81	2.86	29.52	4.29	41.90	210
Age >50	24.00	0.00	12.00	2.00	18.00	8.00	36.00	50
Single women	37.47	1.55	7.32	3.33	34.37	3.33	12.64	451
Married women	17.86	0.97	5.44	3.11	23.88	4.66	44.08	515

Note: EITC regions correspond to: (I) phase-in region, (II) kink between the phase-in and plateau region, (III) plateau region, (IV) kink between plateau and phase-out region, (V) phase-out region, (VI) maximum allowable earnings, and (VII) above the maximum allowable earnings limit. See appendix table 3A.1 for a precise definition of these regions.

region (and beyond). We next turn to a discussion of those impacts on skill formation and hours worked, modifying the simple models developed in section 2 to accommodate specific features of the EITC program. We extend the models to a multi-period setting in section 4.

3.3   *Allowing for endogenous tax-subsidy rates*

First, consider the income-maximizing Ben Porath model. Tax rates are endogenous under the EITC, so the agent's problem becomes:

$$\max_{I} V = [RH_0(1 - I)(1 + S_a)] \cdot 1(RH_0(1 - I) < a)$$
$$+ [RH_0(1 - I) + S_b] \cdot 1(a \le RH_0(1 - I) < b)$$
$$+ [RH_0(1-I)(1 - S_c) + S_b + S_c b] \cdot 1(b \le RH_0(1-I) < c)$$
$$+ [RH_0(1 - I)] \cdot 1(RH_0(1 - I) \ge c)$$
$$+ \left[\frac{RH_1(1 + S_a)}{1 + r} \right] \cdot 1(RH_1 < a)$$

$$+ \left[\frac{RH_1 + S_b}{1+r} \right] \cdot 1(a \leq RH_1 < b)$$

$$+ \left[\frac{RH_1(1 - S_c) + S_b + S_c b}{1+r} \right] \cdot 1(b \leq RH_1 < c)$$

$$+ \left[\frac{RH_1}{1+r} \right] \cdot 1(RH_1 \geq c) \tag{3.9}$$

subject to the human capital production function, $F(I)$, where $1(A) = 1$ if A is true; $1(A) = 0$ otherwise.

This ungainly expression captures the essential features of the EITC program. First, it induces a non-differentiable reward function, and, second, it introduces a non-concavity to the problem. For payoff function V, we are not guaranteed that V is everywhere concave; that is, for $\bar{I} = \lambda I_1 + (1 - \lambda) I_2$ and $0 \leq \lambda \leq 1$, the following may not hold:

$$V(\bar{I}) \geq \lambda V(I_1) + (1 - \lambda) V(I_2).$$

Appendix B formally demonstrates how non-concavity can arise for persons starting in the phase-out region. This potential non-concavity leads to multiple local optima in some cases, and requires non-local methods for solving and estimating the model. (The problem becomes even more difficult when more periods are added to the model, as in section 4.)

All of the other skill accumulation models are similarly plagued by this problem. In the Becker–Ben Porath model with leisure, the budget constraint has to be revised to account for the schedule in the following way:

$$\begin{aligned}
A_0 &+ [RH_0(1 - I - L_0)(1 + S_a)] \cdot 1(RH_0(1 - I - L_0) < a) \\
&+ [RH_0(1 - I - L_0) + S_b] \cdot 1(a \leq RH_0(1 - I - L_0) < b) \\
&+ [RH_0(1 - I - L_0)(1 - S_c) + S_b + S_c b] \\
&\quad \cdot 1(b \leq RH_0(1 - I - L_0) < c) \\
&+ [RH_0(1 - I - L_0)] \cdot 1(RH_0(1 - I - L_0) \geq c) \\
&+ \left[\frac{RH_1(1 - L_1)}{1+r} \right] \cdot 1(RH_1(1 - L_1) < a) \\
&+ \left[\frac{RH_1(1 - L_1) + S_b}{1+r} \right] \cdot 1(a \leq RH_1(1 - L_1) < b) \\
&+ \left[\frac{RH_1(1 - S_c) + S_b + S_c b}{1+r} \right] \cdot 1(b \leq RH_1(1 - L_1) < c) \\
&+ \left[\frac{RH_1(1 - L_1)}{1+r} \right] \cdot 1(RH_1(1 - L_1) \geq c). \tag{3.10}
\end{aligned}$$

An analogous modification is required for the learning-by-doing model. The endogeneity of the tax-subsidy parameters under the EITC coupled with the non-differentiability and non-concavity of the model greatly complicates both theoretical and empirical analysis.

4   A multi-period model

We now present models of on-the-job training and learning-by-doing in a multi-period setting. We present a heuristic analysis of the dynamic impacts of the EITC on labor supply and skill formation in both models. In most cases, as in the simple two-period models previously examined, the effect of the EITC on hours worked and skill accumulation is ambiguous and depends on the balance of many offsetting forces. However, the two canonical learning models produce very different predictions about the effects of the EITC on skill formation. Rather than formally derive all of the properties of these models, we discuss the main implications of such a derivation to guide the simulations and estimation reported below.

Both models discussed in this section assume that individuals choose sequences of consumption, C, and leisure, L, to maximize total (discounted) lifetime utility. In the OJT model, individuals will also choose investment in skills, I, as discussed below. Government policy is described by flat income (or wage) tax rates, τ, and the Earned Income Tax Credit, $S(.)$, which is a function of pre-tax labor earnings, W. Labor earnings depend on the amount of time spent working and the human capital level, H, so that $W = H(1 - I - L)$. This efficiency units assumption normalizes human capital in terms of the pre-tax hourly wage rate. After-tax interest rates are denoted by r.

If utility is time-separable and individuals have single-period preferences $U(C, L)$ and time discount factor δ, we can write the individual maximization problem as[13]

$$V(H, A) = \max_{C,L,I}\{U(C, L) + \delta V'(H', A')\}$$

subject to the asset (A) accumulation equation

$$A' = (1 + r)A + (1 - \tau)W(1 - L - I) + S(W) - C,$$

the somewhat more general human capital equation

$$H' = H + F(H, I, 1 - I - L),$$

and the time constraints $0 \leq I + L \leq 1$ and $0 \leq I, L \leq 1$. We allow for the possibility that both work and investment time raise skill levels and also

---

[13] Let x' denote next period's value for any variable or function x.

allow for human capital to be self-productive. We ignore the market for jobs with different learning content, leaving its development for another occasion. As suggested above, such a model would likely produce impacts somewhere between those of the two pure models presented here. We assume that workers live through age T and that human and physical capital have no value at the end of life, so $\partial V_{T+1}/\partial H_{T+1} = \partial V_{T+1}/\partial A_{T+1} = 0$, where V_{T+1} is the value function in period $T+1$, and, at birth, individuals are endowed with an initial skill level, H_0, and assets, A_0. We assume that $U(C, L)$ is separable, increasing and concave in both of its arguments.

4.1   On-the-job training

The model of on-the-job training posits that skills are acquired only through costly time investments, I, so:

$$\frac{\partial F}{\partial I} > 0, \quad \frac{\partial^2 F}{\partial I^2} < 0, \quad \frac{\partial F}{\partial (1 - I - L)} \equiv 0.$$

We also assume that $\partial F/\partial H \geq 0$ throughout, so that human capital is self-productive.

The EITC schedule, $S(W)$, is not differentiable and also produces a non-convex budget set for individuals. As previously noted, this feature greatly complicates the analysis. Individuals can potentially choose bundles of investment and labor supply that place them at a point of non-differentiability (a, b or c). Non-convexity of the budget set also implies that more than one set of (C, I, L) may satisfy local conditions for a maximum.

Fortunately, the qualitative conclusions of the two-period model with fixed period-specific tax and subsidy rates continue to hold in a more general lifecycle setting. The value of human capital depends positively on the number of hours worked in the future. In addition, since human capital also helps to produce further human capital, the more individuals intend to work in the future, the more they gain from raising their skill level. Alternatively, if individuals do not intend to work in the future, there is no value to investing in human capital.[14] Therefore, to the extent that the EITC increases hours worked, it also increases the marginal return to human capital and skill investment.

There are three effects operating. The first two effects of the EITC on human capital investment can be broadly categorized as follows. First, there is an *income effect* – the EITC increases total lifetime wealth like

---

[14] If, as in Heckman (1976), the marginal utility of leisure depends positively on human capital, human capital has value even when there is no work.

a lump-sum subsidy, which encourages the consumption of leisure and discourages work. This tends to reduce investment in skills.[15] Second, there is a compensated *substitution effect*. By altering net wage rates, the EITC induces a substitution effect (in the opposite direction to the income effect) on hours worked. This has an impact on investment through current and future hours worked. There is also a *direct effect* of the EITC on the marginal costs of and returns to investment. Direct effects are the only ones operating in an income-maximizing model. A positive marginal subsidy rate raises the marginal cost of investment by raising the opportunity cost of time, but it also increases the return to investment in skills by raising future net wage rates.

We explore each of these effects for individuals with different lifecycle earnings profiles. As in the simple two-period model, any labor force entry induced by the EITC program raises skill formation compared with what it would be if an individual never worked. First, consider individuals whose labor earnings would be less than a in figure 3.1 at all ages in the absence of the EITC. They face a positive marginal subsidy for each hour they work, which increases their net wage rate. Standard income and substitution effects would govern labor supply decisions – income effects would discourage work and substitution effects would encourage work. Depending on which effect dominates, individuals may work more or less. If the substitution effect dominates the income effect (that is, individuals have upward-sloping labor supply curves), individuals would work more in response to the EITC. As a result, the returns to human capital investment would increase and individuals would respond by investing more in their skills. Direct effects on investment would be offsetting, since the marginal returns and marginal costs increase by exactly the same proportion. Thus, the net result is that under these conditions agents would invest more and experience greater wage growth.

Individuals whose incomes are between a and b throughout their careers (in the absence of the EITC) would receive a lump-sum subsidy of S_b during each period of work (once again, assuming momentarily that the EITC did not alter their incentives enough to move them off the plateau region). In this case, there would be only income effects on labor supply operating through the lump-sum subsidy and no direct effects on the marginal costs and returns to investment. The EITC unambiguously discourages labor supply and human capital investment through the income effect.[16]

---

[15] In Heckman (1976), wealth effects on labor supply do not translate into effects on investment, because human capital increases the marginal value of leisure at the same rate it increases wage rates.

[16] In fact, the EITC might discourage investment enough to lower earnings to keep people at kink a.

Next, examine the effects of the EITC on individuals whose earnings would increase from the [0, *a*) region to the [*a*, *b*) region as they age.[17] Wealth effects again tend to discourage work and investment. Income effects operating through higher wage rates in the phase-in region also discourage work and investment, whereas substitution effects have the opposite effect. Finally, the marginal costs of investment are increased at ages when the worker is in the phase-in region of the EITC; however, the marginal returns to investment are increased by a lesser amount, since net wage rates are higher for only a fraction of future work years. At the last age for which earnings are less than *a*, the marginal costs for investment are raised by the marginal subsidy rate, whereas the marginal returns to investment in skills are unaffected by the EITC since the marginal subsidy rate falls to zero in the plateau region. Unless substitution effects on labor supply are substantial in early periods, we should expect to observe reductions in investment in response to the EITC. We should also expect to observe a discontinuity in investment and hours worked profiles when individuals move into the plateau region, since the marginal cost of investment and leisure declines discontinuously. Finally, we might also observe individuals reducing their investment and hours worked profiles enough to keep income below (or at) *a* for many years.

The effects of the EITC on investment and labor supply for individuals always within the phase-out region are different yet again. Wealth effects from the lump-sum income adjustment serve to discourage labor supply and investment. In addition, a lower marginal wage rate causes the agent to favor leisure if substitution effects dominate income effects. The direct effects on marginal investment costs and returns are the opposite of those that arise during the phase-in region of the schedule. Both marginal costs and returns are directly reduced by the EITC, exactly canceling each other out so the direct effect is zero. Thus, the net effect on investment and hours worked depends on the balance of income and substitution effects. For upward-sloping labor supply curves, we would expect reductions in hours worked and investment for individuals who stay within the phase-out region. As above, the EITC may reduce investment and work enough to push early earnings into the plateau region.

For those moving from the plateau to the phase-out region of the EITC schedule, investment and hours worked are likely to be lower than they would be without the tax credit. Again, income effects discourage work and investment. Substitution effects operate as just described during the phase-out region. The increase in effective marginal tax rates associated with moving from the plateau to the phase-out region directly affects

---

[17] Recall that labor earnings are generally increasing with age in the absence of the EITC.

the marginal returns and costs of investment like a progressive tax. The marginal costs of investment are unaffected while in the plateau region of the schedule; however, during later earnings periods when the individual's income places him or her in the phase-out region, the marginal returns to investment are reduced. Thus, holding labor supply constant, the EITC would tend to reduce investment in human capital at early ages.[18] The disincentive effects may be so great as to reduce investment and work such that earnings never escape the plateau region.

Finally, we examine the effects of the EITC on individuals whose earnings would normally begin in the phase-out region and would increase to the point that they no longer qualified to receive any credit (moving from [b, c) to c and beyond.) Income and substitution effects all operate as discussed above while earnings are in the phase-out region. The marginal costs of investment are reduced while in the phase-out portion of the schedule, since reductions in earnings caused by increases in investment are partially offset by a higher subsidy. However, the marginal returns do not decline equiproportionally, because no loss in subsidy is experienced when labor income increases during years when individuals earn more than c. For inelastic labor supply, the direct effects of the EITC on investment should dominate indirect effects through hours worked, so investment is encouraged by the EITC. It is possible to observe declines in hours worked and increases in investment in response to the EITC for these higher-income workers. To the extent that the EITC directly encourages investment and thereby raises skill levels and wage rates later in life, it likely results in increased hours worked at older ages.

It is important to remember that investment, consumption and hours worked are all jointly determined. Policy impacts on one dimension affect the other dimensions indirectly. We have highlighted three primary effects of the EITC on investment and labor supply decisions. The balance of these effects and the interrelationships among them are an empirical question we address below. The EITC is likely to discourage investment among low-income workers starting on the first phase of the constraint and to encourage investment among workers moving from the phase-out region to beyond the schedule.

4.2   Learning-by-doing

We next explore a basic experience-based model of learning-by-doing. We ignore costly time investments, I, and concentrate on the effects of

---

[18] To the extent that the level of human capital increases the marginal returns to investment, investment may also decline once individuals reach the phase-out region (holding hours worked constant) owing to reductions in earlier investment.

hours worked, $h = 1 - L$, on human capital accumulation, assuming

$$\frac{\partial F}{\partial I} \equiv 0, \quad \frac{\partial F}{\partial h} > 0, \quad \frac{\partial^2 F}{\partial h^2} < 0.$$

Again, we consider the case where human capital is self-productive in producing skill, so $\partial F / \partial H \geq 0$.

We first present a brief description of individual behavior in the absence of the EITC. When $\delta^{-1} = 1 + r$, consumption and the marginal value of assets are constant over the life cycle. In the learning-by-doing model, there are two changing forces acting on leisure which operate in opposite directions over the life cycle. As before, increasing human capital increases wages. This force implies declining leisure and increasing labor supply with age. On the other hand, the marginal value of additional labor market experience and human capital declines with age, since there are fewer future years to reap the benefits of higher wages. This second force tends to cause labor supply to decline with age. The net effect is ambiguous and will inevitably depend on the exact nature of the skill production process and preferences.

The EITC affects the marginal value of an additional hour of work today for future earnings and the increase in future earnings due to an increase in work in the current period. As with the OJT model, we discuss the effects of the EITC on labor supply and skill formation for workers with different lifetime earnings paths.

First, consider workers whose earnings would place them in the phase-in region of the EITC schedule if their labor supply paths were held at their non-EITC levels. Additional work increases the current subsidy, so substitution effects operate to increase hours worked. Income effects operate in the opposite direction, discouraging work. An increase in work today raises future skill levels and labor income. So, as long as labor earnings remain less than a, an increase in hours worked today will also increase the amount of subsidy received in the future (holding future hours worked constant). Of course, the balance of income and substitution effects on future labor supply will also have an impact on the future returns to current work, since hours worked in the future affect the current marginal value of additional human capital. For upward-sloping labor supply curves, the phase-in region of the EITC unambiguously increases both the current and future returns to work. As a result, labor supply and skill acquisition increase at all ages. This prediction is in sharp contrast to the negative effects on skill formation that are expected when learning is acquired through OJT. Increases in labor supply and skill may push incomes above a and into the plateau region of the EITC.

The effects of the EITC on individuals with earnings in the plateau region are unambiguous. As in the OJT model, pure substitution effects are absent. Only income effects operate through the marginal valuation of wealth, causing individuals to work less at all ages. As a result, skill levels and labor incomes are reduced.

For individuals moving from the phase-in to the plateau region of EITC, all of the previously mentioned effects become relevant. Income effects discourage work at all ages. Income and substitution effects are important at early ages when income is below a, but, after tax and subsidy, skill prices are unchanged once incomes reach the plateau region. Assuming substitution effects dominate income effects, the current returns to work are raised by the EITC in the phase-in region. However, future returns are largely unaffected by the EITC, since the subsidy is unaffected by increases in labor income in the plateau region. The EITC encourages skill formation for those in the first phase by raising the current returns to work. When coupled with the negative wealth effects over the plateau region, we should expect smaller effects of the EITC on labor supply and skill formation for individuals moving beyond the phase-in region than we observe for those remaining in that region.

Whereas the phase-in region encourages work and skill formation by raising the current and future returns to an hour of work, the phase-out region has the exact opposite effect. It reduces the net wage rate, which reduces both the current and future returns to work. The lump-sum transfer of wealth also serves as a disincentive to work. As long as labor supply curves slope upward, individuals with incomes in the phase-out stage of the EITC schedule will work less and produce fewer skills than they would in the absence of the EITC.

The same is true for individuals moving from the plateau region to the phase-out region. Income effects operate to discourage work. Whereas the current returns to work at early ages are largely unaffected by income and substitution effects, the future returns to current work are diminished by the EITC. This is because increases in work today raise future wage rates. The resulting increases in future earnings are partially offset by a reduction in the income subsidy when labor income exceeds b. As a result, labor supply declines and less skill is acquired.

Finally, work and skills are discouraged for individuals moving off the EITC schedule from the phase-out region (again, assuming upward-sloping labor supply curves). Wealth effects discourage work. While in the phase-out region, current returns from work are reduced by the EITC, since, for each additional dollar earned, a fraction of the tax credit is lost. Future returns are largely unaffected, because no subsidy is received in periods when labor income is above c. So, whereas those moving from the plateau to the phase-out region work less because the future returns to work are diminished, workers beginning in the phase-out region work fewer hours because the current returns are lower.

As long as labor supply curves are upward sloping, the EITC tends to encourage work and skill formation for the lowest-income workers – those who spend some of their lives in the phase-in region of the schedule. For all other workers with incomes always above a, the EITC discourages work and reduces the accumulation of skills. Individuals in the phase-out region of the EITC are most discouraged from work, because it reduces both the current and future returns to skills.

4.3   Comparing OJT and LBD

The two pure models of skill formation sometimes predict quite different responses of investment to the EITC. In the OJT model, the EITC has little effect on skill formation for workers in the phase-in region (though, if substitution effects dominate for labor supply, the EITC will raise investment and work for affected persons), whereas the LBD technology produces positive effects on skill formation. For individuals moving off the EITC schedule from the phase-out region, the OJT model predicts an increase in skill accumulation, whereas the LBD model predicts a decline. The effects on learning are reversed in both models for individuals moving from the phase-in region to the plateau region. Workers with earnings in other regions of the EITC schedule respond with reductions in skill acquisition in both models, though the magnitudes of those responses likely differ.

As was true for the two-period models, few sharp analytical predictions about the magnitudes of these effects can be made without some knowledge of parameter values for preferences and the skill production technology. We turn next to an initial empirical exploration using specific versions of both human capital models, exploring the effects of the EITC on skill formation and labor supply.

5   Grounding the model in data

The appropriate way to estimate the impact of the EITC program on earnings and labor supply is to estimate the model imposing the full constraints from the EITC schedule and from economic theory. We do not undertake the formidable task of full structural estimation in the presence of the EITC in this chapter, leaving that for another occasion. Instead, in this chapter we estimate parameters for individual preferences and skill functions using data from a time period when the EITC was a small-scale program for low-skilled workers. The empirical results we offer are necessarily more illustrative than definitive, but they provide some guidance on the likely magnitudes of the effects of the EITC on skill formation.

Responses to the EITC depend critically on where individuals lie on the EITC schedule. We therefore consider a number of different types of workers. In particular, we use data on wages and hours worked from the 1980 March CPS to estimate preference and human capital production parameters for women classified by race (black and white) and education (less than ten years, ten–eleven years and twelve years of schooling). The EITC provided only modest assistance in the early 1980s and was primarily designed as an offset for the social security payroll tax for low-income workers.

Because the EITC schedule is not everywhere differentiable and does not yield a convex budget set, simple methods for solving the individual's problem cannot be used for our simulations. To simplify the problem, we break the life cycle into ten periods. Beginning at age 18, individuals are grouped by five-year periods through age 67. See appendix 3C for an explicit discussion of the algorithm used to solve the optimization problem and to guard against local optima.

We now present the empirical specification for individual preferences and human capital production technology that we use in our calibration and simulations. We assume the following separable utility function

$$U(C, L) = \frac{C^{\gamma+1}}{\gamma + 1} + \psi \frac{L^{\sigma+1}}{\sigma + 1}, \tag{3.11}$$

where γ and σ are both strictly negative and ψ is positive. We choose the conventional Ben Porath (1967) human capital production function for our OJT model:

$$H' = H + B(IH)^\alpha,$$

where $B > 0$ and $0 < \alpha < 1$. Heckman, Lochner and Taber (1998) present some evidence in support of this form of the OJT model for men and women. There is less discussion in the empirical literature about the specification of the learning-by-doing function. One interpretation of a "Mincer" earnings function writes current earnings as a quadratic in cumulative work experience:

$$H = H_0 + \beta_0 X + \beta_1 X^2,$$

where $X = \sum_{\tau=1}^{t-1} h(\tau)$ represents total work experience accumulated to date t. We expect $\beta_0 > 0$ and $\beta_1 < 0$, which would yield increasing and concave wage profiles.[19]

---

[19] Shaw (1989) fits such a model. Altug and Miller (1998) estimate a more general model in which both employment and work hours produce skill. Our specification differs from Mincer's because we use levels of wages whereas he uses logs.

The quadratic in experience earnings function is familiar from the Mincer (1974) model, although his justification for the specification is as an approximation to the Ben Porath (1967) model. In a single cross-section of wages, it is impossible to distinguish between the two models and, in practice, labor economists treat these models interchangeably despite their often contradictory implications about the effects of wage subsidies on skill formation.

Unfortunately, the available data do not allow us to identify all of the parameters of the model because we lack information on consumption and wealth holdings. Since the EITC targets low-income workers, initial assets, A_0, are assumed to be zero for all individuals. We assume $\gamma = -0.9$, yielding an intertemporal elasticity of substitution for consumption of 1.11. We take perfect credit markets as our base case environment and assume an interest rate of $r = 0.6105$, which corresponds to an annual interest rate of 10 percent (each period represents five years). We assume a rate of time preference, $\delta = 0.6219$, which yields slightly rising consumption profiles. These values are consistent with the parameters reported by Browning, Hansen and Heckman (1999).

We use weighted non-linear least squares to estimate the remaining parameters of both human capital models. We estimate separate parameters, Θ, for each category of worker, minimizing

$$\sum_{i=1}^{n} \sum_{t=1}^{10} \left[Q_t^w (w_{i,t} - w_t(\Theta))^2 + Q_t^h (h_{i,t} - h_t(\Theta))^2 \right],$$

where $w_{i,t}$ and $h_{i,t}$ are wage rates and hours worked[20] for individual i of age t from the CPS, and $w_t(\Theta)$ and $h_t(\Theta)$ are wage rates and share of time worked (which includes time spent working and investing in skills in the OJT model) predicted by the model for a person age t, with the parameter vector Θ defining preferences and the human capital production function. In our OJT model, Θ includes ψ, σ, B, α and H_0; in our LBD model, Θ includes ψ, σ, β_0, β_1 and H_0. The weights Q_t^w and Q_t^h are equal to the inverse of the variance of wages and hours worked (respectively) for each demographic group analyzed.[21]

Tables 3D.1 and 3D.2 in appendix 3D present the estimated parameter values for both models. The ψ parameter determines how much

---

[20] We use total hours worked divided by 5,840 (corresponding to 16 hours a day) to express hours in an amount corresponding to a share of available time.

[21] If hours worked and wages in each period are measured with independent and normally distributed errors with zero mean, this is equivalent to maximum likelihood. The parameter estimates are similar when different weights are used. We do not claim optimality for the estimator.

an individual values leisure relative to consumption, and σ determines the intertemporal elasticity for labor supply. The estimates from the OJT model suggest that labor supply is quite inelastic for all types, as seen by the large negative values for σ. Estimates of σ from the LBD model also show inelastic labor supply, although they are generally smaller than the OJT estimates. These estimates are within the range of estimates found in other studies of intertemporal labor supply elasticities (see Browning, Hansen and Heckman, 1999, for a recent summary of estimated labor supply elasticities in the literature). Tables 3D.3 and 3D.4 reveal that our LBD specification tends to fit the data better (in terms of the weighted sum of square errors criterion) for more educated women, while the OJT specification fits the data better for less educated women.

There is considerable heterogeneity in estimates of the human capital production parameters across groups, reflecting differences in lifecycle earnings profiles. Initial stocks of human capital are greatest for highschool graduates. Patterns for other parameters are not so easily detected. In the LBD model, initial skill levels are more homogeneous across all groups (ranging from 2.9 to 3.8 compared with 3.0 to 4.2 in the OJT model). Estimates of β_0 tend to be greater for the more educated workers, reflecting greater returns to experience. The difference between the two sets of H_0 estimates is due to on-the-job investment in the OJT model. Although initial earnings are quite similar across all groups – note the similarity in H_0 estimates in the LBD specification – the steeper wage profiles among more educated workers implies that investment levels are greater for them in the OJT specification. Greater investment among more educated women suggests that their initial human capital levels are larger than their initial wage levels. So, even though initial wages are similar across education groups, initial skill levels vary more in the OJT specification owing to differences in early on-the-job investments. A major difference between the two models lies in the estimated elasticity of intertemporal substitution in leisure demand with respect to the wage, which is the same as the Frisch elasticity in the separable preference specification we use.

6   Simulating the effects of the EITC

In this section, we use the estimated models to simulate the effects of the 1994 EITC schedule (for families with two children) on individual decisions over the life cycle using the parameter values described in the previous section. Since we examine the effects of the program only on a single worker, we implicitly assume that there is no other source of

Table 3.5 *Estimated lifecycle progression through the EITC schedule (OJT simulations based on 1994 EITC schedule for two children)*

	Initial EITC region	Final EITC region
Whites		
<10 years of school	Phase-in/plateau kink	Plateau
10–11 years of school	Phase-in	Phase-out
12 years of school	Plateau	Plateau/phase-out kink
Non-whites		
<10 years of school	Phase-in	Phase-in/plateau kink
10–11 years of school	Phase-in	Plateau
12 years of school	Plateau	Phase-out

labor income (i.e. from a spouse). We begin by analyzing the effects of the EITC on skill formation from the OJT model. We then simulate the effects from the LBD model.

6.1   On-the-job training

The effects of the EITC depend on an individual's earnings profile. Table 3.5 reports the EITC region for the initial and final earnings levels for less educated women,[22] who tend to begin their careers in the phase-in or plateau region and finish in the plateau or phase-out region.

To show the heterogeneity in impacts of the EITC, we focus on two classes of women with low levels of education. In particular, we study the effects of the EITC on human capital investment, leisure, skill levels, wage rates and wage incomes for white females with twelve years of education and non-white females with less than ten years of schooling. As shown in table 3.5, they represent, respectively, workers who move from the plateau region to the phase-out region (or kink between the plateau and phase-out region) and workers who spend their entire careers in the phase-in region. The previous section suggests that the EITC will have differential impacts on investment and labor supply among these subgroups of women.

We first consider the effects of the EITC on the investment (I) of women who would work even in the absence of the EITC, considering

[22] The earnings levels are computed for our OJT simulations when individuals face the EITC schedule. The regions differ only slightly if we consider earnings in the absence of the EITC.

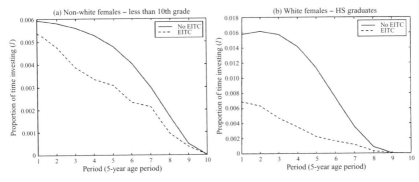

Figure 3.2 *Simulated effects of EITC on investment (OJT model)*

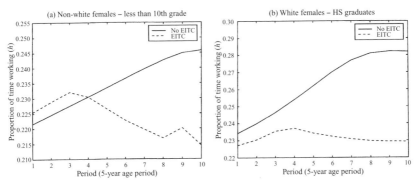

Figure 3.3 *Simulated effects of EITC on hours worked (OJT model)*

entry effects later. As predicted, figure 3.2 reveals that investment is reduced by the introduction of the EITC for both types of female workers. The solid lines represent investment paths in the absence of the EITC; the dotted lines report investment paths after introducing the EITC.

Hours worked for these workers are presented in figure 3.3. Without the EITC, hours worked would generally rise with age. With the EITC in place, however, lifecycle profiles for work hours are substantially flatter, even falling over later years. Hours worked increase for the less educated non-white females while their earnings remain in the phase-in section; however, as earnings reach or move into the plateau region, hours worked decline owing to the wealth effects induced by the lump-sum subsidy. The discontinuity occurs as they reach a kink between different regions of the schedule. For white high-school graduates, hours worked initially rise

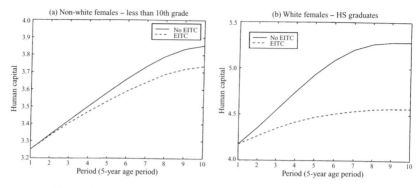

Figure 3.4 *Simulated effects of EITC on human capital (OJT model)*

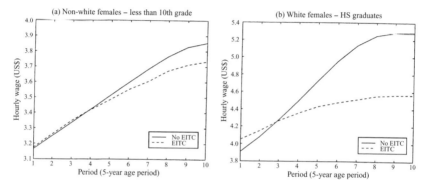

Figure 3.5 *Simulated effects of EITC on wage rates (OJT model)*

until earnings reach the kink between the plateau and phase-out regions. At that point, hours worked decline owing to the high marginal subsidy rate, keeping earnings right at the kink.

Figure 3.4 shows the cumulative effects of on-the-job investments on human capital levels. As could be predicted from figure 3.2, white female high-school graduates experience the largest impact of the EITC on skills. Human capital levels are reduced by more than 10 percent at the end of their careers. Reductions are smaller, but noticeable, for the less educated non-white women.

The resulting effects of the EITC on lifecycle wages can be seen in figure 3.5. Wage profiles flatten as investment declines. Notice that the initial effects on wages, which rise initially as investment rates decline, do not reflect the long-term effects. This suggests the importance of a dynamic analysis. Finally, the combined effects of the EITC on investment,

Table 3.6 *Effects of EITC (OJT model)*

	Change in present value of earnings (percent)	Change in present value of earnings (US$'000)	Present value of received subsidies (US$'000)
Whites			
<10 years of school	−6.32	−4.68	20.61
10–11 years of school	−1.97	−1.29	18.91
12 years of school	−9.25	−8.65	20.61
Non-whites			
<10 years of school	−0.13	−0.09	19.69
10–11 years of school	−0.79	−0.49	18.26
12 years of school	−8.68	−8.29	20.30

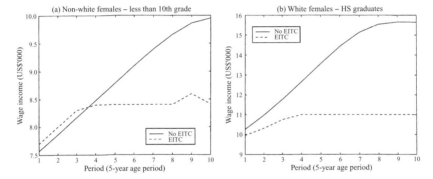

Figure 3.6 *Simulated effects of EITC on wage income (OJT model)*

hours worked and skill levels are translated into impacts on wage income, as seen in figure 3.6. The impacts on wage income are generally exaggerated versions of the impacts on wage rates. Both figures show how workers maintain earnings at a kink in the EITC by adjusting hours of work and investment in skills.

The impacts on lifetime earnings can be seen in table 3.6. The EITC reduces labor market earnings for all workers, with the largest effects observed for the more educated women, who begin their careers in the plateau region. The total lifetime amount of subsidy uneducated women receive is large, reaching US$20,000 in present value. For high-school graduates, nearly half of the subsidy is offset by a decline in labor earnings. Thus, the program reduces hours of work among workers and also reduces their skill levels. For the majority (the number of qualifying high-school graduates far exceeds the number of dropouts), it replaces earnings

Table 3.7 *Annual compensation necessary to make people indifferent between employment and non-employment (OJT simulations based on 1994 EITC schedule for two children)*

	Without EITC (US$'000)	With EITC (US$'000)
Whites		
<10 years of school	5.40	5.39
10–11 years of school	4.84	4.79
12 years of school	6.70	6.69
Non-whites		
<10 years of school	4.95	4.95
10–11 years of school	4.49	4.47
12 years of school	7.52	7.48

with income from "welfare." Most of these earnings declines reflect increases in leisure, because decreases in skills are generally offset by reductions in investment costs.

In most cases, the short-term effects of the EITC are very different from the long-term impacts. For the first few periods, the least educated women increase their hours worked and only slightly reduce investment in response to the EITC. Wages increase initially. The long-term impacts are far different. Investment declines still further and hours worked fall precipitously. Skill levels and wage rates also decline substantially. This reveals the dangers of using short-term responses to predict the long-term consequences of the EITC on individual well-being. Only a dynamic analysis such as the one we adopt can shed light on the long-term outcomes we might expect.

Thus far, we have examined the effects of the EITC only on those who would have worked in the absence of the program. As suggested by the analysis of Eissa and Liebman (1996), the EITC may also encourage individuals to work who otherwise would not. Table 3.7 reports the annual compensation required to make each of the demographic groups we analyze indifferent between working and not working. These calculations compare the utility of full-time leisure and a constant annual income with the income and leisure associated with working for each group. The table reveals that uneducated women can be easily induced to stay out of the labor market for small sums of "welfare" payments. The EITC only marginally reduces those sums, suggesting small entry effects should be expected.

Table 3.8 *Employment rates and average human capital levels (OJT simulations based on 1994 EITC schedule for two children)*

	Percent of population	Employment rate (percent)	Average human capital	Average supplied human capital
Whites				
<10 years of school	3.27	41.88	1.59	0.40
10–11 years of school	2.80	54.80	2.32	0.55
12 years of school	15.86	72.83	3.56	0.94
Non-whites				
<10 years of school	0.74	37.61	1.35	0.32
10–11 years of school	0.87	45.83	1.71	0.41
12 years of school	3.01	68.19	3.42	0.96

Note: Human capital averages (both potential and supplied) are lifetime averages of levels obtained in the simulations for each group, assuming an equal distribution of workers across all age groups. They are inclusive of non-workers, who we assume have potential skill levels equal to H_0 and supply zero skills to the market.

To estimate the total effect of the EITC program on skills, it is necessary to consider potential entry effects. Eissa and Liebman (1996) estimate that the 1986 expansion of the EITC increased employment of single women with children by about 3 percentage points. We explore the consequences for skill investment of a range of potential employment effects (1–7 percent) to determine the total impact of the EITC on average skill levels.[23]

Table 3.8 reports employment rates based on the 1994 March CPS and average human capital (both potential, H, and utilized, $H(1 - I - L)$) as estimated above, assuming an equal distribution of workers across all age groups. Utilized human capital reflects earnings. The reported average human capital levels are inclusive of non-workers, who are assumed to have potential skill levels equal to H_0 and to supply zero skills to the market. Skill and skill supplied to the market increase with education levels.

In table 3.9, we use our estimated preference and human capital parameters to examine the effects of increasing employment on skill formation, using a range of values for the estimated entry effect. Column 1 reports the raw difference in average lifetime skill levels for workers and

[23] In principle, one could estimate the employment effects using table 3.7 and a distribution of potential welfare (or other income) payments to workers. The entry effect will depend on (1) how much the EITC raises the annual compensation necessary to make individuals indifferent between working and not working; and (2) how many individuals are currently at the margin.

Table 3.9 *Effects of EITC on potential skill levels (OJT simulations based on 1994 EITC schedule for two children)*

	Difference in average human capital between workers and non-workers (1)	Change in average human capital owing to changes in					
		Extensive margin (entry)				Intensive margin (those who work with or without EITC)	
		Increase in employment				Unweighted (6)	Weighted (by employment rate) (7)
		1 percent (2)	3 percent (3)	5 percent (4)	7 percent (5)		
Whites							
<10 years of school	0.2765	0.0028	0.0083	0.0138	0.0194	−0.0518	−0.0217
10–11 years of school	0.9527	0.0095	0.0286	0.0476	0.0667	−0.0977	−0.0535
12 years of school	0.2675	0.0027	0.0080	0.0134	0.0187	−0.4471	−0.3256
Non-whites							
<10 years of school	0.2847	0.0028	0.0085	0.0142	0.0199	−0.0603	−0.0227
10–11 years of school	0.6368	0.0064	0.0191	0.0318	0.0446	−0.1144	−0.0524
12 years of school	0.7835	0.0078	0.0235	0.0392	0.0548	−0.3095	−0.2110

	Average human capital (no EITC)	Increase in employment			
		1 percent	3 percent	5 percent	7 percent
Net effects on average human capital for all less educated women	3.0485	−0.2250	−0.2167	−0.2085	−0.2003

Note: Human capital averages are lifetime averages of levels obtained in the simulations for each group, assuming an equal distribution of workers across all age groups. They are inclusive of non-workers, who we assume have potential skill levels equal to H_0. The values assumed for increase in employment denote percentage points of increase.

non-workers. We assume that those who do not work remain at their initial skill levels throughout their lives, whereas those induced to work by the EITC accumulate skills using the technology estimated in this paper following the human capital accumulation paths depicted in figure 3.4. Columns 2–5 report the estimated impact on human capital of increasing employment by different percentage points. These entry effects increase the average skill level in the economy by anywhere from 0.003 to 0.070 for different women (note that these are differences in *potential* wage rates). These must be balanced against the disincentive effects on those who are already working, as reported in columns 6 and 7. Column 6 reports the change in skills for workers attributable to the EITC, while column 7 weights that amount by the employment rate for the particular group. When determining the total effect on average skill levels for any demographic group, simply add the effect on skill from increased employment (from one of columns 2–5) to the effect on current workers (column 7).

Based on the evidence in the literature, a plausible upper bound entry effect is a 3–5 percentage point increase. For dropouts, the skill accumulation effects at the intensive and extensive margins are of similar magnitudes. For all but white women with ten to eleven years of schooling, the negative effects at the intensive margin outweigh the positive entry effects for entry effects as large as 7 percent. Clearly, estimating the impact of the EITC on average skill levels requires knowledge of both employment effects and the effects on current workers. Both effects are important and they operate in different directions.

The bottom panel of table 3.9 predicts how a universal EITC program (regardless of spousal earnings and child status) would affect the skill levels of women with twelve years of schooling or less, using various assumptions about the program's impact on labor-force entry. In this panel, we weight the effects of the EITC for each group including employment effects and those for current workers by the proportion of the population in that group (as reported in table 3.8). Overall, the EITC reduces potential skill levels by about −0.2 (7 percent) among low-educated women, even if entry effects are extremely large.

Table 3.10 repeats these calculations for skills supplied to the market (earnings $= H(1 - I - L)$ for workers and zero for non-workers) rather than total skills, H. The positive impacts of the EITC owing to entry are generally greater when compared with the average levels of utilized skill (reported in table 3.8). The effects at the intensive margin for workers are more similar in the two tables. The net impact of the EITC on aggregate utilized human capital is negative (about −10 percent), even when employment effects are large, since the effects on high-school graduates

Table 3.10 *Effects of EITC on skills supplied to the market (OJT simulations based on 1994 EITC schedule for two children)*

	Difference in average supplied human capital between workers and non-workers (1)	Change in average supplied human capital owing to changes in						
		Extensive margin (entry) Increase in employment				Intensive margin (those who work with or without EITC)	
		1 percent (2)	3 percent (3)	5 percent (4)	7 percent (5)	Unweighted (6)	Weighted (by employment rate) (7)
Whites							
<10 years of school	0.8558	0.0086	0.0257	0.0428	0.0599	−0.0919	−0.0385
10–11 years of school	0.8893	0.0089	0.0267	0.0445	0.0622	−0.1225	−0.0671
12 years of school	1.0286	0.0103	0.0309	0.0514	0.0720	−0.2631	−0.1916
Non-whites							
<10 years of school	0.7903	0.0079	0.0237	0.0395	0.0553	−0.0555	−0.0209
10–11 years of school	0.8105	0.0081	0.0243	0.0405	0.0567	−0.0909	−0.0416
12 years of school	1.1659	0.0117	0.0350	0.0583	0.0816	−0.2427	−0.1655

	Average supplied human capital (no EITC)	Increase in employment			
		1 percent	3 percent	5 percent	7 percent
Net effects on average human capital for all less educated women	0.8000	−0.1370	−0.1172	−0.0973	−0.0774

Note: Supplied human capital averages are lifetime averages of levels obtained in the simulations for each group, assuming an equal distribution of workers across all age groups. They are inclusive of non-workers, who we assume have potential skill levels equal to H_0 and supply zero skills to the market. The values assumed for increase in employment denote percentage points of increase.

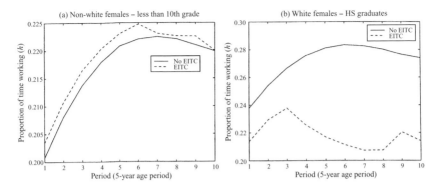

Figure 3.7 *Simulated effects of EITC on hours worked (LBD model)*

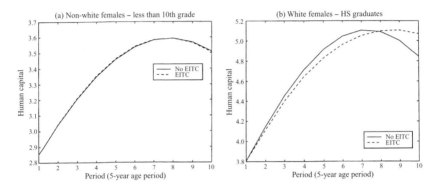

Figure 3.8 *Simulated effects of EITC on human capital (LBD model)*

dominate those for lesser-educated female workers. So, plausible estimates of the impact of the EITC on employment suggest that the EITC
would decrease both potential and utilized skill levels among women with
no college experience.

6.2   Learning-by-doing

The effects of the EITC on skill formation among those who would work
in the presence or absence of the program are much smaller in our estimated LBD specification. Even though hours worked are substantially
reduced for white female high-school graduates, as seen in figure 3.7,
human capital accumulation is not (see figure 3.8). The least educated
non-white females are encouraged to work by the EITC, since they spend

Table 3.11 *Estimated lifecycle progression through the EITC schedule (LBD simulations based on 1994 EITC schedule for two children)*

	Initial EITC region	Final EITC region
Whites		
<10 years of school	Phase-in	Plateau
10–11 years of school	Phase-in/plateau kink	Phase-out
12 years of school	Plateau	Phase-out
Non-whites		
<10 years of school	Phase-in	Phase-in
10–11 years of school	Phase-in/plateau kink	Plateau
12 years of school	Phase-in/plateau kink	Plateau/phase-out kink

their careers in the phase-in region where both future and current returns to work are rewarded by the credit. Table 3.11 shows where along the EITC schedule individuals begin and end their working careers. Most of the entries are similar to those discussed for the OJT model (table 3.5).

The small effects of the program on skill formation are largely the result of the specification of the skill acquisition function. In our specification, human capital is a function of cumulative hours worked. If human capital peaks at some level of total hours worked within the span of possible values, then fewer hours worked each year mean that the critical level is reached later in life. Therefore, wages and skills peak later, but the height of the peak is the same. Since we specify earnings (and skills) as a quadratic function of total experience, and earnings peak at around age 45–50 for most workers, reductions in hours worked caused by the EITC (or its expansion) simply cause a worker's earnings to peak at a later age. The EITC does not reduce hours enough that earnings never reach their peak. If the influence of past hours worked on current skill production depreciated quickly, we would find larger effects of the EITC on skill formation, since earnings need not peak or may peak at a different level. In any case, impacts on skills should be negative for all workers who do not spend part of their careers in the phase-in region. That is a universal feature of a learning-by-doing model.

Wages are the same as skill levels in the LBD model. Figure 3.9 illustrates the weak estimated effect of marginal hours of work on hourly wages. Huge changes in hours of work are required to change hourly

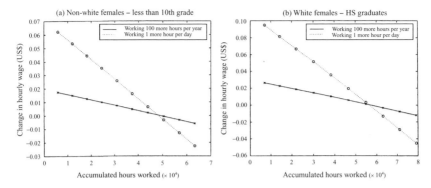

Figure 3.9 *Changes in hourly wages owing to increases in hours worked (LBD model)*

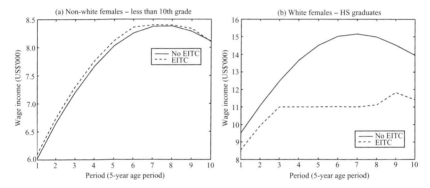

Figure 3.10 *Simulated effects of EITC on wage income (LBD model)*

wages by more than a few cents for most workers. Also notice that, beyond a certain threshold, additional work reduces skills owing to the quadratic specification in total accumulated experience. Because human capital levels are largely unaffected by the program, the effects of the EITC on wage earnings, as shown in figure 3.10, are essentially the result of adjustments in current hours of work. Only non-white females with less than ten years of education earn more as a result of the EITC program.

Table 3.12 translates these earnings effects into the lifetime present value of earnings. Earnings reductions are typically much larger than those predicted from the OJT model; for high-school graduates, reductions in earnings are more than one-half the supplement to earnings

Table 3.12 *Effects of EITC when imposed (LBD model)*

	Change in present value of earnings (percent)	Change in present value of earnings (US$'000)	Present value of received subsidies (US$'000)
Whites			
<10 years of school	−4.34	−3.12	20.18
10–11 years of school	−12.71	−10.38	20.59
12 years of school	−14.20	−13.25	20.60
Non-whites			
<10 years of school	1.26	0.70	16.90
10–11 years of school	−13.30	−10.91	20.61
12 years of school	−15.26	−13.87	20.58

Table 3.13 *Annual compensation necessary to make people indifferent between employment and non-employment (LBD simulations based on 1994 EITC schedule for two children)*

	Without EITC (US$'000)	With EITC (US$'000)
Whites		
<10 years of school	5.10	5.08
10–11 years of school	4.01	3.98
12 years of school	5.39	5.36
Non-whites		
<10 years of school	3.61	3.59
10–11 years of school	4.03	4.02
12 years of school	4.50	4.45

offered by the EITC. For the least educated women, however, the EITC substantially augments earnings with little offset from changes in behavior. The least educated non-white women actually experience increases in labor earnings.

Table 3.13 shows the welfare compensation necessary to make workers indifferent between working and not working in our LBD specification. As in the OJT model, the required sums are small, and the EITC only marginally changes those reservation values. Table 3.14 is the LBD analog of table 3.8, reporting employment rates and average skill levels for

Table 3.14 *Employment rates and average human capital levels (LBD simulations based on 1994 EITC schedule for two children)*

	Percent of population	Employment rate (percent)	Average human capital	Average supplied human capital
Whites				
<10 years of school	3.27	41.88	1.54	0.39
10–11 years of school	2.80	54.80	2.39	0.64
12 years of school	15.86	72.83	3.43	0.94
Non-whites				
<10 years of school	0.74	37.61	1.27	0.28
10–11 years of school	0.87	45.83	1.81	0.50
12 years of school	3.01	68.19	3.16	0.90

Note: Human capital averages (both potential and supplied) are lifetime averages of levels obtained in the simulations for each group, assuming an equal distribution of workers across all age groups. They are inclusive of non-workers, who we assume have potential skill levels equal to H_0 and supply zero skills to the market.

the different women. Tables 3.15 and 3.16 examine the impacts of the EITC on average skills in the economy at the extensive margin (entry effects) and at the intensive margin (for workers). The entry effects are similar to those produced by the OJT model. Impacts on the potential skills of workers (at the intensive margin) are generally small and positive, whereas effects on skills actually supplied to the market are large and negative, as observed with the OJT model. Average potential human capital levels are predicted to increase with the introduction of the EITC, since entry effects dominate. However, utilized skills are predicted to decline for all but the least educated, as the negative effects of the EITC on workers dominate positive entry effects. Although the entry effects on skill formation are quite similar to those found for the OJT model, changes in potential skill among workers caused by the EITC are typically much smaller than in the OJT model. This could have been anticipated from a comparison of the strong effect of the EITC on human capital in the OJT model (figure 3.4) and the weak effect in the LBD model (figure 3.8). The EITC, therefore, is predicted to have slightly larger impacts on average potential skill levels when the LBD model is used. In contrast, the LBD model often produces more negative impacts on the utilized skills of workers than the OJT model (compare the final columns of tables 3.10 and 3.16). This is largely owing to the substantial effects of the EITC on hours worked in the LBD model. In both models, however, the effects of

Table 3.15 *Effects of EITC on potential skill levels (LBD simulations based on 1994 EITC schedule for two children)*

	Difference in average human capital between workers and non-workers (1)	Change in average human capital owing to changes in					
		Extensive margin (entry)				Intensive margin (those who work with or without EITC)	
		Increase in employment				Unweighted (6)	Weighted (by employment rate) (7)
		1 percent (2)	3 percent (3)	5 percent (4)	7 percent (5)		
Whites							
<10 years of school	0.6441	0.0064	0.0193	0.0322	0.0451	0.0186	0.0078
10–11 years of school	0.7197	0.0072	0.0216	0.0360	0.0504	−0.0015	−0.0008
12 years of school	0.9035	0.0090	0.0271	0.0452	0.0632	−0.0039	−0.0028
Non-whites							
<10 years of school	0.5198	0.0052	0.0156	0.0260	0.0364	0.0011	0.0004
10–11 years of school	0.5485	0.0055	0.0165	0.0274	0.0384	0.0219	0.0100
12 years of school	0.9857	0.0099	0.0296	0.0493	0.0690	0.0194	0.0132

	Average human capital (no EITC)	Increase in employment			
		1 percent	3 percent	5 percent	7 percent
Net effects on average human capital for all less educated women	2.9436	0.0094	0.0262	0.0430	0.0598

Note: Human capital averages are lifetime averages of levels obtained in the simulations for each group, assuming an equal distribution of workers across all age groups. They are inclusive of non-workers, who we assume have potential skill levels equal to H_0. The values assumed for increase in employment denote percentage points of increase.

Table 3.16 *Effects of EITC on skills supplied to the market (LBD simulations based on 1994 EITC schedule for two children)*

	Difference in average supplied human capital between workers and non-workers (1)	Change in average supplied human capital owing to changes in					
		Extensive margin (entry) Increase in employment				Intensive margin (those who work with or without EITC)	
		1 percent (2)	3 percent (3)	5 percent (4)	7 percent (5)	Unweighted (6)	Weighted (by employment rate) (7)
Whites							
<10 years of school	0.8558	0.0086	0.0257	0.0428	0.0599	−0.0762	−0.0319
10–11 years of school	0.9450	0.0094	0.0283	0.0472	0.0661	−0.2183	−0.1196
12 years of school	1.0266	0.0103	0.0308	0.0513	0.0719	−0.2572	−0.1874
Non-whites							
<10 years of school	0.7389	0.0074	0.0222	0.0369	0.0517	+0.0062	+0.0023
10–11 years of school	0.9109	0.0091	0.0273	0.0455	0.0638	−0.1762	−0.0807
12 years of school	1.0186	0.0102	0.0306	0.0509	0.0713	−0.3025	−0.2063

	Average supplied human capital (no EITC)	Increase in employment			
		1 percent	3 percent	5 percent	7 percent
Net effects on average human capital for all less educated women	0.8033	−0.1446	−0.1249	−0.1052	−0.0855

Note: Supplied human capital averages are lifetime averages of levels obtained in the simulations for each group, assuming an equal distribution of workers across all age groups. They are inclusive of non-workers, who we assume have potential skill levels equal to H_0 and supply zero skills to the market. The values assumed for increase in employment denote percentage points of increase.

the EITC on the total utilized skills of women with low levels of education are dominated by the negative effects on workers even when employment effects are quite large. For small entry effects (of 1 percentage point), impacts on skills supplied to the market (i.e. earnings) are as large as 18 percent of average levels for the LBD model, whereas the OJT model predicts slightly smaller responses.

6.3   *Accounting for lifecycle eligibility owing to children*

Thus far, we have focused on the impacts of the EITC ignoring other family income or the number of qualifying children. The simulation results presented in the previous sections compare the case of extending the EITC to all workers against removing the EITC for all workers.

The EITC has different schedules based on the number of children living in the household. This seemingly harmless qualification can drastically affect estimated behavioral responses to the EITC, since families cannot expect to receive the credit (or at least the larger credit for parents) for their entire working careers unless they continue to have qualifying children. In general, families can expect to receive the credit for only twenty to thirty years, depending on how many children they have and how they space them. Additional sources of family income alter the analysis in a predictable way to reduce eligibility. We focus on the less obvious effects of current child requirements.

Modifying the analysis to account for limited time periods of EITC qualification substantially changes the implications for workers ending their careers in the phase-in or phase-out regions of the EITC. If termination of EITC eligibility as a result of failure to meet the child requirement occurs in the phase-in region, future returns to investment in skills are no longer subsidized. Only costs of investment are increased, so the disincentive effects reduce skills. In our simulations, the EITC has only moderate negative impacts on investment for the least educated women owing to income effects on labor supply. It will have substantially larger negative impacts on their skill formation if they cannot receive the benefits from increased subsidy levels later in their careers, as would be the case if their children grow too old for them to qualify for the credit. On the other hand, for workers ending their careers in the phase-out region, termination of the credit owing to aging children removes the tax on returns to investment that causes more-educated female workers to scale back their investments. For workers who end their careers with earnings too high to qualify for the credit, the child restriction is of little consequence.

7   Evidence on OJT versus LBD

We have, thus far, discussed the varied impacts of the EITC on skill formation and wage growth using two standard human capital models. The OJT and LBD models predict opposite effects on investment and wage growth. Although changes in the EITC over time could potentially be used to test which model better represents the skill formation process, the complexity of the program makes this extremely difficult to do in practice.

In Heckman and Lochner (2002), we use data from the Seattle and Denver Income Maintenance Experiments to estimate the effects of a short-term (three years) increase in marginal income tax rates on wage growth. These experiments, conducted in the 1970s, randomly assigned low-income families to different negative income tax schedules (for three to five years), which included marginal tax rates ranging from 50 percent to 80 percent. Although both models of human capital formation predict that the short-term income transfers and high marginal tax rates associated with the experiment should, at least temporarily, reduce labor supply, the OJT and LBD models predict opposite effects on skill formation and wage growth.[24] As discussed in section 2.1, the OJT model predicts that a short-term increase in income tax rates will encourage human capital investment and increase wage growth, whereas the LBD model predicts the opposite. The estimates by Heckman and Lochner (2002) suggest that wage growth rates were about 10 percent lower among male treatments facing the negative income tax schedules than among male controls facing the standard US federal tax schedule. This finding suggests that wage growth decreases with increases in short-term tax rates, which is consistent with the theory of learning-by-doing and not with on-the-job training.

8   Conclusions

The EITC has been justified on the grounds that it transfers income to the working poor, particularly struggling mothers, without substantially reducing their incentives to work. It also stimulates non-workers to work. This chapter has explored the impact of the EITC on incentives to work and accumulate skills in two different models of human capital formation. Correct specification of the skill formation process is critical to understanding the effects of the EITC on skills, because different models

---

[24] Results in Robins and West (1980a,b) empirically support the prediction for labor supply.

produce very different predictions of its effects on skill formation. Theory is ambiguous about the effects of the EITC on skill formation, so it is necessary to undertake an empirical analysis of the question.

In order to measure the empirical effects of the EITC, preference and human capital production parameters for two canonical models of skill formation were estimated from the wage and hours worked profiles of less educated working women using the 1980 CPS. Those parameters were then used to predict individual responses in labor supply and investment caused by introduction of the EITC.

We found that in a training model in which skills are produced by costly time investments (OJT), the EITC encourages skill investment for workers who begin their careers in the phase-out region and end their careers above the EITC income cut-off. Time spent working is much lower during the phase-out region and slightly higher beyond that region. None of the less educated women we studied earn this much. Among female high-school dropouts and graduates who spend their careers within the income limits of the EITC schedule, the EITC substantially reduces investment and skill formation. Labor supply is initially higher for workers facing the EITC schedule, but the lifecycle profile is flatter and hours worked are lower later in the life cycle.

Using our estimated experience-based learning-by-doing model of skill formation, we found very different impacts from the EITC. Whereas labor supply is generally reduced by the EITC (by as much as 20 percent in some periods for working women in the phase-out and plateau regions), the effects of the EITC on skill formation are quite small. Skills marginally increase among the least educated dropouts, whose earnings remain within the phase-in region of the schedule.

Impacts of the EITC on skill formation at the extensive (or entry) margin are essentially the same for both skill models. To the extent that the EITC raises employment rates by making work more attractive, it also raises skill levels. For any given increase in work rates, the increase in human capital supplied to the market from increased employment does not depend much on how those skills are formed. In the OJT model, the impacts on skill formation of the EITC for entrants and for those who would work under any event, are of the same order of magnitude but of the opposite sign. Marginal changes among workers tend to dominate, causing the EITC to decrease potential and utilized skills among less educated women. For the LBD model, the entry effects on the formation of potential market skills are much stronger than the effects on those who would work in the presence or absence of the program, whose human capital is only marginally affected. The greatest differences between models of skill formation are found for workers at the intensive margin deciding how much to work and invest in additional skills. When considering utilized skills, the two models are largely in agreement, predicting negative impacts of the EITC on average earnings levels. We estimate declines as large as 18 percent of current average utilized skill levels if entry effects are small.

The empirical evidence presented in this chapter can be regarded only as suggestive rather than as definitive. Like the rest of the literature, we have not yet produced a reliable estimate of the effect of the EITC program on employment among those who would not work in its absence. Our estimated entry effects are simply educated guesses about plausible magnitudes of the response. However, unless the true entry effects are extremely large, negative effects of the EITC on workers are likely to dominate the positive effects through induced entry.

Much more empirical work is required to determine the exact mechanism of skill formation and how learning opportunities are priced in the market. We have compared two simple specifications. The EITC has large effects on training but weak effects on labor supply in an OJT model. It has little effect on skills and larger labor supply impacts when studied within the LBD model we employ.

A more general model of skill formation that recognizes the existence of markets for jobs and that derives explicit solutions for the prices of jobs with different learning opportunities would be desirable. We have demonstrated the importance of knowing the exact mechanism by which skills are produced and how jobs with different learning content are priced. The exact specification of preferences and skill formation requires much further study before we can be sure which model is more appropriate.

At our current level of understanding, the evidence shows that the EITC has a negative impact on the average skill levels of less educated women. (However, it may have large negative effects on other groups of workers, as shown in Heckman, Lochner and Cossa, 1999.) This is because the positive impacts owing to entry are typically dominated by the negative effects on those who would work in the presence or absence of the EITC program. Furthermore, some workers respond to the EITC by increasing their skill levels, whereas others reduce their skills. In the empirically plausible range, the program reduces earnings among less educated women. This effect operates primarily through (long-term) labor supply disincentives. The EITC may have substantial effects on most workers, while having only a minor effect on average skill and wage levels. Econometric methods that identify only the mean effects of programs such as the EITC miss the larger picture.

Appendix 3A

Table 3A.1 *Definition of EITC regions for CPS calculations*

Region	Income range
I (phase-in)	$W < 0.95\,a$
II (first kink)	$0.95\,a \leq W < 1.05\,a$
III (plateau)	$1.05\,a \leq W < 0.95\,b$
IV (second kink)	$0.95\,b \leq W < 1.05\,b$
V (phase-out)	$1.05\,b \leq W < 0.95\,c$
VI (third kink)	$0.95\,c \leq W < 1.05\,c$
VII (no credit)	$1.05\,c \leq W$

Note: The values of a, b, c are obtained from table 3.1.

Appendix 3B: non-concavity of the reward function in the Ben Porath model in the presence of an EITC program

For simplicity, set $R = 1$, $r = 0$, $H_0 = 1$. Then consider $V(I)$ for a program where there is either a phase-out range or a no-program range. For $I > k$, we assume that a person is in the phase-out range (branch 3). For $I \leq k$, we assume that a person is in the no-program range (no tax or subsidy). Using τ as the phase-out tax rate, we may write $V(I)$ for two values of I_1 and I_2, which in the second period place the individual in the no-EITC zone.

$$V(I_1) = (1 + \tau)(1 - I_1)1(I_1 > k) + (1 - I_1)1(I_1 \leq k) + F(I_1)$$

$$V(I_2) = (1 + \tau)(1 - I_2)1(I_2 > k) + (1 - I_2)1(I_2 \leq k) + F(I_2).$$

We can always find such values of I_1 and I_2. (This is trivial if the agent starts in the no-program range.) Provided investment is sufficiently productive, we can move the agent from the phase-out range to the no-program range. This requires that we find values of I_1 such that $(1 - I_1) < c$, $F(I_1) + 1 > c$ so $1 - c < I_1$, $F(I_1) > c - 1$. Assuming F is monotonically increasing, $\text{Max}\,\{1 - c, F^{-1}(c - 1)\} < I_1$. Then letting $\bar{I} = \lambda I_1 + (1 - \lambda)I_2, 0 \leq \lambda \leq 1$,

$$\begin{aligned} V(\bar{I}) &= (1 + \tau)(1 - \bar{I})1(\bar{I} > k) + (1 - \bar{I})1(\bar{I} \leq k) + F(\bar{I}) \\ &= \tau(1 - \bar{I})1(\bar{I} > k) + (1 - \bar{I}) + F(\bar{I}). \end{aligned}$$

Next, we obtain

$$\lambda V(I_1) + (1-\lambda)V(I_2)$$
$$= \lambda\tau(1-I_1)1(I_1 > k) + \lambda(1-I_1) + \lambda F(I_1)$$
$$\quad + (1-\lambda)\tau(1-I_2)1(I_2 > k) + (1-\lambda)(1-I_2) + (1-\lambda)F(I_2)$$
$$= (1-\bar{I}) + \tau(\lambda(1-I_1)1(I_1 > k))$$
$$\quad + \tau((1-\lambda)(1-I_2)1(I_2 > k))$$
$$\quad + \lambda F(I_1) + (1-\lambda)F(I_2).$$

$V(I)$ is concave if

$$V(\bar{I}) \geq \lambda V(I_1) + (1-\lambda)V(I_2),$$

or

$$\tau(1-\bar{I})1(\bar{I} > k) + F(\bar{I}) \geq \tau[\lambda(1-I_1)1(I_1 > k))$$
$$\quad + ((1-\lambda)(1-I_2)1(I_2 > k)] + \lambda F(I_1) + (1-\lambda)F(I_2).$$

Clearly, $F(\bar{I}) - \lambda F(I_1) - (1-\lambda)F(I_2) \geq 0$ by concavity in $F(I)$. However, it is not necessarily true that for $\tau > 0$

$$(1-\bar{I})1(\bar{I} > k) \geq [\lambda(1-I_1)1(I_1 > k)$$
$$\quad + (1-\lambda)(1-I_2)1(I_2 > k)]. \tag{3.12}$$

Provided $I > 0$, it is possible that $\bar{I} < k$, but either I_1 or $I_2 > k$. Then the concavity condition may or may not hold. Thus, for certain ranges of values of investment, we may obtain concavity of the reward function, whereas for others we do not. If investment is sufficiently productive, the contribution of $F(\bar{I}) - \lambda F(I_1) - (1-\lambda)F(I_2)$ may offset the non-concavity arising from the jump in the indicator functions.

Appendix 3C: solution algorithm for individual optimization problem

Problems with discontinuities and a non-convex budget set require that non-standard solution methods be employed in solving the individual's optimization problem. This is why we reduce the lifecycle problem to ten periods. Because gradient methods cannot be used, we use the direct search complex algorithm DBCPOL in Fortran 77 to solve simultaneously for all consumption, leisure and investment (for the OJT model) values when maximizing lifetime utility subject to the appropriate human and physical capital accumulation constraints. In the OJT model, this amounts to trying a path for investment and leisure. Calculating the

Table 3D.1 *Parameter values for the OJT model*

	ψ	σ	B	α	H_0
Whites					
<10 years of school	0.8901	−5.3879	0.8558	0.6015	3.4585
10–11 years of school	0.8971	−6.4344	0.7270	0.3122	3.1871
12 years of school	0.8947	−5.0882	1.8262	0.8473	4.1736
Non-whites					
<10 years of school	0.7751	−6.4974	0.9285	0.6098	3.2512
10–11 years of school	0.8907	−6.0751	0.9656	0.5064	2.9811
12 years of school	0.5194	−6.3269	1.3129	0.6186	3.9263

Table 3D.2 *Parameter values for the LBD model*

	ψ	σ	H_0	β_0	β_1
Whites					
<10 years of school	0.9555	−5.1475	3.0491	1.2586	−0.4397
10–11 years of school	3.0723	−1.3047	3.6451	1.2862	−0.3928
12 years of school	1.9320	−2.5976	3.8051	1.5468	−0.4592
Non-whites					
<10 years of school	1.5521	−4.8080	2.8516	1.0161	−0.3479
10–11 years of school	2.8638	−1.1183	3.4269	1.0245	−0.3375
12 years of school	2.8248	−1.3371	3.6644	1.7231	−0.5218

optimal consumption path given this investment and leisure path is trivial. Then, total lifetime utility is found. These steps are iterated using
the DBCPOL algorithm until the maximizing consumption, leisure and
investment profiles are found. We use multiple starting values for each
profile to determine whether the optimization procedure produces global
optima. Reasonable starting values for investment and leisure generally
produce a global optimum. In particular, when the EITC is not imposed
we use the optimal paths for leisure and investment as initial guesses, and
we always find that this leads to a global optimum. A similar procedure
is used for the LBD model, dropping investment I.

Appendix 3D: parameter estimates

This appendix reports the parameter estimates and goodness of fit for the
models used in the chapter. Tables 3D.1 and 3D.2 report the parameter
estimates for the OJT and LBD models, respectively. The weighted sums

Table 3D.3 *Goodness of fit (OJT model):*
weighted sum of squared differences

	Wages	Hours	Total
Whites			
<10 years of school	16.34	74.86	91.20
10–11 years of school	63.97	201.01	264.98
12 years of school	150.16	134.43	284.59
Non-whites			
<10 years of school	8.92	24.92	33.84
10–11 years of school	46.11	93.95	140.06
12 years of school	49.00	96.13	145.13

Table 3D.4 *Goodness of fit (LBD model):*
weighted sum of squared differences

	Wages	Hours	Total
Whites			
<10 years of school	18.04	78.06	96.10
10–11 years of school	118.15	178.90	297.05
12 years of school	52.91	91.14	144.05
Non-whites			
<10 years of school	12.13	36.98	49.11
10–11 years of school	64.02	114.98	179.00
12 years of school	19.66	19.93	39.59

of squared errors are reported in tables 3D.3 and 3D.4, along with a decomposition of those errors into the contribution of errors in predicting hours and wages.

References

Altug, S. and R. Miller (1990). "Household Choices in Equilibrium," *Econometrica* **58**(3): 543–570.

(1998). "The Effects of Work Experience on Female Wages and Labor Supply," *Review of Economic Studies* **65**(222): 45–67.

Becker, G. (1964). *Human Capital.* New York: Columbia University Press.

Ben Porath, Y. (1967). "The Production of Human Capital and the Life Cycle of Earnings," *Journal of Political Economy* **75**(4): 352–365.

Browning, M., L. Hansen and J. Heckman (1999). "Micro Data and General Equilibrium Models," in J. Taylor and M. Woodford (eds.), *Handbook of Macroeconomics*. Amsterdam: North-Holland Press.

Eissa, N. and J. Liebman (1996). "Labor Supply Response to the Earned Income Tax Credit," *Quarterly Journal of Economics* **111**(2): 605–637.

Heckman, J. (1971). "Three Essays on Household Labor Supply and the Demand for Market Goods," Ph.D. dissertation, Princeton University, chapter 1.

——— (1976). "Life-Cycle Model of Earnings, Learning, and Consumption," *Journal of Political Economy* **84**(4): S11–S44.

Heckman, J. and L. Lochner (2002). "Distinguishing between On-the-Job Training and Learning-by-Doing Models of Skill Formation," Working Paper, University of Rochester.

Heckman, J., L. Lochner and R. Cossa (1999). "Wage Subsidies and Skill Formation: A Study of the Earned Income Tax Credit," Working Paper.

Heckman, J., L. Lochner and C. Taber (1998). "Explaining Rising Wage Inequality: Explorations with a Dynamic General Equilibrium Model of Labor Earnings with Heterogeneous Agents," *Review of Economic Dynamics* **1**(1).

Heckman, J., L. Lochner, J. Smith and C. Taber (1997). "The Effects of Government Policy on Human Capital Investment and Wage Inequality," *Chicago Policy Review* **1**(2): 1–40.

Killingsworth, M. (1982). "Learning by Doing and Investment in Training: A Synthesis of Two Rival Models of the Life Cycle," *Review of Economic Studies* **49**(2): 263–272.

Lochner, L. (1998). "A Life-Cycle Model of Human Capital and Crime: Estimating Deterrent Effects of Wage and Education Subsidies," Ph.D. dissertation, University of Chicago.

Mincer, J. (1974). *Schooling, Experience and Earnings*. New York: Columbia University Press.

Phelps, N. (1997). *Rewarding Work*. Cambridge, MA: Harvard University Press.

Robins, P. and R. West (1980a). "Program Participation and Labor-Supply Response," *Journal of Human Resources* **15**(4): 499–523.

——— (1980b). "Labor-Supply Response over Time," *Journal of Human Resources* **15**(4): 499–523.

Rosen, S. (1972). "Learning and Experience in the Labor Market," *Journal of Human Resources* **7**(3): 326–342.

Shaw, K. (1989). "Lifecycle Labor Supply with Human Capital Accumulation," *International Economic Review* **30**: 431–456.

Weiss, Y. (1972). "On the Optimal Lifetime Pattern of Labour Supply," *Economic Journal* **82**(328): 1293–1315.

4 Unemployment vouchers versus low-wage subsidies

J. Michael Orszag and Dennis J. Snower

1 Introduction

In both Europe and the United States policy makers have been searching for new labor market measures that keep unemployment low *and* avoid large disparities in income. This chapter examines two policy proposals that have this aim: (1) unemployment vouchers[1] and (2) low-wage subsidies.[2] The unemployment vouchers are targeted exclusively at the unemployed (especially the long-term unemployed) and are provided for only a limited period of time. The low-wage subsidies, on the other hand, are granted to all low-wage earners regardless of their employment history and are of limitless duration.

Naturally, the impact effects of unemployment vouchers and low-wage subsidies are quite different. Because unemployment vouchers are targeted typically at the long-term unemployed whereas low-wage subsidies are targeted at the low-wage employed, it may be tempting to think that the two policies address different government objectives, namely, that the unemployment vouchers fight *unemployment* whereas the low-wage subsidies combat *working poverty*. This impression is misleading, however. Both policies affect the incentives to work.[3] Thus both policies influence both unemployment and working poverty.

The unemployment vouchers are meant to reduce unemployment and inequality by stimulating the employment of those who are currently long-term unemployed; the low-wage subsidies pursue these dual objectives by promoting the employment of the working poor. Broadly speaking, the former promotes equity by reducing unemployment and the latter reduces unemployment by promoting equity.[4]

[1] See, for example, Snower (1994, 1997); Orszag and Snower (1998, 1999, 2000).
[2] The case for low-wage subsidies has been argued most elegantly in Phelps (1997b). See, furthermore, Hoon and Phelps (1997) and Phelps (1997a).
[3] They also have quite different effects on the incentives to acquire human capital; but this important topic lies beyond the scope of this chapter.
[4] Both policy approaches share some important advantages. They both are potentially able to alleviate a wide variety of market failures that lead to excessive labor costs and thereby

The effectiveness of the policies in stimulating employment versus alleviating poverty depends on the degree to which their incidence falls on employers versus employees. If the major influence of the policies is to reduce the wages paid by employers, then they will do more to stimulate employment than to alleviate working poverty. On the other hand, if their major influence is to raise the wages of the target group, then they will have a greater effect on mitigating working poverty than stimulating employment.[5]

The big question is how large these relative influences are. Our analysis indicates that the relative effectiveness of the two policies depends on workers' prospective wage growth. The more upwardly mobile workers are (that is, the more their wages rise with employment duration), the more effective will unemployment vouchers be relative to low-wage subsidies. Conversely, the greater the danger that workers come to be trapped in dead-end jobs with flat wage profiles, the more effective will low-wage subsidies be relative to unemployment vouchers.

The chapter is organized as follows. Section 2 discusses the underlying ideas that drive the conclusions of our analysis. Section 3 presents our model of labor market behavior.[6] In section 4 we solve a specific example of the model. In section 5, we examine the effectiveness of given hiring subsidies and employment vouchers in this context. Section 6 discusses the optimal employment subsidy and shows how this depends on the tenure structure of wages. Section 7 concludes.

2   Underlying ideas

As our analysis will show concretely, an unemployed person's incentive to find work depends on the "penalty" for not finding a job. This penalty

depress labor demand (such as the market failures highlighted in the adverse selection, moral hazard, insider–outsider and union theories of labor market activity). Moreover, both are more flexible tools for reducing unemployment and stimulating employment than discretionary labor market policies, such as public sector employment or discretionary subsidies to groups of workers with particular characteristics.

[5] In practice, the policies may generally be expected to affect both the wages employers pay and those employees receive, and the relative magnitudes of these effects will depend on such factors as the relative bargaining strength of employers and employees, the elasticity of labor supply with respect to the policies, the effect of the policies on other welfare state entitlements, and the gap between employers' recruitment and retention rates.

[6] The model draws its inspiration from a labor market model developed by Phelps (1994: ch. 15), which we have applied to the analysis of unemployment accounts in Orszag and Snower (1997). Our innovations here include the incorporation of job search, extension to more than two states to incorporate duration effects of employment and unemployment, incorporation of targeting of employment subsidies, development of the production side of the model and analysis of policies that satisfy a government budget constraint and/or an inequality constraint.

is the difference between the present value of becoming employed and the present value of remaining unemployed. Similarly, an employee's incentive to put effort into the job (in order to reduce the chances of losing the job) depends on the penalty of job loss, which is the difference between the present value of remaining employed and the present value of becoming unemployed.

In this context, low-wage subsidies (LWSs) – financed through payroll taxes on high-wage employees and through unemployment benefits forgone[7] – have a straightforward influence on work incentives. Supposing that the high-wage employees are skilled whereas the low-wage employees are unskilled, the LWSs raise the present value of unskilled employment and, with it, the penalty for not finding and keeping an unskilled job. They also reduce the present value of skilled employment, thereby reducing the penalty for not finding and keeping a skilled job. The overall influence on employment is ambiguous.[8]

By contrast, unemployment vouchers (UVs) – financed through payroll taxes on current employees and through the unemployment benefits forgone – have a different sequence of intertemporal effects. Suppose that the vouchers are targeted at people who have previously been long-term unemployed and are received in the first few periods of employment. Then the UVs raise the present value of long-term unemployment (which qualifies people for the vouchers) and of short-term employment (when the voucher payments accrue), but, if payroll taxes rise to finance vouchers, this will reduce the present value of long-term employment. Thus the vouchers raise the penalty for long-term unemployed people for not finding jobs and raise the penalty for short-term employed people for job loss, but they may reduce the corresponding penalty for the long-term employed. Once again, the overall influence on employment is ambiguous.[9]

Thus the question is not whether LWSs and UVs can always guarantee more employment – they cannot – but in what circumstances they are effective and on what their relative impact depends. Our analysis indicates that a particularly important phenomenon in this respect is the prospective rate of wage growth.

---

[7] These are unemployment benefits that do not have to be paid for unemployed people who find jobs.

[8] It depends on such factors as the relative magnitudes of skilled and unskilled employment, the wage differential between these two types of employment and the relative influence of job search on the probability of finding unskilled versus skilled jobs.

[9] It depends on such factors as the relative magnitudes of long-term and short-term unemployment, the responsiveness of the hiring probability to changes in job search and the responsiveness of the firing probability to changes in work effort.

The greater the growth rate of an individual's real wage with respect to job tenure, the more effective UVs become relative to LWSs. The reason is straightforward. The greater the rate of real wage growth, the greater is the employee's incentive to work hard so as to avoid job loss, and the less the UVs reduce the employee's penalty from job loss. Consequently, for high rates of real wage growth, the UVs will raise the hiring rates of the long-term unemployed without significantly reducing the retention rates of the currently employed workers. In contrast, the greater an individual's real wage growth, the smaller is the influence of LWSs on an individual's incentive to seek and keep work. The high rates of wage growth provide the dominant incentives in these regards, making it more difficult for LWSs to play an employment-promoting role.

These considerations suggest that LWSs and UVs should not be seen as alternatives to one another, but might fruitfully be implemented together. The LWSs could help promote the employment of unskilled workers in dead-end jobs with flat intertemporal wage profiles, whereas the UVs could encourage employment in longer-term, career jobs with steeper profiles.

Finally, the chapter will investigate the relative strengths and weaknesses of these two policies by addressing a simple question: For any given equity-efficiency objective (concerning living standards, unemployment and wage disparities), what is the optimal dynamic structure of employment subsidies? Specifically, what is the optimal size distribution, duration and targeting of employment subsidies?

Addressing this question turns out to be a straightforward and effective way of evaluating the relative appropriateness of the two approaches above. The low-wage subsidy approach is appropriate whenever the optimal employment subsidies (for a given equity-efficiency objective) are (a) limitless over the duration of subsequent employment, (b) constant in magnitude across unemployment and employment durations, and (c) targeted at all workers receiving low wages. On the other hand, the unemployment voucher approach is appropriate whenever the optimal employment subsidies are (a) limited over the duration of subsequent employment, (b) variable in magnitude across unemployment and employment durations (for example, rising with the duration of unemployment and falling with the duration of subsequent employment), and (c) targeted at the unemployed and particularly the long-term unemployed. Not surprisingly, it turns out that the question has no unconditional answer. The main contribution of the chapter is to identify which economic circumstances favor which policy.

The question above tends to have been ignored in the analytical literature of labor market policies because the comparative analyses of these policies are generally undertaken in the context of static models[10] or deterministic dynamic models.[11]

The static models that are typically used in policy evaluations[12] are very problematic. These studies evaluate employment policies by assessing such statistics as how many people in the targeted group got jobs within a specified period of time (typically a quarter or a year), how many of these people would have gained employment without the policy within that period, how many incumbent employees (outside the target group) were displaced by the targeted workers within that period, and how many non-employed people outside the target group were left jobless within that period even though they would have found jobs in the absence of the policy. This framework inevitably focuses on short-run policy effects, largely ignoring the longer-run dynamic repercussions. Although the empirical evaluations do occasionally distinguish between short-run and long-run elasticities of labor demand, they generally do not examine the effects of the policy on the transition rates between employment and unemployment and between high-wage and low-wage jobs, and thus they are unable to evaluate the effects of the policy once the associated lagged adjustment processes have worked themselves out.[13]

On the other hand, the existing dynamic models of employment policies, such as those used in Millard and Mortensen (1997) and Hoon and Phelps (1997), have not been sufficiently detailed to permit the analysis of the critical issues identified above, namely the optimal size distribution, duration and targeting of the policies. It is these issues, we have argued, that provide the acid test for judging the relative merits of unemployment vouchers and low-wage subsidies. In addition, these models have made some strategic simplifying assumptions (such as risk neutrality in Millard and Mortensen, 1997, and workers being fully insured against job loss in Hoon and Phelps, 1997) that not only are critical in evaluating the relative merits of unemployment vouchers and low-wage subsidies, but are not applicable in a world where workers face imperfect capital markets and where the existing job security legislation and unemployment benefit system provide imperfect insurance.

To analyze policies that are meant to reduce unemployment and working poverty, it is necessary (at bare minimum) to use models that examine

[10] See, for example, Layard, Nickell, and Jackman (1991: 490–492) and Snower (1994).

[11] See, for example, Millard and Mortensen (1997), using the matching model of Mortensen and Pissarides (1994), and Hoon and Phelps (1997), using the turnover training model in Phelps (1994) and Hoon and Phelps (1992).

[12] See, for example, NERA (1997, 1995), Martin Hanblin Research (1996), Woodbury and Spiegelman (1987) and Institute for Employment Studies (1994).

[13] The implications of this problem are examined in Orszag and Snower (2000).

the effects of these policies on people's transitions between employment and unemployment and between high-wage and low-wage jobs. Much of the existing literature is based on models that focus on one or the other of these transitions but not both.[14] This chapter examines both transitions, as well as the interaction between them.[15]

Furthermore, it is important to keep in mind that unemployment and working poverty become especially severe social problems only when they are concentrated among a minority of people, trapped in these states for long durations. Thus policies addressing these problems must be analyzed through models that explicitly take account of how people's labor market behavior depends on their duration in various labor market states. Whereas the existing policy literature largely ignores this important issue, this chapter represents an attempt to take some salient duration influences into account.

3   The dynamic structure of the model

There are many skill types of worker in our model but workers enter the labor market with a given skill type so we focus our attention here on the decisions of a worker in a given skill group. Each worker of a given skill type in our model can pass through various labor market states, as illustrated in figure 4.1. All workers die (leave the labor force permanently) with probability d each period. A worker who has been unemployed for j periods is hired with probability h_j; otherwise, the worker will either die or be unemployed for $j + 1$ periods the next period. An employee who has been employed for i periods faces a probability f_i of becoming unemployed, a probability d of dying and a probability $1 - f_i - d$ of retaining a job and becoming employed for $i + 1$ periods.

Let l_{ju} be the leisure of an unemployed worker who has been unemployed for j periods; let $h_j(l_{ju})$ be the associated hiring rate; and let b be the unemployment benefit. Let $u(b, l_{ju})$ be the unemployed worker's associated instantaneous utility, and let $V(j, u)$ be the present value of being unemployed for duration j.

The unemployed individual's problem is to solve:

$$V(j, u) = \max_{l_{ju}} u(b, l_{ju}) + \beta(h_j(l_{ju})V(1, e)$$
$$+ (1 - h_j(l_{ju}))V(j + 1, u)). \tag{4.1}$$

---

[14] For instance, Millard and Mortensen (1997) and Hoon and Phelps (1997) consider the former, but not the latter, transitions.
[15] For example, high-wage jobs tend to be associated with larger retention rates than low-wage jobs.

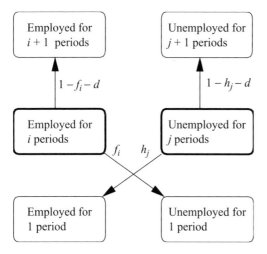

Figure 4.1 *The structure of the model*

The resulting first-order condition is

$$u_{l_{ju}} = -\beta h'_j(l_{ju})[V(1, e) - V(j + 1, u)]. \tag{4.2}$$

In other words, the marginal utility of leisure must be set equal to the discounted marginal hiring propensity $(-\beta h'_j)$ times the penalty for not finding a job $(V(1, e) - V(j + 1, u))$. Since there is diminishing marginal utility of leisure, the optimal level of leisure depends inversely on the penalty for job loss.

The decision-making problem of an employed worker may be expressed along analogous lines. Let l_{ie} be the leisure of a worker who has been employed for $i < I$ periods and $f_i = f_i(l_{ie})$ be that worker's separation rate. Let w_i be the pre-tax wage and w_i^* be the after-tax wage.

Then, since the worker makes decisions based on the after-tax wage w_i^*, his or her current utility is $u(w_i^*, l_{ie})$, $u_{12} \geq 0$. Moreover, let $V(i, e)$ be the present value associated with being employed for duration i, and $V(1, u)$ be the value of becoming unemployed. The worker's decision-making problem is to solve

$$V(i, e) = \max_{l_{ie}} u(w_i^*, l_{ie})$$
$$+ \beta(f_i(l_{ie})V(1, u) + (1 - f_i(l_{ie}) - d)V(i + 1, e)). \tag{4.3}$$

The associated first-order condition is

$$u_{l_{ie}} = \beta f_i'(l_{ie})[V(i + 1, e) - V(1, u)]. \tag{4.4}$$

Here, the marginal utility of leisure must be set equal to the discounted marginal firing propensity $(-\beta f_i')$ times the penalty for job loss $(V(i+1,e) - V(1,u))$. Once again, diminishing marginal utility of leisure implies that the optimal level of leisure depends inversely on the penalty for job loss.

For individuals employed for I periods or unemployed for J periods, the optimization problems and first-order conditions are similar to the ones given above, with one exception. The exception concerns boundary conditions: Unemployment spells of more than J periods and employment spells of more than I periods are treated together (e.g. $V(I+1,e) = V(I,e)$ and $V(J+1,u) = V(J,u)$).

According to equations (4.2) and (4.4), the primary inducement that leads workers to look for jobs and to work hard on the job is the difference between the value of being employed and unemployed. Policies that increase this difference for both the employed and the unemployed will stimulate employment.

4   A specific analytical example

We now consider a specific example of the model above, with linear hire and separation rate functions:

$$h_j(l_{ju}) = \theta_j(1 - a l_{ju}) \tag{4.5}$$

$$f_i(l_{ie}) = \phi_i l_{ie}. \tag{4.6}$$

(Microfoundations for these functions are provided in appendix 4C.)

These functions are reduced forms and we focus here on the worker's decisions, given the parameters of the hiring and firing functions that are under the firm's control. For these hiring and firing functions, let us derive the worker's leisure decision when unemployed (l_{ju}) and employed (l_{ie}). Suppose that the unemployed and employed workers have the same instantaneous utility function,

$$u(c,l) = \frac{(c^\alpha l^{1-\alpha})^\gamma}{\gamma}, \tag{4.7}$$

where c is the consumption and l is the leisure of any worker. Since workers are assumed to consume all their current income, $c = b$ for an unemployed worker (where b is the unemployment benefit) and $c = w_i^*$ for an employed worker (where w_i^* is the after-tax wage), and b_j and w_i^* are predetermined when the workers make their leisure decisions.

Substituting the derivatives of (4.7) and (4.5) into (4.2), we obtain the optimum interior choice of leisure when unemployed as:[16]

$$
l_{ju} = \left[\frac{\beta a \theta_j}{1 - \alpha} (V(1, e) - V(j + 1, u)) \right]^{\frac{1}{(1-\alpha)\gamma - 1}} b_j^{-\frac{\alpha\gamma}{(1-\alpha)\gamma - 1}} \tag{4.8}
$$

for $1 \leq j < \mathcal{J}$ and:

$$
l_{\mathcal{J}u} = \left[\frac{\beta a \theta_j}{1 - \alpha} (V(1, e) - V(\mathcal{J}, u)) \right]^{\frac{1}{(1-\alpha)\gamma - 1}} b_{\mathcal{J}}^{-\frac{\alpha\gamma}{(1-\alpha)\gamma - 1}} . \tag{4.9}
$$

For those employed, the first-order conditions (4.4) and our specific functional forms lead to a solution for leisure when employed of[17]

$$
l_{ie} = \left[\frac{\beta \phi}{1 - \alpha} (V(i + 1, e) - V(1, u)) \right]^{\frac{1}{(1-\alpha)\gamma - 1}} [w_i^*]^{-\frac{\alpha\gamma}{(1-\alpha)\gamma - 1}} \tag{4.10}
$$

for $1 \leq i < I$ and:

$$
l_{Ie} = \left[\frac{\beta \phi}{1 - \alpha} (V(I, e) - V(1, u)) \right]^{\frac{1}{(1-\alpha)\gamma - 1}} [w_I^*]^{-\frac{\alpha\gamma}{(1-\alpha)\gamma - 1}} . \tag{4.11}
$$

These first-order conditions are then substituted back into the optimal value equations and a solution for the value function is derived. From the value function solution, hire and fire rates are determined using equations (4.5) and (4.6). In appendix 4A, we solve this model in closed form (albeit with some strong parameter restrictions, but for arbitrary I and $\mathcal{J}$) and we show that the solution when the parameters of the model are duration independent is:

$$
V(i, e) = \bar{V}(e) = \left[\frac{\left(1 + \frac{F_2}{1 - F_1} \right)}{\left[\frac{G_0}{1 - G_1} - \frac{F_0}{1 - F_1} \right]} \right]^{\frac{z}{z-1}} \frac{G_0}{1 - G_1} \tag{4.12}
$$

$$
V(j, u) = \bar{V}(u) = \bar{V}(e) - \left[\frac{\left(1 + \frac{F_2}{1 - F_1} \right)}{\left[\frac{G_0}{1 - G_1} - \frac{F_0}{1 - F_1} \right]} \right]^{\frac{1}{z-1}} \tag{4.13}
$$

[16] The hire rate in (4.5) must lie between 0 and $1 - d$. This implies that

$$
\frac{1}{a} \left[1 - \frac{1 - d}{\theta_j} \right] \leq l_j \leq \frac{1}{a}.
$$

[17] The hire rate in (4.10) must lie between 0 and $1 - d$ so that $0 \leq l_{ie} \leq \frac{1-d}{\phi_i}$.

where $z - 1 = \frac{1}{(1-a)\gamma - 1} < 0$

$$F_0 = b^{\frac{-a\gamma}{(1-a)\gamma-1}} (\beta a\theta)^{\frac{(1-a)\gamma}{(1-a)\gamma-1}} \left[\frac{1}{1-\alpha}\right]^{\frac{1}{(1-a)\gamma-1}} \left(\frac{1}{\gamma}\left[\frac{1}{1-\alpha}\right] - 1\right)$$

$$F_1 = \beta(1-d),\ F_2 = \beta\theta$$

$$G_0 = (w^*)^{\frac{-a\gamma}{(1-a)\gamma-1}} (\phi\beta)^{\frac{(1-a)\gamma}{(1-a)\gamma-1}} \left[\frac{1}{1-\alpha}\right]^{\frac{1}{(1-a)\gamma-1}} \left(\frac{1}{\gamma}\left[\frac{1}{1-\alpha}\right] - 1\right) \text{ and}$$

$$G_1 = \beta(1-d).$$

Although this is a closed-form solution, its structure is rather complex and it is useful to consider the properties of the model with respect to variations in parameters, before proceeding to consider optimal duration-dependent policy. To determine such baseline parameters, we let the period of analysis be one quarter and select a coefficient of relative risk aversion of 10, $\alpha = 0.8$, $\beta = 0.98$, $\phi = 0.7$, $a = 1.0$, $\theta = 0.75$, $b = 0.4$, $w^* = 1.5$, $d = 0.005$. In this case, the baseline unemployment rate is 8.4 percent, the fire rate is 1.6 percent and the hire rate is 23.5 percent.

To evaluate the reasonableness of these parameters, we define the long-term unemployed to be those unemployed for at least a year (four periods). As shown in appendix 4B, if the transition rate out of unemployment is a constant h, then the steady-state proportion of people who are unemployed for more than x periods is $(1 - h)^x$. Thus, the fraction of the unemployed who are long-term unemployed is $(1 - h)^4$. In the United Kingdom, roughly 36 percent of the unemployed have been jobless for over a year: $(1 - h)^4 = 0.36$, where h is deadweight (the hire rate in the absence of vouchers). This suggests that, under our Markov assumptions, the deadweight parameter is 0.2254, which is very close to our hire rate of 23.5 percent.

Furthermore, it can be shown that, if the rate of outflow from unemployment is h, then the mean duration of an unemployment spell is $1/h$.[18] Our separation rate of 0.016 thus corresponds to an average job tenure of roughly ten years (which is well below the average tenure of fifteen years reported for UK men by Burgess and Rees, 1994).

The effects of important parameter variations are shown in figures 4.2–4.5. Figure 4.2 shows the effects of simultaneous changes of wages and employer firing propensity (ϕ). A higher wage clearly raises the reward

---

[18] To see this, observe that $(1 - f)^x v_0^s$ is the number of people who have been employed for x periods, where v_0^s is the steady-state number of entrants to employment. The probability of being fired after x periods is therefore $f(1 - f)^{x-1}$. Thus, the mean duration of unemployment is $\sum_{x=1}^{\infty} xf(1 - f)^{x-1}$. Noting that the mean duration of employment is f times $\sum_{x=1}^{\infty} (1 - f)^x = 1/f - 1$, we arrive at the result by differentiation.

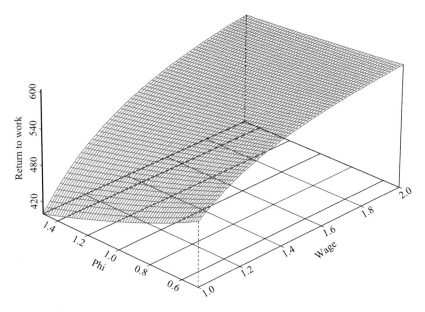

Figure 4.2 *The effect of changes in wages and employer firing propensity (φ) on the reward to work*

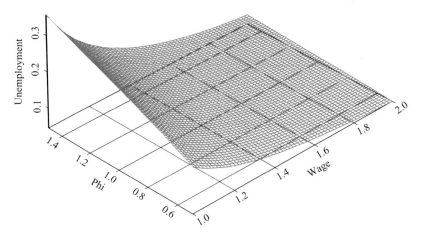

Figure 4.3 *The effect of changes in wages and employer firing propensity (φ) on unemployment*

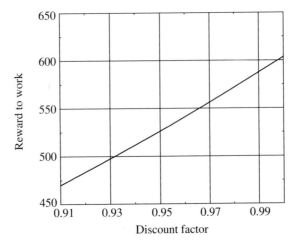

Figure 4.4 *The effect of changes in the discount factor on the reward to work*

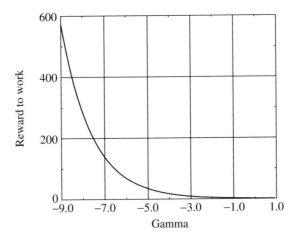

Figure 4.5 *The effect of changes in risk aversion (γ) on the reward to work*

to work, whereas a higher employer firing propensity (higher ϕ) lowers the reward to work; there is also some complementarity between higher wages and less monitoring because workers are willing to trade off lower wages for less strenuous working conditions. Figure 4.3 depicts the corresponding effects of changes in ϕ and wages on aggregate unemployment. A rise in wages increases the reward to work and lowers unemployment, whereas the opposite is true for an increase in ϕ.

Two of the most important factors in determining the reward to work are the discount factor and risk aversion. Figure 4.4 shows that a higher discount factor raises the reward to work. This is because, given a profile of wages and benefits, workers who have less time-preference see greater gains from working. Figure 4.5 shows that higher relative risk aversion (higher γ) increases the reward to work. Risk-averse workers attach a higher utility penalty to losing their jobs and hence the reward to work is higher in utility terms for risk-averse workers.

5   The effects of unemployment vouchers and low-wage subsidies

The analytical solution from the previous section only holds under the restrictive condition of duration-independent parameters and hence does not enable the practical analysis of duration-dependent employment policy. We therefore solve our model numerically, taking into account the constraints that hire and fire rates must be between 0 and $1 - d$.

We compare the economic implications of the following two policies:

- **unemployment vouchers:** Unemployed workers, upon receiving a job, receive a two-year voucher;
- **low-wage subsidies:** Low-skill (low-wage) workers receive a subsidy of unlimited duration.

We examine the influence of these two policies on two types of worker:

- **"dead-end workers":** These workers are trapped indefinitely in low-wage (low-productivity) jobs, on account of their irremediably low skills.
- **"upwardly mobile workers":** These workers experience a rise in their wages after a period of on-the-job experience, on account of either on-the-job training or market power acquired within the firm.

As we shall see, the two policies have radically different effects on these two groups.

5.1   Dead-end workers

We compare a two-year voucher of 50 percent of the initial wage and a wage subsidy of 7.2 percent. Both have equivalent effects on the government budget.

Figure 4.6 shows the effects of the voucher on the value of employment and figure 4.7 shows the effects of a low-wage subsidy. Figures 4.8 and 4.9 show the corresponding effects on the value of unemployment.

The direct effect of the voucher is to raise the value of employment for workers and encourage workers to find jobs. However, it does so more at short durations than at long durations. At long employment durations,

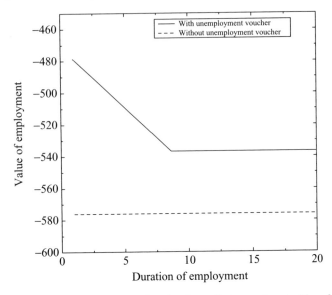

Figure 4.6 *The value to dead-end workers of being employed with and without an unemployment voucher*

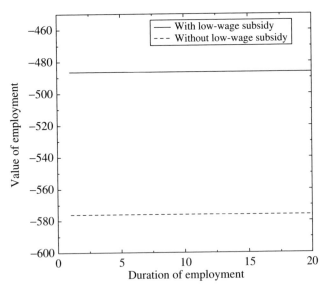

Figure 4.7 *The value to dead-end workers of being employed with and without a wage subsidy*

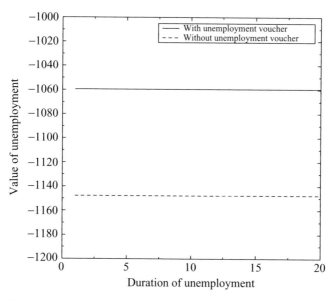

Figure 4.8 *The value to dead-end workers of being unemployed with and without an unemployment voucher*

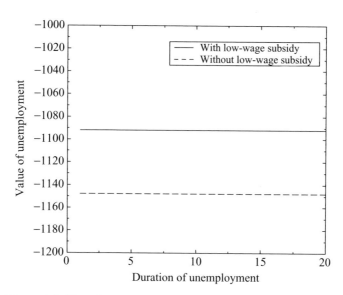

Figure 4.9 *The value to dead-end workers of unemployment at different durations with a low-wage subsidy*

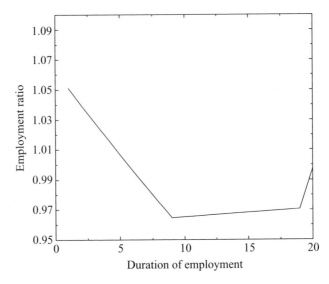

Figure 4.10 *Change in employment at different durations with an unemployment voucher*

the value of employment still rises because workers who are long-term employed and become unemployed will have access to a voucher. On the other hand, the low-wage subsidy has the same effect on the value of employment at all durations. Both the unemployment voucher and the low-wage subsidy increase the value of unemployment, but the voucher does so more because the voucher payments are front-loaded. The increase in the value of unemployment is an indirect effect that reduces the incentives for workers to stay in their current job, which works against the direct effects of unemployment vouchers and wage subsidies in reducing unemployment.

The unemployment voucher and the low-wage subsidy have differential effects on the duration distribution of employment and unemployment. The unemployment voucher reduces the number of long-term unemployed, whereas the low-wage subsidy has a bigger effect on encouraging long-term employment. In figures 4.10 and 4.11 we plot the effects of the unemployment voucher on the ratios of employment and unemployment before and after the policy. Figures 4.12 and 4.13 are the corresponding plots for the low-wage subsidy. The unemployment voucher results in unemployment of 7.8 percent compared with a steady-state baseline unemployment rate of 8.4 percent. However the low-wage subsidy is more effective, reducing the unemployment rate to 7.3 percent.

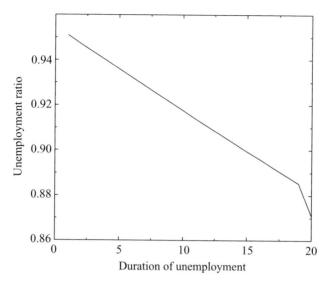

Figure 4.11 *Change in unemployment at different durations with an unemployment voucher*

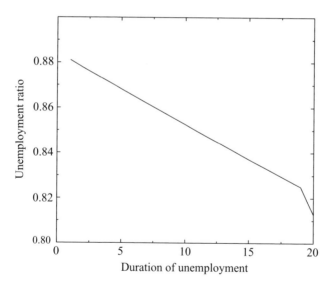

Figure 4.12 *Change in unemployment at different durations with a low-wage subsidy*

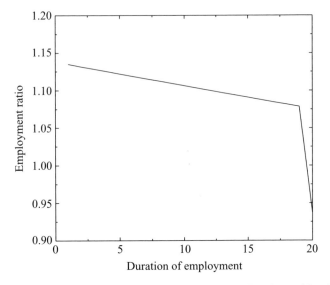

Figure 4.13 *Change in employment at different durations with a low-wage subsidy*

The reason for this difference is straightforward. As the figures above show, the low-wage subsidies imply that the discounted value of remaining employed remains constant as the duration of employment increases. By contrast, the unemployment vouchers imply that this discounted value falls as duration increases over the first two years of employment. The lesser unemployment influence of the unemployment vouchers thus arises because workers perceive lower values to remaining in work and therefore their separation rates rise with their duration of employment.

5.2   Upwardly mobile workers

The relative effectiveness of the two policies is quite different when workers are upwardly mobile. These workers, as noted, receive a significant reward to experience some time after entering their jobs. For instance, the long-term unemployed often experience a jump in earnings after they demonstrate their ability to work. In these circumstances, the disadvantage of the unemployment voucher policy is small, because the wage increase discourages workers from quitting their jobs in their first two years of employment.

To model this effect in a simple way, we assume that an unemployed person receives a wage of 1.0 for the first two years after gaining

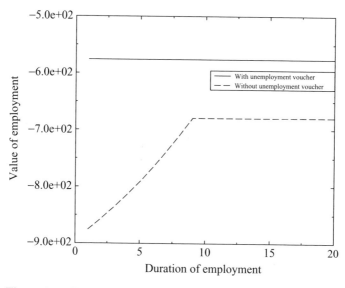

Figure 4.14 *The value to upwardly mobile workers of being employed with and without an unemployment voucher*

employment, and then experiences a wage increase to 1.50. We consider an unemployment voucher of 0.50 and a low-wage subsidy of 0.077, which have similar budgetary impacts.

Figure 4.14 shows, for instance, the effect of the unemployment voucher on the value of employment and figure 4.15 shows the effect on the value of unemployment.

The direct effect of the voucher again is to raise the value of employment for workers and to encourage workers to find jobs. However, it does so more at short durations than at long durations. Consequently, in contrast to the dead-end worker case, the discounted value of employment does not fall in the initial two years, so that workers are encouraged to stay in work. Both the unemployment voucher and the low-wage subsidy increase the value of unemployment, but the voucher does so more because the voucher payments are front-loaded.[19] As the baseline unemployment rate is 10.0 percent, the unemployment voucher reduces unemployment to 8.4 percent, whereas the low-wage subsidy reduces it to 8.7 percent. The unemployment voucher and the low-wage subsidy again have differential impacts on the duration distribution of employment

---

[19] The increase in the value of unemployment is an indirect effect that reduces the incentives for workers to stay in their current jobs, which works against the direct effects of unemployment vouchers and wage subsidies in reducing unemployment.

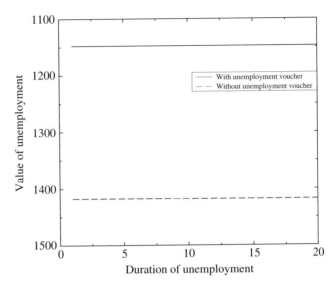

Figure 4.15 *The value to upwardly mobile workers of being unemployed with and without an unemployment voucher*

and unemployment. The unemployment voucher reduces the number of long-term unemployed, whereas the low-wage subsidy has a bigger effect in encouraging long-term employment.

The increase in the value of unemployment is an indirect effect that reduces the incentives for workers to stay in their current jobs, which works against the direct effects of unemployment vouchers and wage subsidies in reducing unemployment. The more upwardly mobile workers expect to be (that is, the more workers expect their wage to increase in the future), the more effective the voucher is likely to be.

6   Optimal subsidy policy

It remains to examine optimal subsidies. We focus on two optimization criteria:
- minimization of the number of long-term unemployed (those unemployed for more than two years);
- maximization of the aggregate welfare of low-skill, low-wage groups (Benthamite).

The first criterion will more likely tend to lead to policies that stimulate most the welfare of the unemployed or the short-term employed by providing them with incentives to find jobs, whereas the second criterion

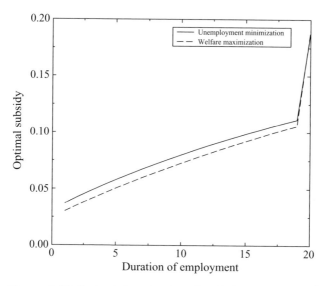

Figure 4.16 *Optimal duration-dependent balanced-budget payroll policy with flat wages*

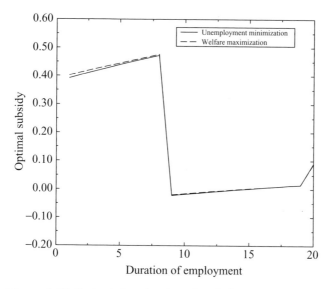

Figure 4.17 *Optimal duration-dependent balanced-budget payroll policy with increasing wages*

seems to lead more naturally to policies that affect all workers. (We also have considered other criteria, such as maximization of the welfare of the short-term employed (Rawlsian) or minimization of aggregate unemployment, but the results do not differ significantly from the two criteria above.)

For our optimization exercise, the government budget constraint is that the total expenditure on employment subsidies to the target skill group is less than or equal to its total savings on unemployment benefits plus the amount the government receives in payroll taxes from other groups of workers and other budgetary sources:

$$\sum_{i=1}^{n_i} \tilde{n}_e(i)v(i) \le \sum_{j=1}^{n_j} \left(b(j)\tilde{n}_u(j) - b^o(j)\tilde{n}_u^o(j) \right) + g,$$

where $\tilde{n}_e(i)$ are the number of eligible workers employed for i periods, $v(i)$ is the subsidy paid to them, $\tilde{n}_u(j)$ are the number of workers whose unemployment is of duration j eligible for benefits, $b(j)$ are the unemployed benefits paid, $\tilde{n}_u^o(j)$ are the number of workers whose unemployment is of duration j originally eligible for benefits, $b^o(j)$ are the original level of benefits paid, and g is the level of government spending.

For the dead-end worker case, the optimal subsidy is shown in figure 4.16. For the upwardly mobile worker case, the corresponding optimal subsidy is shown in figure 4.17. Note that the optimal subsidy for the upwardly mobile worker is very close to an unemployment voucher, whereas the optimal subsidy for the dead-end worker case is closer to a low-wage subsidy.[20] Our results therefore suggest that the optimal policy depends tightly on the wage prospects of the newly employed.

7   Conclusion

This chapter has examined the effectiveness of unemployment vouchers and low-wage subsidies. Our analysis indicates that, if workers are upwardly mobile (that is, they experience wages that will increase after a period of employment), unemployment vouchers are likely to be more effective than low-wage subsidies both in terms of maximizing the welfare of low-skill workers and also in terms of minimizing unemployment. On the other hand, if workers are trapped indefinitely in dead-end jobs with flat wage profiles, low-wage subsidies perform better.

---

[20] The optimal subsidy curve is actually upward sloping to incentivize workers to stay in their jobs.

Appendix 4A: a closed-form analysis of the basic consumer model

Substituting equations (4.8)–(4.11) into the value function equations (4.1) and (4.3), we obtain

$$V(j, u) = \frac{b_j^{-\frac{\alpha\gamma}{(1-\alpha)\gamma-1}}}{\gamma} \left(\frac{\beta a\theta_j}{1-\alpha}\right) [V(1, e) - V(j+1, u)]^{\frac{(1-\alpha)\gamma}{(1-\alpha)\gamma-1}}$$
$$+ \beta(1-d)V(j+1, u) + \beta [V(1, e)$$
$$- V(j+1, u)] \cdot \theta_j \cdot (1-\alpha) \left(\frac{\beta a\theta_j}{1-\alpha}\right)^{\frac{1}{(1-\alpha)\gamma-1}}$$
$$\times [V(1, e) - V(j+1, u)]^{\frac{1}{(1-\alpha)\gamma-1}} b_j^{-\frac{\alpha\gamma}{(1-\alpha)\gamma-1}} \quad (4.14)$$

for $j < \mathcal{J}$. Collecting terms in the $V(.)$, equation (4.14) can be rewritten as

$$V(j, u) = F_{0j} [V(1, e) - V(j+1, u)]^{\frac{(1-\alpha)\gamma}{(1-\alpha)\gamma-1}} + F_{1j} V(j+1, u)$$
$$+ F_{2j} [V(1, e) - V(j+1, u)], \quad (4.15)$$

where

$$F_{0j} = b_j^{\frac{-\alpha\gamma}{(1-\alpha)\gamma-1}} (\beta a\theta_j)^{\frac{(1-\alpha)\gamma}{(1-\alpha)\gamma-1}} \left[\frac{1}{1-\alpha}\right]^{\frac{1}{(1-\alpha)\gamma-1}} \left(\frac{1}{\gamma}\left[\frac{1}{1-\alpha}\right]-1\right) \quad (4.16)$$

$$F_{1j} = \beta(1-d) \quad (4.17)$$
$$F_{2j} = \beta\theta_j. \quad (4.18)$$

Similarly, for the employed:

$$V(i, e) = \frac{(w_i^*)^{\frac{-\alpha\gamma}{(1-\alpha)\gamma-1}}}{\gamma} \left(\frac{\beta\phi_j}{1-\alpha}\right)^{\frac{(1-\alpha)\gamma}{(1-\alpha)\gamma-1}}$$
$$\times [V(i+1, e) - V(1, u)]^{\frac{(1-\alpha)\gamma}{(1-\alpha)\gamma-1}}$$
$$+ \beta(1-d)V(i+1, e) - (\beta\phi_j)^{\frac{(1-\alpha)\gamma}{(1-\alpha)\gamma-1}} \cdot$$
$$\times [V(i+1, e) - V(1, u)]^{\frac{(1-\alpha)\gamma}{(1-\alpha)\gamma-1}}$$
$$\times \left(\frac{1}{1-\alpha}\right)^{\frac{1}{(1-\alpha)\gamma-1}} (w_i^*)^{\frac{-\alpha\gamma}{(1-\alpha)\gamma-1}} \quad (4.19)$$

for $i < I$. As with equation (4.14) this can be rewritten in a manner similar to (4.15):

$$V(i, e) = G_{0i} \left[V(i + 1, e) - V(1, u) \right]^{\frac{(1-\alpha)\gamma}{(1-\alpha)\gamma - 1}} + G_{1i} V(i + 1, e), \tag{4.20}$$

where

$$G_{0i} = (w_i^*)^{\frac{-\alpha\gamma}{(1-\alpha)\gamma-1}} (\phi_i \beta)^{\frac{(1-\alpha)\gamma}{(1-\alpha)\gamma-1}} \left[\frac{1}{1-\alpha} \right]^{\frac{1}{(1-\alpha)\gamma-1}} \left(\frac{1}{\gamma} \left[\frac{1}{1-\alpha} \right] - 1 \right) \tag{4.21}$$

$$G_{1i} = \beta(1 - d). \tag{4.22}$$

For those unemployed for J periods, the equation is

$$V(J, u) = F_{0J} \left[V(1, e) - V(J, u) \right]^{\frac{(1-\alpha)\gamma}{(1-\alpha)\gamma - 1}} + F_{1J} V(J, u) + F_{2J} \left[V(1, e) - V(J, u) \right], \tag{4.23}$$

where

$$F_{0J} = b_J^{\frac{-\alpha\gamma}{(1-\alpha)\gamma-1}} (\beta a \theta_J)^{\frac{(1-\alpha)\gamma}{(1-\alpha)\gamma-1}} \left[\frac{1}{1-\alpha} \right]^{\frac{1}{(1-\alpha)\gamma-1}} \left(\frac{1}{\gamma} \left[\frac{1}{1-\alpha} \right] - 1 \right) \tag{4.24}$$

$$F_{1J} = \beta(1 - d) \tag{4.25}$$
$$F_{2J} = \beta\theta_J. \tag{4.26}$$

For those employed for I periods, the value function follows:

$$V(I, e) = G_{0I} \left[V(I, e) - V(1, u) \right]^{\frac{(1-\alpha)\gamma}{(1-\alpha)\gamma - 1}} + G_{1I} V(I, e), \tag{4.27}$$

where

$$G_{0I} = (w_I^*)^{\frac{-\alpha\gamma}{(1-\alpha)\gamma-1}} (\phi_I \beta)^{\frac{(1-\alpha)\gamma}{(1-\alpha)\gamma-1}} \left[\frac{1}{1-\alpha} \right]^{\frac{1}{(1-\alpha)\gamma-1}} \left(\frac{1}{\gamma} \left[\frac{1}{1-\alpha} \right] - 1 \right) \tag{4.28}$$

$$G_{1I} = \beta(1 - d). \tag{4.29}$$

Equations (4.15), (4.20), (4.23) and (4.27) together form a $J + I$ system of non-linear equations in $J + I$ unknowns.

Constant coefficients

We will try to solve this system in one special case of constant parameters (for example, $F_{0j} = F_0$, $F_{1j} = F_1$, $F_{2j} = F_2$, $G_{0i} = G_0$, $G_{1i} = G_1 \ \forall i, j$). We define

$$z = \frac{(1-\alpha)\gamma}{(1-\alpha)\gamma - 1} \tag{4.30}$$

$$\Delta_i V_e = V(i, e) - V(1, u) \tag{4.31}$$

$$\Delta_j V_u = V(1, e) - V(j, u). \tag{4.32}$$

Now consider the equation for those who have been employed for I periods:

$$(1 - G_1)V(I, e) = G_0 \left[\Delta_I V_e \right]^z \tag{4.33}$$

so that

$$\Delta_I V_e = \left[\frac{(1-G_1)}{G_0} V(I, e) \right]^{\frac{1}{z}}. \tag{4.34}$$

The individual employed $I - 1$ periods solves

$$V(I - 1, e) = G_0 \left[\Delta_I V_e \right]^z + G_1 V(I, e). \tag{4.35}$$

Using (4.34), equation (4.35) becomes

$$V(I - 1, e) = G_0 \left[\frac{(1-G_1)}{G_0} V(I, e) \right] + G_1 V(I, e) = V(I, e). \tag{4.36}$$

Since $V(I - 1, e) = V(I, e)$, $\Delta_{i-1} V_e = \Delta_i V_e$ and

$$V(I - 2, e) = G_0 \left[\frac{(1-G_1)}{G_0} V(I, e) \right] + G_1 V(I - 1, e) = V(I, e). \tag{4.37}$$

Continuing this procedure, we find that $V(i, e) = V(I, e)$ for all i.

In a similar manner, we consider the equation for those who have been unemployed for J periods:

$$(1 - F_1)V(J, u) = F_0 \left[\Delta_J V_u \right]^z + F_2 \Delta_J V_u. \tag{4.38}$$

Now, compare with the equation for those unemployed $\mathcal{J} - 1$ periods:

$$V(\mathcal{J} - 1, u) = F_0 \left[\Delta_{\mathcal{J}} V_u \right]^z + F_2 \Delta_{\mathcal{J}} V_u + F_1 V(\mathcal{J}, u). \qquad (4.39)$$

Using (4.38), we have

$$V(\mathcal{J} - 1, u) = (1 - F_1) V(\mathcal{J}, u) + F_1 V(\mathcal{J}, u) = V(\mathcal{J}, u). \qquad (4.40)$$

To show that this continues to work:

$$V(\mathcal{J} - 2, u) = F_0 \left[\Delta_{\mathcal{J}-1} V_u \right]^z + F_2 \Delta_{\mathcal{J}-1} V_u + F_1 V(\mathcal{J} - 1, u), \qquad (4.41)$$

but, since $V(\mathcal{J} - 1, u) = V(\mathcal{J}, u)$, $\Delta_{\mathcal{J}-1} V_u = \Delta_{\mathcal{J}} V_u$ and

$$V(\mathcal{J} - 2, u) = F_0 \left[\Delta_{\mathcal{J}} V_u \right]^z + F_2 \Delta_{\mathcal{J}} V_u + F_1 V(\mathcal{J}, u), \qquad (4.42)$$

which equals $V(\mathcal{J} - 1, u)$. We let $\bar{V}(u) = V(j, u)$ and $\bar{V}(e) = V(i, e)$. We define

$$\Delta \bar{V} = \bar{V}(e) - \bar{V}(u). \qquad (4.43)$$

We have

$$(1 - F_1) \bar{V}(u) = F_0 [\Delta \bar{V}]^z + F_2 \Delta \bar{V} \qquad (4.44)$$

$$(1 - G_1) \bar{V}(e) = G_0 [\Delta \bar{V}]^z. \qquad (4.45)$$

We note from equations (4.44) and (4.45):

$$\bar{V}(u) = \frac{F_0}{1 - F_1} [\Delta \bar{V}]^z + \frac{F_2}{1 - F_1} \Delta \bar{V} \qquad (4.46)$$

$$\bar{V}(e) = \frac{G_0}{1 - G_1} [\Delta \bar{V}]^z. \qquad (4.47)$$

Subtracting (4.46) from (4.47), we obtain

$$\left(1 + \frac{F_2}{1 - F_1} \right) \Delta \bar{V} = \left[\frac{G_0}{1 - G_1} - \frac{F_0}{1 - F_1} \right] [\Delta \bar{V}]^z, \qquad (4.48)$$

so that, if $\Delta \bar{V}$ is non-zero (which is true if $\bar{V}(u)$ is bounded),

$$\left(1 + \frac{F_2}{1 - F_1} \right) = \left[\frac{G_0}{1 - G_1} - \frac{F_0}{1 - F_1} \right] [\Delta \bar{V}]^{z-1} \qquad (4.49)$$

and[21]

$$\Delta \bar{V} = \left[\frac{\left(1 + \frac{F_2}{1-F_1}\right)}{\left[\frac{G_0}{1-G_1} - \frac{F_0}{1-F_1}\right]} \right]^{\frac{1}{z-1}}. \tag{4.50}$$

From (4.47) we obtain

$$\bar{V}(e) = \left[\frac{\left(1 + \frac{F_2}{1-F_1}\right)}{\left[\frac{G_0}{1-G_1} - \frac{F_0}{1-F_1}\right]} \right]^{\frac{z}{z-1}} \frac{G_0}{1 - G_1} \tag{4.51}$$

$$\bar{V}(u) = \bar{V}(e) - \Delta \bar{V}. \tag{4.52}$$

Appendix 4B: the fraction of long-term unemployed

This appendix derives the fraction of long-term unemployed in a Markov model with constant transition rates. The difference equations for unemployment:

$$v_{t,x} = (1 - h)v_{t-1,x-1}$$

have the solution $v_{t,x} = (1 - h)^x v_{t-x,0}$ for $t > x$, where the term $v_{t-x,0}$ is the number of entrants to unemployment x periods ago. The total number of unemployed v_x^s of duration x in steady state is:

$$\sum_{x=0}^{\infty}(1 - h)^x v_0^s = \frac{v_0^s}{h}, \tag{4.53}$$

where v_0^s is the number of entrants to unemployment (and the superscript 's' denotes the steady state).

The number unemployed for duration greater than or equal to y is

$$\sum_{x=y}^{\infty}(1 - h)^x v_0^s = v_0^s \sum_{x=0}^{\infty}(1 - h)^{x+y}$$

$$= v_0^s(1 - h)^y \sum_{x=0}^{\infty}(1 - h)^x \tag{4.54}$$

$$= \frac{v_0^s(1 - h)^y}{h}.$$

---

[21] We note from (4.30) that:

$$z - 1 = \frac{1}{(1 - \alpha)\gamma - 1} < 0,$$

implying boundedness.

The ratio of (4.54) to (4.53) is $(1 - h)^y$. This calculation assumes duration-independent transition rates and a steady state.

Appendix 4C: microfoundations of the hiring and separation functions

This appendix provides illustrative microfoundations for the hiring and separation activities described in general terms above. The hiring and separation activities are influenced by the behavior of both the workers and the firms. We focus on the workers' influence in this example.

To motivate the hire rate, we consider that workers going to interviews at a firm face a hire rate of ω_j, which is known to the workers. Workers have a time endowment of 1 when unemployed and obtaining an interview takes c units of time. Workers who do one interview are hired with a probability ω_j; if they are not hired (with probability $1 - \omega_j$), they may proceed to a second interview and be hired with a probability ω_j. The probability ω_j is determined by the firm's profit-maximizing behavior, described later.

Thus each worker's hiring rate (the total probability of being hired) is

$$h_j = \omega_j \sum_{k=0}^{N-1} (1 - \omega_j)^k = 1 - (1 - \omega_j)^N. \tag{4.55}$$

This hiring rate may now be expressed in terms of the unemployed worker's leisure. The worker's total time endowment (to be split between leisure and job search) is 1, and N interviews take δN units of time, where δ is a positive constant. Thus, leisure when unemployed is $1 - \delta N$, so that $N = (1 - l_{ju})/\delta$. Hence

$$h_j(l_{ju}) = 1 - (1 - \omega_j)^{\frac{1-l_{ju}}{\delta}}, \tag{4.56}$$

which is decreasing in the leisure when unemployed. A linear approximation to equation (4.56) is:

$$h_j(l_{ju}) = 1 + \log(1 - \omega_j)\frac{(l_{ju} - 1)}{\delta}, \tag{4.57}$$

which can be rewritten as

$$h_j(l_{ju}) = \theta_j(1 - a l_{ju}). \tag{4.58}$$

We shall use this linear hiring function in the ensuing analysis.

Next consider a simple, illustrative way to motivate the firing rate. Suppose that output per worker is given by the production function $q_i = \epsilon/l_{ie}$, where ϵ is a random variable uniformly distributed between 0 and α (a positive constant), iid across workers. Let the firm have a threshold level of output $\bar{q}_i$ below which it fires the employee and above which it retains him. This threshold level is determined in the firm's profit maximization problem, considered later. Then the firing rate (the probability of firing a worker) is $f = (\bar{q}l_{ie}/\alpha)$. Thus the firing rate can be expressed simply as

$$f_i(l_{ie}) = \phi_i l_{ie},\qquad(4.59)$$

where $\phi_i = \bar{q}/\alpha$.[22]

References

Burgess, S. and H. Rees (1994). "Lifetime Tenure and Transient Jobs: Job Tenure in Britain 1975–1991," CEPR Discussion Paper 1098, December.
Hoon, H.T. and E.S. Phelps (1992). "Macroeconomic Shocks in a Dynamized Model of the Natural Rate of Unemployment," *American Economic Review* **82**: 889–900.
  (1997). "Payroll Taxes and VAT in a Labor-Turnover Model of the Natural Rate," *International Tax and Public Finance* **41**: 185–201.
Institute for Employment Studies (1994). "Evaluation of Workstart Pilots," Discussion Paper, London.
Layard, R., S. Nickell and R. Jackman (1991). *Unemployment: Macroeconomic Performance and the Labour Market*. Oxford: Oxford University Press.
Martin Hanblin Research (1996). "A Report on Workstart," Discussion Paper, London.
Millard, S.P. and D. Mortensen (1997). "The Unemployment and Welfare Effects of Labour Market Policy: A Comparison of the U.S. and U.K.," in D. Snower and G. de la Dehesa (eds.), *Unemployment Policy: Government Options for the Labour Market*, 545–572. Cambridge: Cambridge University Press.
Mortensen, D. and C. Pissarides (1994). "Job Creation and Job Destruction in a Theory of Unemployment," *Review of Economic Studies* **61**: 397–415.
NERA (1995). "OECD Wage Subsidy Evaluation," Discussion Paper, London.
  (1997). "Right to Work Assessment," Discussion Paper, London.
Orszag, J.M. and D. Snower (1997). "From Unemployment Benefits to Unemployment Support Accounts," paper presented at the conference "Rethinking the Welfare Society," La Coruna, Spain.
  (1998). "A Continuum Model of Employment and Unemployment: An Overview," in Holger Wolt (ed.), *Contemporary Economic Development Revisited: Macroeconomic Policy and Financial Systems*, vol. 5. London: Macmillan.
  (1999). "Youth Unemployment and Government Policy," *Journal of Population Economics* **12**(2): 197–213.
  (2000). "A Macro Theory of Employment Vouchers," *German Economic Review* **1**(4): 385–419.

[22] Another way of justifying equation (4.6) is as a technological relationship between the monitoring of workers and separations. Alternatively, it may be justified in terms of a quitting model (such as in Phelps, 1994; Hoon and Phelps, 1992); workers who wish to quit supply little effort and it is for the firm to raise the wage in order to induce them to supply more labor.

Phelps, E. (1994). *Structural Slumps: The Modern Equilibrium Theory of Unemployment, Interest and Assests.* Cambridge, MA: Harvard University Press.

(1997a). "Wage Subsidy Programmes: Alternative Designs," in D. Snower and G. de la Dehesa (eds.), *Unemployment Policy: Government Options for the Labour Market.* Cambridge: Cambridge University Press.

(1997b). *Rewarding Work: How to Restore Participation and Self-Support to Free Enterprise.* Cambridge, MA: Harvard University Press.

Snower, D. (1994). "Converting Unemployment Benefits into Employment Subsidies," *American Economic Review, Papers and Proceedings* **84**(May): 65–70.

(1997). "The Simple Economics of Benefit Transfers," in D. Snower and G. de la Dehesa (eds.), *Unemployment Policy: Government Options for the Labour Market.* Cambridge: Cambridge University Press.

Woodbury, S. and R. Spiegelman (1987). "Bonuses to Workers and Employers to Reduce Unemployment: Randomized Trials in Illinois," *American Economic Review* **77**: 513–530.

Index

aggregate income 57, 61, 62
Altug, S. 79, 85, 103
asset value, and market equilibrium 55
assets, of firms 26
average wage 57, 61, 62

Becker, Gary 74
Becker–Ben Porath model 13, 75
  see also on-the-job training
    model
Ben Porath, Y. 74, 85, 103, 104
  see also on-the-job training
    model
Binmore, K.G. 53
Black, Sandra 8
Blanchard, O.J. 5, 19
Bok, Derek 9
Brainerd, Elizabeth 8
Browning, M. 104, 105
Burda, M.C. 48
Burgess, S. 140

Cossa, Ricardo 13, 79, 125

Dalton, K. 7
Davidson, K. 71
Davis, S.J. 46
declines in inclusion 3–6
Diamond, P.A. 45, 53
discrimination 1–2, 8
distributive justice 7
Domestic Strategy Group 9
Dréze, Jacques 17
duration of employment subsidy 134, 135
  and balanced-budget payroll policy 79
  effects on dead-end workers 143–8
  effects on upwardly mobile workers
    149–50
  and low-wage subsidy 144, 145, 147,
    148
  and unemployment vouchers 144, 145,
    146, 147, 149, 150

Eagly, Robert V. 28
Earned Income Tax Credit (EITC) 12, 13,
    40, 69, 70, 74, 75, 78, 90
  definition of regions 126
  description of program 89–90
  distribution of earnings 92, 93
  distribution of households 91
  effects of subsidy 74–7
    on distribution of low-educated
      female workers 78
    on female high-school graduate
      workers 92
    on incentives to work 123–5
    on individuals who would otherwise
      not work 110
    on labour supply and investment
      76–7
    on low-education female workers
      78–9, 90–2
    on promotion of skill formation 76,
      95
    on reduction in skill formation 76
  effects on human capital investment
    96–8
    direct effect 97
    income effect 96, 97, 98
    substitution effect 97, 98
  effects on investment and labor supply
    98–9, 103, 107
  and family income 90
  qualifying children 91, 122
  total effect on skills 111–15
  with addition of labor–leisure
    choice 76
  see also learning-by-doing model;
    on-the-job training model
education, investment in 38
Eissa, N. 110
employment creation 13
employment expansion 39
  long-run 18–19
employment flexibility 11

employment subsidy 8, 13, 39, 49, 62, 65, 67–9
  compared with wage subsidy 63–4
  marginal effects 63–4, 66
  optimization criteria 150–2
  and unemployment 64, 66
employment tax 49
  see also wage tax

Felli, Ernesto 7
female low-skill workers, in Mortensen–Pissarides model
  distribution of 131–2
  impact of EITC 78–9
  wages and hours worked 78
firing cost 7, 53, 54, 62
firing rate 158
firing tax 48, 49
  effects on unemployment 59, 69
forgone leisure 79
fraction of long-term unemployed 157–8
Freeman, Richard B. 16
Friedman, M. 45

Gottschalk, P. 8
government responses to inclusion problem 11–13
graduated employment subsidy 13
Greenwood, J. 5, 6

Haltiwanger, J. 46
Hamermesh, Daniel 17
Hansen, L. 104
Haveman, Robert 17
Heckman, James 13, 38, 74, 79, 82, 96, 97, 103, 104, 123, 125
high-skill workers in Mortensen–Pissarides model 62
  average wage 63
  employment subsidy effects 65
  hiring subsidy effects 65
  subsidy-tax effects 68
  unemployment rate 63, 64
hiring costs, in Nash bargain 53
hiring function 158
hiring subsidy 39–40, 49, 62, 65, 70
  and balanced-budget condition 33
  effects on aggregate income 67
  effects on average wage 67
  effects on unemployment 66, 69
  increase in 59
  long-run effects 33
  marginal effects 66–7
Hobhouse, L.T. 7

home production 49
Hoon, Hian Teck 5, 13, 17, 50, 131, 135, 136, 137, 159
Hosios, A.J. 61
Hurd, Michael 17

incentives to work
  low-wage subsidies 133
  penalty 132
  unemployment vouchers 133
incentive-wage condition 18, 25, 29, 31, 33, 34
inclusion failure
  and social effects 8–11
  and transfer payments 9–10
  and underground economy 10
inclusion frontier 4
Independent Women's Forum of Washington DC 8
individual optimization problem 127–8
insider-wage contract 70
Institute for Employment Studies 135
interest rate 17–22
  and employment expansion 39
  and labor supply 41
  and tax-subsidy policy 35–6
  and wage subsidies 21–2

Jackman, R. 5, 17, 135
job availability, in Davidson–Woodbury model 72
job creation 48
  costs 48, 49, 52, 54, 56
  and market equilibrium 55
  see also hiring subsidy
job destruction 48, 51
  attributable to shock 46–7
  costs 48, 56
  curve 58
  and market equilibrium 55
jobless rates, in "glorious years" 4–5
jobs, importance of 1
Joyce, M. 8

Kaldor, Nicholas 17
Kanagiris, George 19
Killingsworth, M. 79
Krueger, Alan 28

labor market analysis
  flows approach 44–5
  search and match approach 45
labor-turnover model 23–5
Layard, R. 5, 17, 135
Lazear, E. 48

learning-by-doing (LBD) model 77, 79–80
  compensation 118
  cost of skill acquisition 79
  difference from OJT model 83
  employment rates 119
  estimated lifecycle progression 116
  evidence 123
  goodness of fit 129
  hourly wages 117
  hours worked 115, 119–22
  human capital 103–5, 115
  individual preferences 103–5
  multi-period 95–6
  parameter estimates 128
  parameter values 128
  schooling 88
  skill acquisition function 116
  skill formation 74, 100–2, 115–16, 124
  skill levels 119–22
  specification of equations 81–2
  tax rates 95
  training effectiveness of firms 84–8
  wage subsidies and employment 88,
    116–18
  welfare compensation 29
  without EITC 99
Leibman, J. 110, 111
Lochner, Lance 13, 74, 79, 103, 123, 125
low-skill workers in Mortensen–Pissarides
    model 62
  employment subsidy effects 65
  hiring subsidy effects 65
  subsidy-tax effects 68
  unemployment rate 62, 63
low-wage subsidies, acting with
    unemployment vouchers 134
  effects on dead-end workers 143, 148,
    152
  effects on upwardly mobile workers 143,
    148–50, 152
  and incentives to work 131–2, 133
Luxembourg Summit, the 12

MacLeod, W.B. 50
Malcomson, J. 50
Malinvaud, Edmond 17
marginal training cost 37–8
marginalization 2–3
  negative interactions 7–8
market equilibrium 55–8
market tightness 46, 50, 56, 71
Martin Hamblin Research 135
Millard, S.P. 63, 135, 136
Miller, R. 79, 85, 103
Mincer, J. 103, 104

models, assessment of static and dynamic
    135
Mortensen, Dale 13, 44, 45, 53, 61, 63,
    135, 136
Mortensen–Pissarides model 45–8
  effects of employment and hiring
    subsidies 60–9
  market segmentation 47
  unemployment incidence 47–8
Murray, Charles 16

Nash solution 45, 53
natural rate of unemployment 17
NERA 135
Nickell, S. 5, 135
non-concavity 94
  in Ben Porath model 126–7
non-convexity problem 89, 96

on-the-job training (OJT) model 77, 79
  compensation 110
  difference from LBD model 83
  employment rate 111
  estimated lifecycle progression 106
  evidence 123
  extended model 83
  goodness of fit 129
  hours worked 107
  human capital investment 103–5, 106–8
  increased leisure 110
  individual preferences 103–5
  labor supply elasticity 105
  lifecycle wages 108–9
  lifetime earnings 109
  long-term effects 110
  multi-period 95–9
  parameter estimates 128
  parameter values 128
  schooling 88
  skill formation 96–9, 106–15, 124
  skill levels 108, 109, 112, 114
  specification of equations 80–2
  tax rates 93–5
  training effectiveness of firms 84–8
  wage income 108, 109
  wage subsidies and employment 88
optimal size distribution of employment
    subsidies 134, 135
Orszag, Michael 14, 131, 132, 135
Orszag–Snower model
  closed-form analysis 153–7
  computational solutions
  structure 17, 136–43

Palmer, John 17

payroll tax 61, 63–4, 66
  flat-rate 17–22
  and low-wage subsidy 133
  proportional 17, 18, 19, 28, 34, 36, 39
Pencavel, John 17
personal wealth, and inclusion decline 4
Petrongolo, B. 46
Phelps, Edmund, S. 5, 6, 7, 8, 16, 17, 23,
  45, 49, 50, 74, 79, 131, 132, 135,
  136, 159
Pigou, Arthur 17
Pissarides, Christopher 5, 13, 17, 44, 45,
  46, 53, 61, 135
primary goods 1
private enterprise 10–11
productivity growth, and inclusion decline
  4, 5
productivity slowdown 5
  impact on less advantaged 5–6
Progressive era, the 6, 7

quit rate 17, 18, 24, 28, 29, 30, 35, 36

Rawls, John 1, 7
Rees, H. 140
Robins, P. 123
Roosevelt, Theodore 7
Rosen, S. 77, 80, 85
Rubinstein, A. 53

Saint-Paul, Gilles 7
Samuelson, Paul 7
Schuh, S. 46
Seattle and Denver Income Maintenance
  Experiments 123
self-sufficiency, importance of 1
Shaw, K. 79, 103
skill formation
  cost of 79
  effect of wage subsidies 74–7
  reduction in 76
  specification of process 79
skill investment, cost of 75
Smith, Adam 7
Smith, J. 74
Snower, Dennis J. 14, 17, 40, 131, 132,
  135
social inclusion
  definition 1
  and wage gap 16
social intervention, and inclusion
  deficiency 6–8
social surplus 6–7
social wealth, rise in 5
Spiegelman, R. 135

statutory minimum wage rate 11
Stigler, G.J. 45
Summers, Lawrence 28

Taber, C. 74, 103
targeting, of employment subsidies 134,
  135
tax subsidies 12–13, 25–33
transfer payments 9–10
Tria, Giovanni 7

underground economy 10
unemployment, and incentives 23
unemployment compensation payment
  49
unemployment duration hazard 46
unemployment rate 28, 57, 61, 62, 63
unemployment vouchers 14
  acting with low-wage subsidy 134
  effects on dead-end workers 143, 148,
    152
  effects on upwardly mobile workers 143,
    148–50, 152
  and incentives to work 131–2, 133

vacancy duration hazard 46
vacancy posting costs 48

wage contract 50–1
wage growth
  unemployment vouchers and low-wage
    subsidy 132, 133–4
wage rate
  determination of 3, 53–5
  and less advantaged 38
  see also Nash solution
wage subsidies 16–19, 69
  abuse of 40
  age-specific 77
  flat (constant)
    in closed economy 34–7
    long-run effects 27–30
      on employment 28–9
      on wages 29
    in neoclassical model 19–22
    in open economy 26
    short-run effects 30–1
  graduated 17, 18
    in neoclassical model 19, 21
    in open economy 26
  in LBD model 82
  long-term effects 17, 31–3
    wage effects 32–3
  net budgetary costs 39
  in OJT model 81

wage tax
    age-specific 77
    effects on employment 58–9, 62
    to finance employment subsidy 67–9,
        70
    in LBD model 82
    in OJT model 81
wealth supply 21–2
    in closed economy 34–5
    and tax-subsidy policy 41–2
    and zero-profit curve 36
Weiss, Y. 79
Welch, Finis 8

West, R. 123
Wilson, William J. 16
Wolinsky, A. 53
Woodbury, S.A. 71, 135
work experience 77
    see also learning-by-doing model
worker search intensity 71–2
world real rate of interest, and inclusion
        decline 4, 5

zero-profit curve 18, 25, 27–8, 31, 33, 34,
        36, 38, 41
Zoega, G. 5